A Staircase to Standards Success
for English Language Arts

The Power to Persuade:
Opinion and Argument

Pam Allyn
Executive Director of LitLife and LitWorld

PEARSON

Boston • Columbus • Indianapolis • New York • San Francisco • Upper Saddle River
Amsterdam • Cape Town • Dubai • London • Madrid • Milan • Munich • Paris • Montreal • Toronto
Delhi • Mexico City • São Paulo • Sydney • Hong Kong • Seoul • Singapore • Taipei • Tokyo

Vice President, Editor in Chief: Aurora Martínez Ramos
Acquisitions Editor: Kathryn Boice
Associate Sponsoring Editor: Barbara Strickland
Editorial Assistant: Katherine Wiley
Senior Marketing Manager: Christine Gatchell
Production Editor: Karen Mason
Project Coordination, Editorial Services, and Text Design: Electronic Publishing Services Inc., NYC
Art Rendering and Electronic Page Makeup: Jouve
Cover Designer: Diane Lorenzo and Jenny Hart
Grade Band Opening and Lesson Set Illustrations: Steve Morrison

Text Credits: The Common Core State Standards for the English Language Arts are © Copyright 2010. National Governors Association Center for Best Practices and Council of Chief State School Officers. All rights reserved. Oil Spill Editorial © 2011 Kim-Anh Vo. Reprinted by permission of the author. Words As Free As Confetti a poem from Confetti Poems for Children Text copyright © 1996 by Pat Mora. Permission arranged with LEE & LOW BOOKS INC., New York, NY 10016.

Photo Credits: All photos not credited are courtesy of the author. Illustrations on pages 231–234 © Cora Engelbrecht.

Library of Congress Cataloging-in-Publication Data
Allyn, Pam.
  The power to persuade : opinion and argument / Pam Allyn.
    p. cm. — (Core ready lesson sets for grades 3 to 5 ; bk. 4)
  ISBN-13: 978-0-13-290754-5
  ISBN-10: 0-13-290754-2
  1. Language arts (Elementary)—Curricula—United States.   2. Language arts (Elementary)—Activity programs—United States.   I. Title.
  LB1576.A6144 2013
  372.6—dc23
                                                                                    2012025145

10 9 8 7 6 5 4 3 2 1

ISBN 10: 0-13-290754-2
ISBN 13: 978-0-13-290754-5

About the Author

Pam Allyn is an authority in the field of literacy education and a world-renowned expert in home and school literacy connections. As a motivational speaker, expert consultant, author, teacher, and humanitarian advocating for children, she is transforming the way we think about literacy as a tool for communication and knowledge building.

Pam currently serves as the executive director of LitLife, a national literacy development organization providing research-based professional development for K–12 educators. She founded and leads LitWorld, a groundbreaking global literacy initiative that reaches children across the United States and in more than 60 countries. Her methods for helping all students achieve success as readers and writers have brought her acclaim both in the United States and internationally. Pam is also recognized for founding the highly acclaimed initiative Books for Boys for the nation's most struggling readers.

Pam is the author of 11 books for educators and parents, including the award-winning *What to Read When: The Books and Stories to Read with Your Child—And All the Best Times to Read Them* (Penguin Avery), *Pam Allyn's Best Books for Boys* (Scholastic), and *Your Child's Writing Life: How to Inspire Confidence, Creativity, and Skill at Every Age* (Penguin Avery). Her work has been featured on "Good Morning America," "The Today Show," "Oprah Radio," *The Huffington Post, The New York Times,* and across the blogosphere.

About the Core Ready Series

Core Ready is a dynamic series of books providing educators with critical tools for navigating the Common Core State Standards. The foundational text, *Be Core Ready: Powerful, Effective Steps to Implementing and Achieving the Common Core State Standards*, provides practical strategies for how to implement core ideas to make all students college- and career-ready scholars. The *Core Ready Lesson Sets*, including three grade bands with four books per grade band, provide an easy-to-use way to access and organize all of the content within the standards. Readers see how to take complex concepts related to the standards and turn them into practical, specific, everyday instruction.

Acknowledgments

I thank the team at Pearson for believing in the Core Ready vision. Aurora Martínez is a passionate and radiant leader who makes all things possible. Thanks to Karen Mason for her superb dedication to this work, to Christine Gatchell, Kathryn Boice, and Krista Clark for their great energy, and to Karla Walsh, Carrie Fox, Melinda Durham, Amy Pavelich, and their amazing team at Electronic Publishing Services Inc. for their wonderful care for this project.

Thanks to my colleagues at LitLife, most especially to the dream team on this project: Carolyn Greenberg, Jen Scoggin, Katie Cunningham, and Debbie Lera. They are teachers, leaders, and big thinkers who never forget it is about children first. I am blessed to work with them. Many, many thanks to Flynn Berry, Megan Karges, David Wilcox, Shannon Bishop, Rebekah Coleman, Marie Miller, Erin Harding, Danny Miller, and Jim Allyn for glorious input at every step.

I would like to thank our reviewers who provided valuable feedback: Christine H. Davis, Hillcrest Elementary (Logan, Utah); Wendy Fiore, Chester Elementary School in Connecticut; Keli Garas-York, Buffalo State College in New York; Karen Gibson, Springfield Public Schools in Illinois; Timothy M. Haag, Greater Albany Public Schools, New York; Katie Klaus Salika Lawrence, William Paterson University of New Jersey; Edward Karl Schultz, Midwestern State University (Wichita Falls, TX) Elizabeth Smith, Saint Joseph's College in New York; and Rhonda M. Sutton, East Stroudsburg University in Pennsylvania. Finally, I thank Steve Morrison for his extraordinary illustrations which were, like everything else about everyone who has participated in the creation of this series, so perfect all together.

Contents

Grade 3 *The Reader and Writer's Opinion: A Collaborative Author Study* 1

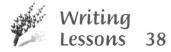

Writing Lessons 38

Grade 4 *Poetry Wars: Reading, Interpreting, and Debating Meaning in Poetry* 64

Reading Lessons 77

Grade 5 *Making the Case: Reading and Writing Editorials* 132

Appendixes

Grade 3 Appendixes

Grade 4 Appendixes

Grade 5 Appendixes

Welcome

Welcome to *The Power to Persuade: Opinion and Argument*. Here you

will find the rich and detailed lesson plans, and the specifics and daily

activities within them, that you can use instantly to make the Core Ready

instruction come to life.

The Four Doors to the Common Core State Standards

We have synthesized the expanse of the Common Core State Standards document into four essential doors to the English Language Arts. These Four Doors organize the CCSS into curriculum, identifying the most critical capacities our students need for the 21st century—skills, understandings, and strategies for reading, writing, speaking, and listening across subject areas. "The Four Doors to the Core" group the CCSS into lesson sets that match the outcomes every college and career-ready student must have. The magic of the Four Doors is that they bring reading, writing, speaking, and listening skills together into **integrated lesson sets**. Rather than face an overwhelming array of individual standards, teachers, students, parents, and administrators together can use the Four Doors to create the kind of curriculum that simplifies the schedule and changes lives. Here are the Four Doors to the Core:

▶ The Road to Knowledge: Information and Research

This Door to the Core—The Road to Knowledge—encompasses research and information and the skills and strategies students need to **build strong content knowledge and compose informational text** as suggested by the Common Core State Standards.

▶ The Power to Persuade: Opinion and Argument

This Door to the Core—The Power to Persuade—encompasses instruction that explores the purposes, techniques, and strategies to **become effective readers and writers of various types of opinion text** as delineated in the Common Core State Standards.

▶ The Shape of Story: Yesterday and Today

This Door to the Core—The Shape of Story—encompasses exploration of a variety of genres with the corresponding craft, structures, and strategies one needs to be a **successful consumer and producer of literary text** as required by the Common Core State Standards.

▶ The Journey to Meaning: Comprehension and Critique

This Door to the Core—The Journey to Meaning—encompasses the strategies and skills our students need to **comprehend, critique, and compose literary text** as outlined in the Common Core State Standards.

Get Ready to Build the Power to Persuade

The Core Door Power to Persuade focuses on the recognition and development of opinion and argument though reading, writing, listening, and speaking. It seeks to foster in students an awareness of purpose and point of view as they examine the views of others and develop their own ideas and voice. Through exploration of literature, poetry, and editorial writing, students will consider their own passions, viewpoints, and evidence at hand as they develop and defend ideas in book reviews, poetry interpretations, and editorials. They will cite specific evidence to justify their ideas. They will practice effective listening, conversation, and oral speaking behaviors as they collaborate to develop their ideas and present to an audience.

Students will consider the power of word choice and structure and employ appropriate vocabulary and transitional phrases to express and link ideas effectively. They will study and practice how to express ideas clearly, cohesively, and concisely in a manner that is appropriate to their audience. They will share their writing and thinking with others orally or using appropriate tools and technologies.

These lesson sets provide a variety of diverse opportunities for our students to say what they are thinking, and to respond to texts, ideas, and discourse in ways that are not only intuitive but also informed. The students take an active role in their own reading, and reveal through writing and speaking their own unique, one-of-a-kind of voice, creating new ideas in the world and practicing for the day when, in the college classroom or workplace, they have to defend an idea or invent a new one.

Walk Through a Lesson Set

This section is meant to take the reader through the major features of the lesson set with snapshots of design elements/icons, etc. to illustrate.

Why This Lesson Set?

This section establishes the rationale for the lesson set and provides helpful background information about the lesson set focus.

Common Core State Standards Alignment

All of the Common Core State Standards addressed in the lesson set are listed here, including the individual grade-level standards.

Essential Skill Lenses
(PARCC Framework)

This table provides specific examples of how in this lesson set, Core Ready students will build the essential skills required by the Partnership for Assessment of Readiness for College and Careers (PARCC), a multi-state coalition that is currently developing Core Standards–aligned assessments that are slated to replace many statewide assessments across the United States. This alignment helps to ensure that Core Ready students will be prepared when states begin to use these assessments.

Core Questions

Core Questions are thought-provoking, open-ended questions students will explore across the lesson set. We expect students' responses to the Core Questions to evolve as their experience and understanding become richer with each

lesson. For best results, post these questions somewhere in your classroom and use them to focus your instruction.

Ready to Get Started?

This is a brief and inspiring pep talk intended to set the stage for teachers and provide insight about learners at this grade level.

Lesson Set Goals

Here you will find a list of goals for student learning summarized in clear language in three to five observable behaviors for each reading and writing lesson set, listed with corresponding Common Core State Standards that the goals address.

Choosing Core Texts

For best practice to occur and for all our students to achieve success, all teaching of reading and writing should be grounded in the study of quality literature. Here you will find lists of books, poems, articles, and other texts for you and your students to use for modeling and close reading to achieve the instructional goals of the lesson set. We also explain the types of texts that will focus and enrich your students' reading and writing during this lesson set. Any text that is used specifically as an exemplar in a lesson appears here in the first list. We also recommend additional texts with similar features and qualities to supplement your work in this lesson set.

Teacher's Notes

This section relays a personal message from us to you, the teacher, meant to give the big picture of what the lesson set is all about, the impact we hope it will have on students, and tips or reminders to facilitate your teaching.

Core Message to Students

This segment speaks directly to students, providing background knowledge and rationale about the lesson set to come. We encourage you to share this message with your students to set the stage for their learning.

Building Academic Language

This section provides a list of key terms and phrases chosen to help your students read, write, listen, and speak during the course of the lesson set. Introduce these terms to your students in context gradually; scaffold their use by making them visible to everyone, with bulletin boards and manipulatives; and encourage students to use the new words as they communicate during your study together. See the glossary at the end of each grade's lesson set for more information about important lesson vocabulary.

Recognition

The successful conclusion of each grade's lesson set is a time for recognition. Find specific suggestions for how to plan meaningful recognition opportunities for your students here.

Assessment

In this section you will find information about where to find assessment tools in every lesson set, along with suggestions specific to that grade.

Also see the Reading Lessons and Writing Lessons sections to find Milestone Performance Assessments for monitoring progress and for standards-aligned reading and writing rubrics.

Core Support for Diverse Learners

Here we provide guidance for how to pace and plan instruction and provide materials that will help all students in your class be successful during the lessons.

Complementary Core Methods

This segment offers specific ideas for how to use key instructional structures (read-aloud, shared reading, shared writing, etc.) to reach the goals of the lessons.

Core Connections at Home

This section suggests ways to keep caregivers at home informed and involved.

The Reading and Writing Lessons

Each set of reading and writing lessons is separated into two sections with the following contents for either reading or writing:

- The Core I.D.E.A. / Daily Instruction at a Glance table

- Reading and writing rubrics aligned to unit goals and Common Core State Standards

- Detailed lesson plans (10 for reading, 10 for writing, and 1 Language Companion Lesson)

What to Look for in the Core I.D.E.A. / Daily Instruction at a Glance Table

Specifies the I.D.E.A. framework stage for each lesson

Lists any extra teacher support found in the lesson:
- Milestone Assessment
- Speaking and listening opportunities
- Suggestions for English Language Learner (ELL) support
- Technology suggestions
- Close reading opportunity

Indicates the lesson number

States the teaching objective of each lesson

Lists the standards that align with the lesson

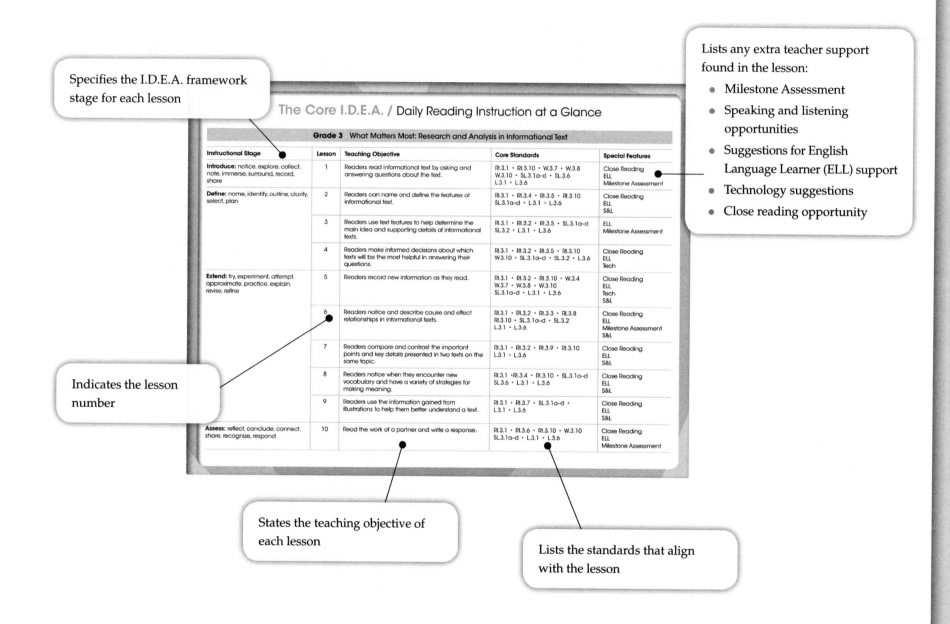

The Core I.D.E.A. / Daily Reading Instruction at a Glance

Grade 3 What Matters Most: Research and Analysis in Informational Text

Instructional Stage	Lesson	Teaching Objective	Core Standards	Special Features
Introduce: notice, explore, collect, note, immerse, surround, record, share	1	Readers read informational text by asking and answering questions about the text.	RI.3.1 · RI.3.10 · W.3.7 · W.3.8 W.3.10 · SL.3.1a–d · SL.3.6 L.3.1 · L.3.6	Close Reading ELL Milestone Assessment
Define: name, identify, outline, clarify, select, plan	2	Readers can name and define the features of informational text.	RI.3.1 · RI.3.4 · RI.3.5 · RI.3.10 SL.3.1a–d · L.3.1 · L.3.6	Close Reading ELL S&L
	3	Readers use text features to help determine the main idea and supporting details of informational texts.	RI.3.1 · RI.3.2 · RI.3.5 · SL.3.1a–d SL.3.2 · L.3.1 · L.3.6	ELL Milestone Assessment
	4	Readers make informed decisions about which texts will be the most helpful in answering their questions.	RI.3.1 · RI.3.2 · RI.3.5 · RI.3.10 W.3.10 · SL.3.1a–d · SL.3.2 · L.3.6	Close Reading ELL Tech
Extend: try, experiment, attempt, approximate, practice, explain, revise, refine	5	Readers record new information as they read.	RI.3.1 · RI.3.2 · RI.3.10 · W.3.4 W.3.7 · W.3.8 · W.3.10 SL.3.1a–d · L.3.1 · L.3.6	Close Reading ELL Tech S&L
	6	Readers notice and describe cause and effect relationships in informational texts.	RI.3.1 · RI.3.2 · RI.3.3 · RI.3.8 RI.3.10 · SL.3.1a–d · SL.3.2 L.3.1 · L.3.6	Close Reading ELL Milestone Assessment S&L
	7	Readers compare and contrast the important points and key details presented in two texts on the same topic.	RI.3.1 · RI.3.2 · RI.3.9 · RI.3.10 L.3.1 · L.3.6	Close Reading ELL S&L
	8	Readers notice when they encounter new vocabulary and have a variety of strategies for making meaning.	RI.3.1 ·RI.3.4 · RI.3.10 · SL.3.1a–d SL.3.6 · L.3.1 · L.3.6	Close Reading ELL S&L
	9	Readers use the information gained from illustrations to help them better understand a text.	RI.3.1 · RI.3.7 · SL.3.1a–d · L.3.1 · L.3.6	Close Reading ELL S&L
Assess: reflect, conclude, connect, share, recognize, respond	10	Read the work of a partner and write a response.	RI.3.1 · RI.3.6 · RI.3.10 · W.3.10 SL.3.1a–d · L.3.1 · L.3.6	Close Reading ELL Milestone Assessment

What to Look for in the Reading and Writing Rubrics

In both the reading and writing lesson sets, we provide a discipline-specific performance rubric, including performance descriptors for four levels of proficiency. A score of 3 ("Achieving") indicates that by the end of the lesson set, a student has demonstrated solid evidence of success with the elements of the task or concept and can perform independently when required by the standards.

Lesson set goals

Standards alignment—the Core standards that match each goal

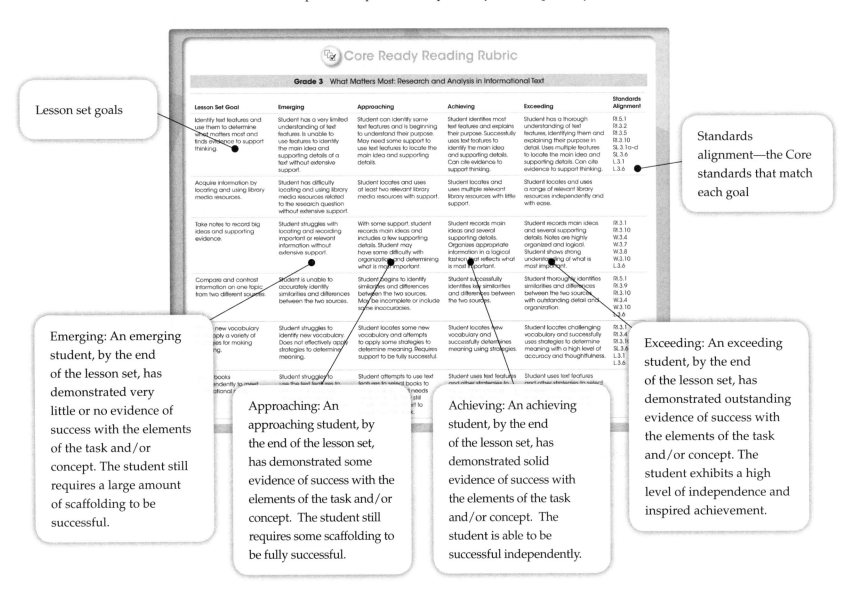

Emerging: An emerging student, by the end of the lesson set, has demonstrated very little or no evidence of success with the elements of the task and/or concept. The student still requires a large amount of scaffolding to be successful.

Approaching: An approaching student, by the end of the lesson set, has demonstrated some evidence of success with the elements of the task and/or concept. The student still requires some scaffolding to be fully successful.

Achieving: An achieving student, by the end of the lesson set, has demonstrated solid evidence of success with the elements of the task and/or concept. The student is able to be successful independently.

Exceeding: An exceeding student, by the end of the lesson set, has demonstrated outstanding evidence of success with the elements of the task and/or concept. The student exhibits a high level of independence and inspired achievement.

What to Look for in the Detailed Lesson Plans

Teaching Objective: A succinct statement that captures the primary focus of the lesson.

Standards Alignment: A list of the standards that the students will practice and apply during the lesson.

Materials: List of the texts, resources, equipment, and so on that you should gather in preparation for the lesson.

Indented text indicates scripted suggestions for what you might say to students.

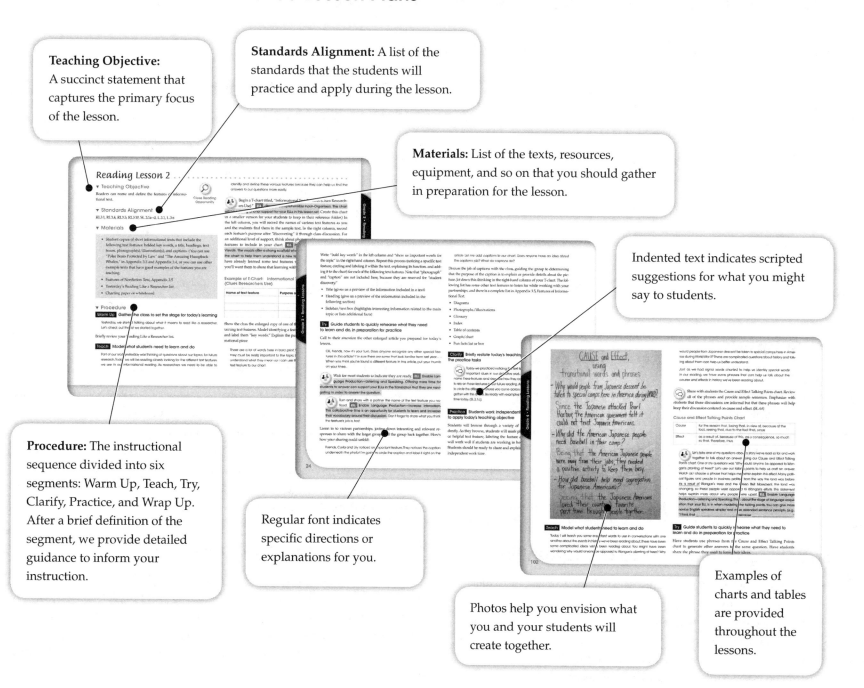

Procedure: The instructional sequence divided into six segments: Warm Up, Teach, Try, Clarify, Practice, and Wrap Up. After a brief definition of the segment, we provide detailed guidance to inform your instruction.

Regular font indicates specific directions or explanations for you.

Examples of charts and tables are provided throughout the lessons.

Photos help you envision what you and your students will create together.

Special Features Marked with an Icon

Look for these icons to help you find the following important elements within each lesson set.

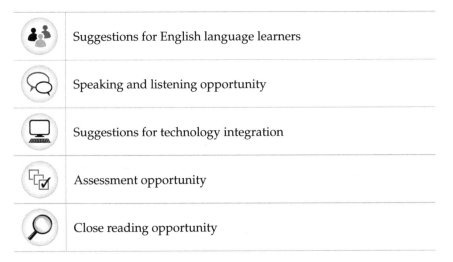

Suggestions for English language learners

Speaking and listening opportunity

Suggestions for technology integration

Assessment opportunity

Close reading opportunity

ELL Support

Across the lesson set, we highlight specific strategies embedded in the lesson to shelter instruction for ELL students. Based on Jim Cummins's *Five Principles for Teaching Content to English Language Learners* (www.pearsonschool.com), these strategies will help ELL students participate successfully in the whole-group lesson and will support the development of their language skills. Wherever you see this icon, you can expect to find which of the 5 Principles is being employed alongside helpful advice and information to support your English Language Learners in any lesson you teach. (See Figure 1 for a complete list with descriptions of the Five Principles for Teaching Content to English Language Learners).

Speaking and Listening Opportunities

Speaking and listening skills are essential for career- and college-ready students, yet these two capacities are frequently underrepresented in classrooms. We have embedded frequent opportunities for students to grow in these areas. Look for the Speaking and Listening icon to see where. Also, see the appendix of any Core Ready lesson set book for a standards-aligned checklist to help you assess student performance in these areas.

Technology Options

The Common Core State Standards require that students use technology strategically and capably, and for today's student, this is essential work across the disciplines. Each lesson set provides several suggestions, marked with the Technology icon, for how to build student technology skills and enhance the lessons with various technological tools. Beside each English Language Arts Goal we list for students, we present both high- and low-tech options for your classroom. Although we strongly advocate using a high-tech approach, we recognize that circumstances of funding, training, or even those annoying times when equipment just refuses to function may make it difficult to rely completely on technology. Therefore, we also suggest a low-tech method to achieve the goal—tools that are easily available and inexpensive or free.

Milestone Assessments

Every lesson set includes several suggested Milestone Performance Assessments to assess students' progress toward the lesson set goals. Each of these performance-based assessments aligns directly with one or more Common Core State Standards for reading or writing. With each milestone assessment, we include a checklist of indicators for you to observe with specific guidelines for where to gather the evidence. See each grade's appendix for "copy and clip" masters of these checklists.

Close Reading Opportunities

Every lesson set includes several lessons that require focused, text-based reading where teachers model and students practice reading closely to determine what the text says explicitly, making logical inferences from it, and citing specific textual evidence when writing or speaking to support conclusions drawn from the text. This icon marks a Close Reading opportunity.

Figure 1 Five Principles for Teaching Content to English Language Learners

1. Identify and Communicate Content and Language Objectives

When presenting content objectives.

- Simplify language (active voice, use same terms consistently)
- Paraphrase
- Repeat
- Avoid idioms and slang
- Be aware of homophones and multiple-meaning words
- Clarify (with simplified language, gestures, visuals)
- Check for understanding

When working with language objectives focus on

- Key content vocabulary
- Academic vocabulary found across the curriculum
- Language form and function essential for the lesson

2. Frontload the Lesson

Provide opportunities to frontload or preteach lesson elements.

- Activate prior knowledge by connecting to students' academic, cultural, or personal experiences
- Build background by explaining new vocabulary or unfamiliar facts and concepts
- Preview text by reviewing visuals, headings, and/or highlighted text
- Set a purpose for reading by clarifying comprehension questions at the end of the lesson
- Make connections by helping students see relationships between the lesson and other aspects of their lives

3. Provide Comprehensible Input

Make oral and written content accessible by providing support.

- Visuals: photos, illustrations, cartoons, multimedia
- Graphics: graphs, charts, tables
- Organizers: graphic organizers, outlines
- Summaries: text, audio, native language
- Audio: recordings, read-alouds
- Audiovisual aids: videos, dramatizations, props, gestures
- Models: demonstrations and modeling
- Experiences: hands-on learning opportunities, field trips

4. Enable Language Production

Structure opportunities for oral practice with language and content.

Listening and speaking

- Make listening input understandable with a variety of support
- Model language
- Allow wait time for students to plan what they say

Reading and writing

- Tailor the task to each student's proficiency level
- Provide support and scaffolding
- Expect different products from students with different levels of proficiency

Increasing interaction

- Provide collaborative tasks so students can work together
- Encourage the development of relationships with peers
- Lower anxiety levels to enable learning, as indicated by brain research

5. Assess for Content and Language Understanding

Monitor progress and provide reteaching and intervention when necessary.

Diagnostic Assessment

- Determine appropriate placement
- Identify strengths and challenges

Formative Assessment

- Check comprehension in ongoing manner
- Use appropriate instruction and pacing

Summative Assessments

- Provide alternative types of assessment when possible, such as projects and portfolios
- Provide practice before administering formal tests

Accommodations

- Provide extra time
- Use bilingual dictionaries
- Offer oral presentation of written material

Source: Jim Cummins, "Five Principles for Teaching Content to English Language Learners." Retrieved from www.pearsonELL.com. Reprinted with permission.

Language Companion Lesson

Each lesson set includes a Language Companion Lesson as a resource and model for explicit teaching of language standards within the context of each lesson set topic.

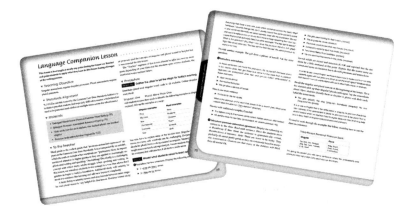

Glossary

A glossary of key terms is provided with each grade's lesson set.

Appendixes

We have provided a variety of resources in the appendixes, including masters for graphic organizers and charts, sample texts for close reading, a Speaking and Listening Performance Checklist, bibliographical information for the research and texts we mention within the lesson sets, Clip-Apart Milestone Performance Assessments that can be copied, and other resources specific to the lesson sets. The Appendixes pages, along with other teaching tools, will be available as downloadable PDFs in the PDToolkit. For information, visit the PDToolkit for Pam Allyn's *Be Core Ready* Series at **http://pdtoolkit. pearson.com.**

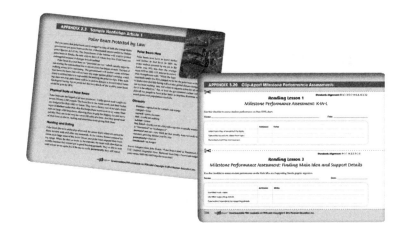

FAQs about the Core Ready Lesson Sets

Q How does Core Ready ensure alignment with the Common Core State Standards?

A We have carefully examined, analyzed, and synthesized the standards to create for all students rich, engaging learning experiences—many of which touch on multiple standards—with the goal that within a single grade level, Core Ready students will experience the full breadth of Core Standards in reading, writing, speaking, and listening. Every grade-level standard in these three areas is listed in one or more of the lessons for that grade level, and most appear in multiple lessons.

As the Common Core document on "Focus and coherence in instruction and assessment" states, not every standard appears as a stand-alone instruction and assessment objective:

> While the Standards delineate specific expectations in reading, writing, speaking, listening, and language, each standard need not be a separate focus for instruction and assessment. Often, several standards can be addressed by a single rich task. (CCSS, p. 5)

We consider every standard we list in the Common Core State Standards Alignment section to be an integral part of what students must do in order to achieve one or more instructional objective of the multifaceted tasks that make up each lesson set.

Q How do you address Foundational Standards for Reading and Language Standards?

A When applicable, Foundational Skills for Reading Standards and Language Standards may be listed with a lesson; however, the full range of Reading Foundations and Language Standards is outside the scope of these lesson sets.

We recommend that teachers plan opportunities for students to build Reading Foundational Skills by exploring grade-level appropriate skills in the context of the core texts from each lesson set and applying this knowledge to their independent reading and writing. Schools may also wish to acquire developmentally appropriate curricular materials specific to this area. *Words Their Way* by Donald Bear et al. is an excellent example of a program that addresses this need.

Regarding the teaching and application of language standards, we stand with the position of the National Council of Teachers of English:

> the use of isolated grammar and usage exercises not supported by theory and research is a deterrent to the improvement of students' speaking and writing and that, in order to improve both of these, class time at all levels must be devoted to opportunities for meaningful listening, speaking, reading, and writing. (NCTE Position Statement on the Teaching of Grammar, 1998–2009)

The primary goal of grammar study is to improve writing and speaking skills. Students acquire such skills best not from isolated drill and practice of grammar rules, but from engagement in authentic language experiences requiring active participation in reading, writing, listening, and speaking.

> The inclusion of Language standards in their own strand should not be taken as an indication that skills related to conventions, effective language use, and vocabulary are unimportant to reading, writing, speaking, and listening; indeed, they are inseparable from such contexts. (CCSS, p. 25)

Q What are the Language Companion Lessons?

A The Core Ready Lesson Sets provide the type of authentic integrated experiences that will help all students expand their language skills.

Explicit instruction in selected language concepts benefits students as they try to navigate the complex rules and requirements of conventional English. To this end, we have provided Language Companion Lessons, one per grade, as resources and models for the explicit teaching of language standards within the context of each lesson set topic.

When choosing teaching objectives for the Language Companion Lessons, we considered a few factors. First, we made sure to include a lesson for each of the standards listed in the Language Progressive Skills, which are specially marked in the standards as being particularly likely to require extended attention over time. The inclusion of these growth-targeted standards will help Core Ready teachers start addressing these important topics.

Second, we made sure that the lesson set and Language Companion Lessons were compatible in focus so that students could immediately connect and apply the language learning to their reading and writing experiences. For example, a lesson on punctuating dialogue would not be a very good match for a lesson set on writing editorials—while dialogue might be included in editorials, it is not very common. A lesson on using domain-specific words would be a better language match for that lesson set. Teaching this lesson will enhance your students' language use during the lesson set. The Language Companion Lessons can also be used as models for teaching other language standards that couple well with the content of the lesson set.

Q How do you address the Common Core State Standard requirements for text complexity (Standard 10)?

A We have reflected the Core requirements by suggesting texts that meet the standards' call for appropriate text complexity for the lesson set grade level. In addition to our own suggestions for grade-level appropriate text, we have used many exemplars from Appendix B of the Common Core State Standards across each lesson set book.

We support the Common Core State Standards' assertion that the ability to read complex text independently and proficiently is essential for high achievement in college and the workplace and important in numerous life tasks. To this end, we also agree with the Core Standards tenet that all students deserve opportunities to read and engage with high-quality literature. We stand firmly, however, by years of research that suggests that students who are learning to read need extended practice (Allington, 2009; Kuhn et al., 2006) with texts that they can read with accuracy and comprehension (Allington, 2012; Ehri, Dreyer, Flugman, & Gross, 2007) in order to improve their abilities. This means time spent reading appropriately leveled text, which may be above, within, or below grade level depending on an individual's needs and skills. This type of differentiation typically takes place in small-group and independent settings.

Q Do I have to use the core texts recommended in the lesson set? What if I can't get a text or I have a different one in mind?

A Although we always provide specific suggestions for texts that we feel will serve you and your students well for each lesson, there is always room to make thoughtful substitutions. Can't find the text cited in the lesson? Already have a great piece in your classroom collection? No problem. Use the description of what to look for in the introduction to guide you to substitute texts you already own or already love.

Q Are teachers required to use the text exemplars listed by the Common Core State Standards in Appendix B?

A The writers of the Core Standards intended the text exemplars as models of appropriate texts for each grade band, not a required list, as stated below:

> The choices should serve as useful guideposts in helping educators select texts of similar complexity, quality, and range for their own classrooms. They expressly do not represent a partial or complete reading list. (Common Core, 2011, p. 2)

We have included some of the Appendix B texts in the lesson sets alongside our own choices of texts that meet the parameters suggested by the exemplars.

Q You include an icon for speaking and listening opportunities and strategies to support ELLs in only some lessons, yet there seem to be lots of speaking and listening and similar ELL strategies in practically every lesson. Why don't you mark every instance with an icon?

A Icons are added where we felt teachers should purposefully focus their instruction and attention on a particular element. Core Ready Lessons are rich with practices that strengthen speaking, listening, and language skills, such as conversing with a classmate, but we do not include an icon in every instance. We hope that by highlighting effective practices in selected lessons, we will increase teachers' awareness of how to build speaking, listening, and language skills in any lesson they teach.

Q **Must the lesson sets be taught in any particular order?**

A Each set of 10 reading and writing lessons has been designed to be modular; that is, the sequence in which you teach the lesson sets may vary in response to local curricular needs, testing schedules, or other factors that influence a school calendar. However, that being said, we offer a suggested set of calendar options for you in our online PDToolkit. We make specific, strongly encouraged suggestions in regard to the K–2 lessons in particular.

Q **Should the individual lessons be taught in the order they appear in the book?**

A Yes. The lessons within the Core Ready lesson sets are arranged in a purposeful sequence that reflects respected models of how students learn, such as the "gradual release of responsibility" model (Pearson and Gallagher, 1993) and "cognitive apprenticeship theory" (Collins, Brown, & Newman, 1989). Across the lessons, the teacher guides the students toward increasing levels of independence with the lesson set goals. The teaching objectives of each lesson generally build on the knowledge gained in the previous lesson and many student products are developed in a series of steps across multiple lessons. Therefore, the lessons are designed to be taught as a set and are best delivered in the sequence we provide.

There are four stages in a Core Ready lesson set: Introduce, Define, Extend, and Assess. We use the acronym I.D.E.A. to refer to this structure. Each stage is described below. For a much more detailed description of these stages, please see the foundational book of this series, *Be Core Ready: Powerful, Effective Steps to Implementing and Achieving the Common Core State Standards.*

▶ **Introduce** The Introduce stage activates students' background knowledge and builds a big-picture understanding of the topic of study.

▶ **Define** The Define stage provides students with essential knowledge, terms, and structures that will guide their learning about the topic across the unit.

▶ **Extend** If you compare the types of lessons found in the Define stage of the unit to a road map to learning, the Extend stage might be likened to a series of guided day trips designed to help students become increasingly independent travelers. This is the phase in which students apply and refine the skills and strategies they need to achieve the goals of the unit.

▶ **Assess** The Assess stage serves to wrap up each lesson set in a meaningful way intended to encourage students to recognize and commit to how they have grown as readers, writers, listeners, and speakers.

Q **Is it important to teach both the reading and the writing lessons?**

A The reading and writing lesson sets are strategically connected, and we have long advocated teaching reading and writing in an integrated manner. That is, what we study with our classes in reading is directly related to what we study in writing. For example, a reading lesson set on successful reading of folktales is taught alongside writing lessons on how to write folktales. Or a set of reading lessons on determining theme in traditional text is accompanied by lessons on theme-related written response to literature.

We have found that the confluence of reading and writing benefits both students and teachers. Each area, reading or writing, helps students be more successful in the other via the natural connections that students make between the two disciplines. A reading experience helps students gain knowledge that helps them develop and enhance the content and structure of connected writing tasks. As students read folktales, for example, they gain a sense of the literary elements, author's purpose, and craft techniques that they will need to consider and include as they write folktales. Likewise, a close study of how to write folktales raises student awareness of what to expect in this genre, leading them be more confident and perceptive readers.

Teachers intuitively understand that such connections help students, but often, curricular materials do not align reading and writing together. Core Ready's dynamically integrated reading and writing lesson sets make it easy for teachers to help students see important connections clearly and immediately. "In reading yesterday, we talked about how folktales usually include magic and fantasy. Today in writing, you begin to imagine how magic and fantasy can be an important part of your original tale."

Because of the close relationship between our reading and writing lesson sets, we strongly recommend that they be taught side by side. Is it possible to teach *just* the reading lessons or *just* the writing lessons? In most cases, with some adjustments, this could be done, but again, we recommend that reading and writing be presented simultaneously to maximize the benefits for students and teachers.

Q You provide a lot of specific guidelines for what teachers should say aloud and do during the lessons. Should I follow those specifications exactly?

A It depends. There are all kinds of cooks out there. Some like to follow the recipe to the letter. Some like to refer to a recipe and immediately improvise with the ingredients and procedure. Others like to follow a recipe exactly the first time, and figure out places they want to modify next time to suit their tastes and needs. It is much the same with teachers and lesson plans. We expect that some teachers will adopt these plans as written and others will adapt them to suit their teaching style, needs, and resources. The quotes and directions are there to model how the teaching *might* go. The most non-negotiable elements by far are the teaching objectives and standards alignment. If you keep your eye on those as your ultimate destinations, there are many roads that will get you there. These lessons are designed to guide you along the way.

Q Are the lessons meant to be taught in one class period? If not, what are your suggestions for timing?

A Each lesson provides guidelines for six instructional segments: Warm Up, Teach, Try, Clarify, Practice, and Wrap Up. As your students become actively engaged in the rich content of the lessons, you are often likely to find that one class period will not be enough time to complete all of these segments thoroughly. It is perfectly OK to split the segments over two or more periods.

We encourage you to use your professional judgment to decide how to allocate your time teaching these lessons. There are, however, a few rules of thumb that will make your teaching more successful:

1. *Make every effort to include all six segments of the lesson.* There is a purposeful flow and gradual release of responsibility embedded in every lesson to guide students to build independence. Skipping sections interrupts this flow and reduces the likelihood that students will achieve the objectives of the lesson.

2. *Don't let the whole-group segments at the beginning of the lesson (Warm Up, Teach, Try, Clarify) eat up all of your time.* As a group, many teachers have a tendency to go on too long with the whole class lesson. Come on— you know we are talking to you! Nearly all of us are guilty of this from time to time. Just one more example, ask a couple more questions to check understanding, address a few more wayward student comments—we've all been there! Try to keep the whole-group instruction sharply focused with a succinct demonstration (Teach) and rehearsal (Try) of the teaching objective. Your students' attention span is limited, and you need to get "off the stage" so that they can get to what is arguably the most important part of the lessons. Which brings us to . . .

3. *Allow ample time for independent practice.* Although courtside instruction and pep talks from the coach are helpful to a budding basketball player, nothing builds a player's skills like playing the game. Likewise, while young readers and writers certainly need your teaching and guidance, what they really need most is to *read* and *write*—eyes on the text, pencils on paper, actively thinking and engaging in the reading and writing process *themselves*. This is where the students get to apply the teaching objective of the lesson on their own using their own texts or writing. This is where they work through the hard stuff of reading and writing that builds capacity, confidence, and stamina—focused practice, collaboration with other learners, making and revising mistakes, making choices, and revising their thinking and understanding of how language works. It is perfectly OK and necessary for you to coach from the sidelines, but if students are to become independent readers and writers, they must have extended time working independently. How much time is "ample" time? Depending on the grade level, we usually allocate about half of the total lesson time to independent practice. So, within 80 minutes spent on all six lesson segments, about 35 to 40 minutes should be in independent practice. Younger students and students who are unaccustomed to working independently will need to build up to longer periods of independent work. While your students are working independently, you may be holding teaching conferences with individual students, working with small groups to differentiate instruction, or making assessment notes to inform your planning.

A variety of options for allocating lesson plan time are in the table on the next page. All are based on a 50-minute class period. If you have more or less time, scale up or scale down the number of minutes accordingly, keeping proportions similar.

Timing Guidelines for a Lesson

	Days (Minutes)	Lesson Segment (Minutes)
A lesson that includes all six segments in one 50-minute session	Day 1 (50)	Warm Up (3), Teach (10), Try (5), Clarify (2), Practice (25), Wrap Up (5)
A lesson that spans 2 days	Day 1 (50)	Warm Up (10), Teach (20), Try (15), Clarify (5)
	Day 2 (50)	Practice (45), Wrap Up (5)
A lesson that spans 3 days with extended time for the independent practice	Day 1 (50)	Warm Up (10), Teach (20), Try (15), Clarify (5)
	Day 2 (50)	Practice (50)
	Day 3 (50)	Additional Practice (40), Wrap Up (10)
A lesson that spans 2 days, plus a reteach based on Milestone Performance Assessment data to allow students more time to achieve the teaching objective	Day 1 (50)	Warm Up (10), Teach (20), Try (15), Clarify (5)
	Day 2 (50)	Practice (45), Wrap Up (5)
	Day 3 (50)	Reteach Based on Milestone Data Warm Up (3), Teach (10), Try (5), Clarify (2), Practice (25), Wrap Up (5)

PD pd TOOLKIT™

Common Core State Standards Alignment

Accompanying *Core Ready for Grades 3–5*, there is an online resource site with media tools that, together with the text, provides you with the tools you need to implement the lesson sets.

The PDToolkit for Pam Allyn's *Core Ready* Series is available free for 12 months after you use the password that comes with the box set for each grade band. After that, you can purchase access for an additional 12 months. If you did not purchase the box set, you can purchase a 12-month subscription at **http://pdtoolkit.pearson.com.** Be sure to explore and download the resources available at the website. Currently the following resources are available:

- Pearson Children's and Young Adult Literature Database
- Videos
- PowerPoint Presentations
- Student Artifacts
- Photos and Visual Media
- Handouts, Forms, and Posters to supplement your Core-aligned lesson plans
- Lessons and Homework Assignments
- Close Reading Guides and Samples
- Children's Core Literature Recommendations

In the future, we will continue to add additional resources. To learn more, please visit **http://pdtoolkit.pearson.com.**

Available in the PDToolkit is a matrix that details the Common Core State Standards alignment for each Core Ready lesson set in all of the Core Ready books. See sample shown below.

Common Core Language Arts Standards Alignment

Standard Number	Standard	The Road to Knowledge (RK)	The Power to Persuade (PP)	The Shape of Story (SS)	The Journey to Meaning (JM)
Reading: Literature					
RL.3.1	Ask and answer questions to demonstrate understanding of a text, referring explicitly to the text as the basis for the answers.	•	•		•
RL.3.2	Recount stories, including fables, folktales, and myths from diverse cultures; determine the central message, lesson, or moral and explain how it is conveyed through key details in the text.	•			
RL.3.3	Describe characters in a story (e.g., their traits, motivations, or feelings) and explain how their actions contribute to the sequence of events.				•
RL.3.4	Determine the meaning of words and phrases as they are used in a text, distinguishing literal from nonliteral language.			•	
RL.3.5	Refer to parts of stories, dramas, and poems when writing or speaking about a text, using terms such as chapter, scene, and stanza; describe how each successive part builds on earlier sections.	•	•		•
RL.3.6	Distinguish their own point of view from that of the narrator or those of the characters.				•
RL.3.7	Explain how specific aspects of a text's illustrations contribute to what is conveyed by the words in a story (e.g., create mood, emphasize aspects of a character or setting).				•
RL.3.8	(Not applicable to literature)				
RL.3.9	Compare and contrast the themes, settings, and plots of stories written by the same author about the same or similar characters (e.g., in books from a series).	•			
RL.3.10	By the end of the year, read and comprehend literature, including stories, dramas, and poetry, at the high end of the grades 2–3 text complexity band independently and proficiently.				•

PD TOOLKIT™ Common Core Language Arts Standards Alignment for Pam Allyn's *Core Ready Lesson Sets: A Staircase to Standards Success for English Language Arts.* Copyright © 2014 Pearson Education, Inc. 1

Grade 3

The Reader and Writer's Opinion:
A Collaborative Author Study

Introduction

The Common Core State Standards ask students in grade 3 to engage with grade-appropriate complex literature. In this lesson set, students will think deeply about their reading in order to uncover the central message or theme, as well as ask and answer questions by explicitly referring to these texts. In addition, this lesson set will push Core Ready learners to compare and contrast the themes, settings, and plots of stories written by the same author.

Fostering deep understanding of text is critical for those of us working with third graders. In this lesson set, students work in collaborative groups that will depend on each member's ability to read with sufficient accuracy and fluency in order to support optimal comprehension. By encouraging students to work in collaborative groups, we as teachers have the opportunity to highlight the importance of reading grade-level texts with purpose and understanding.

In harmony with the speaking and listening standards, this lesson set provides a wide range of opportunities for students to ask and answer questions

Why This Lesson Set?

In this lesson set, students will:

- Read closely to deepen comprehension and compare literary elements across book series

- Develop speaking and listening skills and collaborative abilities by participating in small literature study groups

- Cite specific text evidence to support their ideas and opinions

- Create and deliver an organized presentation on their collaborative group findings

of a fellow classmate to deepen their understanding of the material being read. Using a shared book series, students must continuously report on their reading by clearly sharing their own ideas and relevant details at an understandable pace. A major thrust of this work will be encouraging our students to engage in effective discussions using a variety of activities to foster successful collaboration, such as being prepared, following agreed-upon rules for discussion, and explaining their own understandings in light of the discussion at hand.

Finally, this lesson set allows students to write routinely within a range of time frames. In their reading work, students will be asked to complete several short pieces of writing, including summaries, to deepen their understanding of the material. When writing, students will be asked to compose opinion pieces about their chosen series over a longer period of time. This requires students to carefully organize their work, considering the purpose for their writing as well as the intended audience.

Common Core State Standards Alignment

Reading Standards

RL.3.1 Ask and answer questions to demonstrate understanding of a text, referring explicitly to the text as the basis for the answers.

RL.3.2 Recount stories, including fables, folktales, and myths from diverse cultures; determine the central message, lesson, or moral, and explain how it is conveyed through key details in the text.

RL.3.4 Determine the meaning of words and phrases as they are used in a text, distinguishing literal from nonliteral language.

RL.3.5 Refer to parts of stories, dramas, and poems when writing or speaking about a text, using terms such as *chapter*, *scene*, and *stanza*; describe how each successive part builds on earlier sections.

RL.3.9 Compare and contrast the themes, settings, and plots of stories written by the same author about the same or similar characters (e.g., in books from a series).

RL.3.10 By the end of the year, independently and proficiently read and comprehend literature, including stories, dramas, and poetry, at the high end of the grades 2–3 text complexity band.

RI.3.10 By the end of the year, read and comprehend informational texts, including history/social studies, science, and technical texts, at the high end of the grades 2–3 text complexity band independently and proficiently.

Writing Standards

W.3.1 Write opinion pieces on topics or texts, supporting a point of view with reasons.

a. Introduce the topic or text they are writing, state an opinion, and create an organizational structure that lists reasons.

b. Provide reasons that support the opinion.

c. Use linking words and phrases (e.g., *because, therefore, since, for example*) to connect opinion and reasons.

d. Provide a concluding statement or section.

W.3.4 With guidance and support from adults, produce writing in which the development and organization are appropriate to the task and purpose.

W.3.5 With guidance and support from peers and adults, develop and strengthen writing as needed by planning, revising, and editing.

W.3.6 With guidance and support from adults, use technology to produce and publish writing (using keyboarding skills) as well as to interact and collaborate with others.

W.3.8 Recall information from experiences or gather information from print and digital sources; take brief notes on sources and sort evidence into provided categories.

W.3.10 Write routinely over extended time frames (time for research, reflection, and revision) and shorter time frames (a single sitting or a day or two) for a range of discipline-specific tasks, purposes, and audiences.

Speaking and Listening Standards

SL.3.1 Effectively engage in a range of collaborative discussions (one-on-one, in groups, and teacher-led) with diverse partners on grade 3 topics and texts, building on others' ideas and clearly expressing their own.

a. Come to discussions prepared, having read or studied required material; explicitly draw on that preparation and other information known about the topic to explore ideas under discussion.

b. Follow agreed-upon rules for discussions (e.g., gaining the floor in respectful ways, listening to others with care, speaking one at a time about the topics and texts under discussion).

c. Ask questions to check understanding of information presented, stay on topic, and link their comments to the remarks of others.

d. Explain their own ideas and understanding in light of the discussion.

SL.3.2 Determine the main ideas and supporting details of a text read aloud or information presented in diverse media and formats, including visually, quantitatively, and orally.

SL.3.3 Ask and answer questions about information from a speaker, offering appropriate elaboration and detail.

SL.3.4 Report on a topic or text, tell a story, or recount an experience with appropriate facts and relevant, descriptive details, speaking clearly at an understandable pace.

SL.3.5 Create engaging audio recordings of stories or poems that demonstrate fluid reading at an understandable pace; add visual displays when appropriate to emphasize or enhance certain facts or details.

SL.3.6 Speak in complete sentences when appropriate to task and situation in order to provide requested detail or clarification.

Language Standards

L.3.2 Demonstrate command of the conventions of standard English grammar and usage when writing or speaking.

a. Explain the function of nouns, pronouns, verbs, adjectives, and adverbs in general and their functions in particular sentences.

b. Form and use regular and irregular plural nouns.

c. Use abstract nouns (e.g., *childhood*).

d. Form and use regular and irregular verbs.

e. Form and use the simple (e.g., *I walk; I walked; I will walk*) verb tenses.

f. Ensure subject–verb and pronoun–antecedent agreement.

g. Form and use comparative and superlative adjectives and adverbs, and choose between them depending on what is to be modified.

h. Use coordinating and subordinating conjunctions.

i. Produce simple, compound, and complex sentences.

L.3.2 Demonstrate command of the conventions of standard English capitalization, punctuation, and spelling when writing.

a. Capitalize appropriate words in titles.

b. Use commas in addresses.

c. Use commas and quotation marks in dialogue.

d. Form and use possessives.

e. Use conventional spelling for high-frequency and other studied words and for adding suffixes to base words (e.g., *sitting, smiled, cries, happiness*).

f. Use spelling patterns and generalizations (e.g., word families, position-based spellings, syllable patterns, ending rules, meaningful word parts) in writing words.

g. Consult reference materials, including beginning dictionaries, as needed to check and correct spellings.

L.3.3 Use knowledge of language and its conventions when writing, speaking, reading, or listening.

a. Choose words and phrases for effect.

b. Recognize and observe differences between the conventions of spoken and written standard English.

L.3.6 Acquire and accurately use grade-appropriate conversational, general academic, and domain-specific words and phrases, including those that signal spatial and temporal relationships (e.g., *After dinner that night we went looking for them*).

Essential Skill Lenses (PARCC Frameworks)

The Partnership for Assessment of Readiness for College and Careers (PARCC) is a coalition of more than 20 states that have come together with "a shared commitment to develop an assessment system aligned to the Common Core State Standards that is anchored in college and career readiness" (www.parcconline.org). As part of its proposal to the U.S. Department of Education, PARCC has developed model content frameworks for English language arts to serve as a bridge between the Common Core State Standards and the PARCC assessments in development at the time of this publication. In the grades 3 to 5 lesson sets, we expect students to engage in reading and writing through eight PARCC specified skill lenses that are rooted in the standards. The following table details how each skill lens is addressed across the lesson set (PARCC, 2011).

	Reading	Writing
Cite Evidence	Students will be asked to cite the text as evidence throughout this lesson set. In particular, students will be using text as evidence to support their ideas about theme, as well as during collaborative group discussions about setting and plot.	Students will be expected to cite specific textual evidence as reasoning to support their statement of opinion. Two to three pieces of textual evidence should be used in their work to support the main arguments.
Analyze Content	In this lesson set, students must carefully analyze books within a series to determine the central theme of the various texts. In addition, students will be asked to make comparisons of setting, plot, and theme across texts to draw conclusions about the series.	In the Define portion of the writing lesson set, students will analyze a shared reading to identify the most compelling portions as well as specific elements of persuasive writing.

	Reading	Writing
Study and Apply Grammar and Usage	Students must demonstrate the ability to convey their ideas clearly, using language that is appropriate to the situation and audience.	Students will analyze their own writing to improve its clarity.
Study and Apply Vocabulary	Students will be asked to use key lines and language from their texts as clues to identify the larger theme of the selected work. In addition, specific learning language is included with this lesson set. Students will be exposed to this terminology and will incorporate terms into their speaking and writing.	In this lesson set, students are expected to choose precise language to strengthen their writing. Students will work in collaborative groups to identify weak language, brainstorm stronger word choices, and make changes to their work accordingly.
Conduct Discussions	Students will work in cooperative Core Crews to study a series of books. Students will hold regular group discussions as well as create a shared presentation. Rules and behaviors that foster productive conversation are a crucial element of this study.	Students will continuously engage in conversations to analyze and improve their own writing throughout this lesson set. In addition, students will work in small groups and will be asked to rely on rich conversations with one another to craft a shared piece of persuasive writing to be presented to the group.
Report Findings	Students will be required not only to share their understandings with their specific small group, but also to report the highlights of these conversations back to the larger group. In particular, Core Crews will be asked to present how a specific theme unfolds across their series, using specific examples from the text to support their thinking.	Students will craft and deliver an oral presentation that expresses their collective opinion of the series studied by the group. Presentations must be reported by the group in an organized manner and include an introduction, clear statement of opinion, two or three supporting reasons with textual evidence, and a strong conclusion.
Phonics and Word Recognition	We recommend that teachers plan opportunities for students to build Reading Foundational Skills by exploring grade-level appropriate skills in the context of the Core Texts from each lesson set and applying this knowledge to their independent reading.	We recommend that teachers encourage students to apply Reading Foundational Skills in the context of their daily writing.
Fluency and Stamina	Through shared reading calendars and sustained reading across a series of books, students will improve their fluency and stamina within a specific genre.	Throughout this series study, students will be asked to write across short and long time frames, crafting quick responses and summaries as well as more lengthy persuasive reviews of books. This combination will support students as they develop their skills to write fluently and with purpose in a variety of situations.

Core Questions

Before delving into your teaching, it is important to consider the Core Questions that drive our work in this lesson set. Reading deeply within a series of books and making connections across a number of texts can be a difficult task for many third graders. Focusing on abstract concepts, such as theme, necessitates careful scaffolding as well as sufficient amounts of guided practice with both grade-level texts and texts at each student's appropriate instructional level. These questions should remain at the core of your teaching. Refer back to them often, encouraging your students to share their thinking as it evolves.

- How does reading in a series differ from reading nonseries books by the same author?
- How does studying a series help us get a deeper understanding of setting, plot, and theme?
- What makes an author's series unique?
- What are some common themes in children's literature?
- What types of series, themes, settings, or plots appeal to you as a reader? Why?

Ready to Get Started?

Reading a number of books from a favorite series is fun but also helps us build stamina as readers. We get stronger and faster when we read books in a series because we get the "trick" of the series. We know the characters and come to feel strongly about them. We see how plot twists are similar from book to book in the series. It is wonderful to share this perspective with your third graders and to support their work as they grow as readers, building their capacity to make connections by having a strong and sturdy foundation of a linked set of books, the series, to rely upon.

Lesson Set Goals

Within this lesson set are many goals we want to help our students reach.

Reading Goals

- Contribute meaningfully to conversations with peers to ensure meeting goals and making meaning. (SL.3.1a–d, SL.3.3, SL.3.6, L.3.1, L.3.6)
- Read at least three books from a chosen series. (RL.3.1, RL.3.4. RL.3.9, RL.3.10)
- Infer the theme, setting, and plot of books from within the chosen series, using explicit examples from the text as the basis for answers. (RL.3.1, RL.3.5, RL.3.9, RL.3.10, SL.3.1a–d, SL.3.6, L.3.1, L.3.6)

- Compare and contrast the setting, plot, and theme of books from within the chosen series, using explicit examples from the text as the basis for answers, to draw conclusions about the series. (RL.3.1, RL.3.5, RL.3.9, RL.3.10, SL.3.1a–d, SL.3.6, L.3.1, L.3.6)
- Craft a succinct summary of the series by focusing on story elements. (RL.3.1, RL.3.5, RL.3.9, RL.3.10, W.3.4, W.3.8, W.3.10, SL.3.2, L.3.6)
- Collaborate with peers to create a visual and oral presentation that examines themes, settings, and plots across the chosen series. (RL.3.1, RL.3.9, RL.3.10, SL.3.1a–d, SL.3.3, SL.3.4, SL.3.6, L.3.1, L.3.6)
- Ask and answer questions to demonstrate understanding of a text, referring explicitly to the text as the basis for the answers. (RL.3.1)
- By the end of the year, independently and proficiently read and comprehend a variety of literature at the high end of the grades 2–3 text complexity band. (RL.3.10)
- Write routinely over extended time frames (time for research, reflection, and revision) and shorter time frames (a single sitting or a day or two) for a range of discipline-specific tasks, purposes, and audiences. (W.3.10)
- In collaborative discussions, demonstrate evidence of preparation for discussion and exhibit responsibility to the rules and roles of conversation. (SL.3.1a, SL.3.1b)
- In collaborative discussions, share and develop ideas in a manner that enhances understanding of a topic. Contribute and respond to the content of the conversation in a productive and focused manner. (SL.3.1c, SL.3.1d)
- Speak in complete sentences when appropriate and demonstrate a command of standard English grammar and usage. (SL.3.6, L.3.1)
- Acquire and accurately use grade-appropriate conversational, general academic, and domain-specific vocabulary and phrases. (L.3.6)

Writing Goals

- Take notes on relevant information to use for gathering supporting details. (RL.3.1, RL.3.10, W.3.4, W.3.8, W.3.10)
- Use textual evidence and details to support opinion statements. (RL.3.1, RL.3.10, SL3.1a–d, SL.3.6, L.3.1, L.3.6)

- Craft a well-organized persuasive piece of writing (book review) about a book series that includes a strong introduction and concluding statement and linking words or phrases. (RL.3.1, RL.3.9, RL.3.10, W.3.1a–d, W.3.4, W.3.5, W.3.10, L.3.6)

- With guidance and support from peers and adults, plan, revise, and edit a story, paying close attention to the conventions of standard English and clarity of the story's development. (W.3.5)

- Prepare and publish a final book review. (W.3.6, W.3.10, SL.3.6, L.3.1, L.3.2, L.3.3)

- Ask and answer questions to demonstrate understanding of a text, referring explicitly to the text as the basis for the answers. (RL.3.1)

- Write an organized opinion piece that includes a clear introduction, point of view, supporting reasons, linking words and phrases, and concluding statement. (W.3.1)

- By the end of the year, independently and proficiently read and comprehend a variety of literature at the high end of the grades 2–3 text complexity band. (RL.3.10)

- Write routinely over extended time frames (time for research, reflection, and revision) and shorter time frames (a single sitting or a day or two) for a range of discipline-specific tasks, purposes, and audiences. (W.3.10)

- In collaborative discussions, demonstrate evidence of preparation for discussion and exhibit responsibility to the rules and roles of conversation. (SL.3.1a, SL.3.1b)

- In collaborative discussions, share and develop ideas in a manner that enhances understanding of a topic. Contribute and respond to the content of the conversation in a productive and focused manner. (SL.3.1c, SL.3.1d)

- Speak in complete sentences when appropriate and demonstrate a command of standard English grammar and usage. (SL.3.6, L.3.1)

- Demonstrate knowledge of standard English and its conventions. (L.3.1, L.3.2, L.3.3)

- Acquire and accurately use grade-appropriate conversational, general academic, and domain-specific vocabulary and phrases. (L.3.6)

Choosing Core Texts

This lesson set uses the Clementine series by Sara Pennypacker. Clementine is an engaging character; she is a third grader who has experiences and adventures that third graders can relate to in significant ways. However, please feel free to choose to use a different series for your shared class reading—one that better reflects your preferences as a reader or the interests and tastes of the students in your class. Begin sharing your class series through read-alouds on the first day of this lesson set, if not earlier, so that you can refer to these texts during your teaching.

To prepare for this lesson set, you will need to gather sets of series books that represent a range of reading levels and genres. Consider several key factors when choosing series, including: the instructional reading level of your students, their varied interests and culturally based experiences, as well as the types of books that get them excited about reading. By this time of the year, you know your students well. Take this lesson set as an opportunity to get to know them even better by asking specific questions about their reading interests, identities, and desires. What do *they* want to read? Is there a series of books that they aspire to read? Allowing students to linger in a series of mysteries, spend time with a funny group of characters, or dig into historical fiction is not just a gift; it will also spark the motivation necessary to improve both reading stamina and fluency.

There is a staggering number of exciting series to introduce to your class during this lesson set. With such a wide variety to choose from, it is highly likely that each of your students will be able to find engaging reading that speaks to their particular interests and reading level. Keeping in mind the broad range of interests held by students of different genders, experiences, and cultures, I suggest the following series to support the work in this lesson set.

- Amber Brown series by Paula Danziger
- A to Z Mystery series by Ron Roy
- Black Lagoon Adventures series by Mike Thaler
- Captain Underpants series by Dav Pilkey
- Chet Gecko mystery series by Bruce Hale
- Clementine series by Sara Pennypacker
- Geronimo Stilton series by Geronimo Stilton
- Ghostville Elementary series by Marcia Thornton Jones

- Judy Moody series by Megan McDonald
- Julian series by Ann Cameron and the Huey series by Ann Cameron (about Julian's younger brother)
- Junie B. Jones series by Barbara Park
- Magic Tree House series by Mary Pope Osborne
- Miami series by Patricia McKissack
- Ruby Lu series by Lenore Look
- Secrets of Droon series by Tony Abbott
- The Littles series by John Lawrence Peterson

You will also want to find persuasive book reviews to use as shared texts throughout this lesson set. Be sure to include a range of reviews, including those written by professional organizations and others crafted by children. Following are several sources you may want to consider when collecting these types of texts to share with your class:

- Amazon (www.amazon.com): Amazon includes reviews by publishing houses and other major organizations as well as reviews posted by individuals.
- Kids Book Review (www.kids-bookreview.com): Click on Reviews in the main navigation bar to find a list of reviewed books.
- Kids Reads (www.kidsreads.com): This website has a collection of online book reviews written for children.
- New York Public Library (http://kids.nypl.org/reviews/books/index.cfm): This website has the On-Lion for Kids reviews section.
- Spaghetti Book Club (www.spaghettibookclub.org): This website is full of reviews written and illustrated by children.

A Note about Addressing Reading Standard 10: Range of Reading and Level of Text Complexity

This lesson set provides all students with opportunities to work with texts deemed appropriate for their grade level as well as texts at their specific reading level. Through shared experiences and focused instruction, all students engage with and comprehend a wide range of texts within their grade-level complexity band. I suggest a variety of high-quality complex texts to use within the whole-group lessons and recommend a variety of additional titles under Choosing Core Texts to extend and enrich instruction. During independent practice and in small-group collaborations, however, research strongly suggests that all students need to work with texts they can read with a high level of accuracy and comprehension (i.e., at their developmentally appropriate reading level) in order to significantly improve their reading (Allington, 2012; Ehri, Dreyer, Flugman, & Gross, 2007). Depending on individual needs and skills, a student's reading level may be above, within, or below his or her grade-level band.

Teacher's Notes

Take a moment to remember what it feels like to get completely lost in a series of amazing books. How you cannot wait to get to the bookstore or library to get the next installment and find out what happens. How you feel the themes addressed in the book resonate with your own life and stick with you long after you have put the book down. Isn't that what we want to instill in our students—that love of reading that makes them long for that reading time to begin? Fostering this sort of passion for books means creating spaces and time for children to get lost in other worlds. It also means providing our students with the skills to make meaning from their reading and construct more sophisticated and nuanced opinions about that reading. In this lesson set, you will get to do just that. By asking your students to work in collaborative groups, you will be able to capitalize on their enthusiasm and give them guidance on the core speaking and listening skills necessary to have rich conversations about their reading. However, this lesson set goes beyond just learning to love and talk about a series. This lesson set will help your students delve more deeply into text by giving them the skills for and guided practice with identifying the themes in their reading. It will also push your students to make meaningful connections across texts within a series.

Core Message to Students

Before the first lesson, use the following as a shared reading or read-aloud to set the stage and engage students in discussion about your upcoming study. See Appendix 3.1 for an enlarged version to reproduce and share with students.

> In this lesson set we are going to be making some new friends! We are going to spend time reading within a series of books. A series is a set of books, written by the same author, that share the same characters and same type of stories. Once you read a few books from a series, you'll start to feel like those characters are old friends. You will be working in teams for this lesson set. I've put each of you into a *Core Crew*. Together you will choose and study a series together. It's going to be your job to get to know everything about your series—the settings, the plots, and the themes you might find—so you can prove to the class that your series is the best, the most interesting, the funniest, or the most important for third graders to read.

Questions for Close Reading

The Core Ready lessons include many rich opportunities to engage students in close reading of text that requires them to ask and answer questions, draw conclusions, and use specific text evidence to support their thinking (Reading Anchor Standard 1). These opportunities are marked with a close reading icon. You may wish to extend these experiences using our recommended Core Texts or with texts of your choosing. Use the following questions as a resource to guide students through close reading experiences in any book series.

- What elements (characters, setting, plot patterns, author's style, etc.) do all of the books in this series have in common?
- What elements (characters, setting, plot patterns, author's style, etc.) differ between books in this series?
- How does(do) the main character(s) change or grow across the series?
- What themes or messages seem to be a part of all of the books in the series?
- Would you recommend this series to others? Why? (Be specific.)

Building Academic Language

On the following page is a list of academic language to introduce to your class. Encourage students to use this language regularly in their conversations. Rather than introduce all the terms at once, slowly add them to a learning wall as your teaching unfolds. See the glossary at the end of this chapter for definitions of these terms.

Recognition

At the end of this lesson set, it is important to recognize the hard work done by your students. Upon completion of the reading lesson set, students will share their thinking about a common theme in their series with other students in the class. Recognition of this accomplishment could take the form of a museum walk, in which the entire class (or several interested classes) walks through the various displays or engages with the multimedia presentations in a manner similar to the museum experience. Each Core Crew could select one member to act as a docent as the class filters through. In the writing lesson set, students will compose an individual book review focused on a text from their chosen series, as well as a collaborative piece of persuasive writing that shares the group's

> " A man only learns in two ways, one by reading, and the other by association with smarter people.
>
> —Will Rogers "

opinion of the entire series. You can recognize this hard work in a number of authentic ways, including:

- Posting individual book reviews or collaborative series reviews in the school library for other students to use

- Posting individual book reviews or collaborative series reviews on a children's book review website

- Inviting the school librarian, principal, or other school staff to hear the oral presentations of the series reviews

Core Words

author's purpose	point of view
chapter	problem/conflict
character	series
key events	setting
opinion	solution/resolution
persuade	summary
plot	theme

Core Phrases

- The character(s)/setting in the series stay(s) the same across the series in the following ways.

- The character(s)/setting in the series change(s) across the series in the following ways.

- The plot/setting/theme/main character in (title) differs from (title) in that _____.

- The books in this series are similar in the following ways.

- One theme that emerges in this book is _____.

- A theme that emerges in both books is _____.

- I have determined the theme to be _____.

- This theme is suggested by (evidence from the character, plot events, etc.) _____.

- The evidence for this theme is _____.

- I think this because _____.

- In the book, it states that _____.

Assessment

Assessment in this lesson set is both ongoing and culminating, meaning that as teachers we are constantly observing how students are making meaning and how they are interpreting new material. Throughout this lesson set, look for performance-based assessments, called Milestone Performance Assessments, each marked with an assessment icon. Milestone Performance Assessments are opportunities to notice and record data on standards-aligned indicators during the course of the lesson set. Use the results of these assessments to determine how well students are progressing toward the goals of the lesson set. Adjust the pace of your teaching and plan instructional support as needed.

I also encourage you to use the Reading and Writing Rubrics, also marked with an assessment icon, with each lesson set to evaluate overall student performance on the standards-aligned lesson set goals. In this lesson set, the series book reviews crafted by individual students are an important summative assessment piece that can be analyzed and placed in a portfolio of student work.

In addition, we have provided a speaking and listening checklist (see Appendix 3.10) that provides observable Core Standards–aligned indicators to assess student performance as speakers and listeners. Every Core Ready lesson set offers multiple opportunities to make such observations. Use the checklist in its entirety to gather performance data over time or choose appropriate indicators to create a customized checklist to match a specific learning experience.

Core Support for Diverse Learners

This lesson set was created with the needs of a wide variety of learners in mind. Throughout the day-by-day lessons, you will find examples of visual supports, graphic organizers, highlighted speaking and listening opportunities, and research-driven English language learner supports aimed at scaffolding instruction for all learners. Also, I urge you to consider the areas of challenge with which your students may need guided support. The following sections spotlight important considerations as you move through the lesson sets.

Reading

Choosing texts that are at students' reading levels is essential for their reading success and reading identity. When finding texts, make sure you have various levels represented in your classroom reading collection. Your students or some of your students may benefit from repeated exposure to a lesson's teaching objective over several days. This can be accomplished with the whole class or in small-group settings. In addition, try to incorporate series that appeal to a wide range of student interests—series that excite boys, series that engage girls, series for sports lovers, series for history buffs, series for students who like reading about characters who have experiences similar to their own. Igniting the spark that motivates children to increase their reading stamina and think more deeply about their texts often comes from finding the right book.

Closely monitor your students who are reading below grade level to determine whether they are reading with accuracy and fluency to support comprehension. Encourage students to use context to confirm or self-correct word recognition and understanding and to reread when necessary. Refer to the Common Core Foundational Skills Standards—at both the grade 3 level as well as kindergarten, grade 1, and grade 2 standards—for direct, explicit foundational skills support that your students reading below grade level may need.

Many of the series used in your class will be in chapter book format. Chapter books are layered with multisyllabic words and lengthier sentences that will require teacher support to decode and understand. Refer to our Core Words guide for vocabulary that you may want to frontload with small groups of students. Be cognizant of any unfamiliar or series-specific language embedded within the selections of series you choose for both whole-class teaching as well as independent reading, and preview the texts you provide to students reading below grade level.

As you continue your work with students, use observational notes and reading assessment data to create two to three specific short-term goals for your students with diverse needs. For example, as stated previously, these goals may be related to increasing word accuracy, building vocabulary, improving fluency, or enhancing comprehension. Throughout this lesson set, tailor your individualized and small-group instruction set so that it addresses and evaluates student progress toward these goals.

Writing

Inspired writers are motivated writers. Allowing students to choose the topic of their writing is critical for their ultimate success and their positive development of identity as writers. When immersing your students in a new genre, form, or purpose for writing, be sure to emphasize the meaning and function this particular type of writing may have in their own lives. Many of your students will also benefit from exposure to strong mentor texts and examples of your own writing as well as the experience of sharing their own work—both the final product and writing in process.

Many of your students will benefit significantly from the opportunity to sketch their book or series reviews before adding text. For example, some students will require extra support in writing to move from drawing to writing or to move from story mapping to writing sentences. You can also provide additional scaffolding by having students draw out and organize the various components of their book review. This is especially helpful for visual learners and students who need to "sketch to stretch." Even your most proficient writers can benefit from this step, but many of your resistant writers will feel more comfortable with getting their ideas on paper through drawing first. Some students may have difficulty writing in this persuasive genre, particularly if this is a new genre for them. Specifically, many may struggle with using precise and powerful language. Therefore, activities such as word brainstorms and the use of learning walls become essential.

As your students move from determining their ideas for their book and series reviews to composing their persuasive pieces, provide them a variety of paper choices that are third-grade appropriate. For students with fine motor control issues, providing a variety of paper choices that have handwriting lines with a dotted line in the middle can offer support as letter formation may require significant energy for some writers. Also consider having some students type and electronically publish their reviews rather than handwrite them if that is a medium more conducive to their writing success.

We want our third graders to share their reviews with an audience, and supporting them as developing writers is essential. In addition to providing students with topic choice and the opportunity to draw before writing, we can provide further scaffolding by having students orally rehearse their opinion statements and reasoning to us or to a peer. For some students, the oral rehearsal will provide a springboard to writing. Others will have greater success dictating their reviews to you.

As with the reading lessons, your students may benefit from multiple exposures to a single lesson's teaching objective. This can be done with the whole class or in small-group settings.

English Language Learners

Although it is always our goal as teachers to get to know all of our students deeply both in and out of the classroom setting, this work is perhaps more critical when considering our English language learners. Honoring families' cultural traditions and experiences is important for getting to know and working with your students in meaningful ways.

English language learners are learning about persuasive writing alongside native English speakers in your classroom, but they are also simultaneously learning English. For our English language learners, it is essential to simultaneously develop their ability to easily hold conversations about their reading and writing and build their academic language base. Goldenberg (2008) defines "academic English" as the more abstract, complex, and challenging language that permits us to participate successfully in mainstream classroom instruction. English language learners will over time be responsible for understanding and producing academic English both orally and in writing. However, language acquisition is a process, and our English language learners range in their development of English language acquisition. I urge you to consider your students along a spectrum of language acquisition from students new to this country to those who are proficient conversationally to those who have native-like proficiency.

Refer to the English language learner icons throughout this lesson set for ways to shelter instruction for English language learners. These elements will help English language learners participate successfully in the whole-group lesson and support the development of their language skills. Although these moments during instruction are designed to support English language learners, many schools are adding a separate English language development (ELD) block targeted at oral English language development to further support their students in language acquisition.

Students with growing English proficiency will benefit from a persuasive word wall, which will build vocabulary (refer to the Core Words and Phrases). A sentence word wall that gives them sentence starters to help with conversation will also offer students another layer of support. Some English language learners may benefit from having their own personalized copies of these words to keep in their reading or writing notebooks for quick reference. Visual aids will further support students and guide them on words that are important to this study and what they mean.

Some students will benefit from spending several days on the same teaching objective. You may consider gathering small groups of readers or writers for repeated instruction or using one-on-one conferences as an opportunity to revisit teaching objectives.

Complementary Core Methods

Read-Aloud

Choose a book series for your class to study that you believe will resonate with and excite the largest number of students possible. By mirroring the work of this lesson set during your ritual read-aloud, you provide students with an additional opportunity to practice the more abstract skills, such as determining the theme of a book or series. During your read-aloud, give students the chance to practice the following:

- Identifying the setting and plot (problem, key events, and solution)
- Inferring the theme of the book
- Making connections across texts in the same series by comparing and contrasting the setting, plot, and/or theme
- Stating an opinion about a text in the series, supporting that opinion with evidence from the text

Shared Reading

Finding short texts to share for this lesson set should be a breeze! Shared reading in this lesson set can focus on supporting the work done during the writing portion of this lesson set. Including a variety of reviews about books from the series you are studying as a class will provide students with a group of mentor texts for their own writing work. Be sure to include reviews written by children as well as those written in more formal ways, such as those found on book jackets or on Amazon.

Shared Writing

Shared writing can take on a number of topics during this lesson set. Early in your work, you may want to include shared writing that feels more like a quick-write. For example, lead the class in shared quick-writes focused on the theme of a shared read-aloud. You can also model and practice writing reviews of the books included in the series you are studying as a class.

Core Connections at Home

Use this lesson set as an opportunity to highlight the importance of reading together at home. Send home a list of potential series for students to explore with their families. Create a brief packet of conversation prompts and quick-write ideas to guide parents in their work with their children.

Reading Lessons

The Core I.D.E.A. / Daily Reading Instruction at a Glance table highlights the teaching objectives and standards alignment for all 10 lessons across the four stages of the lesson set (Introduce, Define, Extend, and Assess). It also indicates which lessons contain special features to support ELLs, technology, speaking and listening, and formative (Milestone) assessments.

The following Core Ready Reading Rubric is designed to help you record each student's overall understanding across four levels of achievement as it relates to the lesson set goals. I recommend that you use this rubric at the end of the lesson set as a performance-based assessment tool. Use the Milestone Performance Assessments and checklists as tools to help you gauge student progress toward these goals, reteach, and differentiate as needed. See the foundational book, *Be Core Ready: Powerful, Effective Steps to Implementing and Achieving Common Core State Standards*, for more information about the Core Ready Reading and Writing Rubrics.

The Core I.D.E.A. / Daily Reading Instruction at a Glance

	Grade 3	The Reader and Writer's Opinion: A Collaborative Author Study		

Instructional Stage	Lesson	Teaching Objective	Core Standards	Special Features
Introduce: notice, explore, collect, note, immerse, surround, record, share	1	Collaborative groups have rules and behaviors that help them to run smoothly and be productive.	SL.3.1a–d • SL.3.6 • L.3.1 • L.3.6	ELL Tech S&L
	2	Productive conversations use a series of strategies to stay focused.	RL.3.1 • RL.3.10 • SL.3.1a–d • SL.3.3 • SL.3.6 • L.3.1 • L.3.6	Close Reading ELL S&L
Define: name, identify, outline, clarify, select, plan	3	Collaborative groups set clear goals for their work.	RL.3.1 • RL.3.10 • SL.3.1a–d • SL.3.6 • L.3.1 • L.3.6	Close Reading ELL
	4	Readers can craft succinct summaries of their reading by focusing on story elements.	RL.3.1 • RL.3.5 • RL.3.9 • RL.3.10 • W.3.4 • W.3.10 • SL.3.1a–d • SL.3.2 SL.3.6 • L.3.1 • L.3.6	Close Reading ELL Milestone Assessment
Extend: try, experiment, attempt, approximate, practice, explain, revise, refine	5	Readers can identify the theme(s) of their reading by using a variety of clues to help them.	RI.3.10 • RL.3.1 • RL.3.5 • RL.3.9 • SL.3.1a–d • SL.3.2 • SL.3.4 • SL.3.6 L.3.1 • L.3.6	Close Reading ELL S&L
	6	Readers use explicit examples from the text as evidence to support their thinking about the theme(s) of their books.	RL.3.1 • RL.3.5 • RL.3.9 • RL.3.10 W.3.4 • W.3.10 • SL.3.1a–d • SL.3.6 L.3.1 • L.3.6	Close Reading ELL Milestone Assessment
	7	Readers think deeply about an author's work by comparing the setting, plot, and theme across several books.	RL.3.1 • RL.3.5 • RL.3.9 • RL.3.10 W.3.4 • W.3.10 • SL.3.1a–d • SL.3.6 L.3.1 • L.3.6	Close Reading ELL Milestone Assessment
	8	Readers find out more about the author to make deeper connections to their books.	RL.3.1 • RL.3.9 • RL.3.10 • W.3.4 W.3.8 • W.3.10 • SL.3.1a–d • SL.3.6 L.3.1 • L.3.6	Close Reading Tech ELL
	9	Readers share their ideas with others.	RL.3.1 • RL.3.5 • RL.3.9 • RL.3.10 W.3.4 • W.3.8 • W.3.10 • SL.3.1a–d SL.3.3 • SL.3.4 • SL.3.6 • L.3.1 L.3.6	Close Reading Milestone Assessment ELL S&L Tech
Assess: reflect, conclude, connect, share, recognize, respond	10	Readers reflect on the Core Questions and make plans for their future reading.	RL.3.10 • RL.3.9 • W.3.4 • W.3.10	

 Core Ready Reading Rubric

Lesson Set Goal	Emerging	Approaching	Achieving	Exceeding	Standards Alignment
Contribute meaningfully to conversations with peers to ensure meeting goals and making meaning.	Student shows little or no evidence of contributing meaningfully to conversations with peers.	Student attempts to contribute meaningfully to conversations with peers to ensure they are meeting goals and making meaning. May struggle with some components such as setting goals or applying strategies to get conversations unstuck.	Student contributes meaningfully to conversations with peers to ensure they are meeting goals and making meaning. Successfully applies several strategies to get conversations unstuck or to meet goals.	Student shows an advanced ability to contribute meaningfully to conversations with peers to ensure they are meeting goals and making meaning. Student applies multiple strategies to ensure that the group sets and meets goals and finds ways to get conversations unstuck.	SL.3.1a–d SL.3.3 SL.3.6 L.3.1 L.3.6
Read at least three books from a chosen series.	Student makes little or no attempt to complete the three books from the series, even with significant prompting.	Student reads fewer than three books in the series or needs significant prompting to complete reading.	Student reads three books from a chosen series with little or no prompting.	Student reads more than three books from a chosen series thoroughly and independently.	RL.3.1 RL.3.4 RL.3.9 RL.3.10
Infer the theme, setting, and plot of books from within the chosen series, using explicit examples from the text as the basis for answers.	Student may be beginning to demonstrate understanding of how to identify the theme, setting, and plot in a book but requires significant support to be successful.	Student attempts to infer the theme, setting, and plot of books from within their chosen series. May have some inaccuracies or lack examples from their text.	Student infers the theme, setting, and plot of books within the chosen series. Uses examples from the text to support his or her thinking. Some components may be better developed than others.	Student consistently infers the theme, setting, and plot of books within the chosen series. Uses detailed and thoughtful examples from the text as the basis for his or her answers.	RL.3.1 RL.3.5 RL.3.9 RL.3.10 SL.3.1a–d SL.3.6 L.3.1 L.3.6
Compare and contrast the setting, plot, and theme of books from within the chosen series, using explicit examples from the text as the basis for answers in order to draw conclusions about their series.	Student may be beginning to demonstrate understanding of how to identify the theme, setting, and plot in a book but requires significant support to be successful with comparing and contrasting across series.	Student compares and contrasts the theme, setting, and plot of books from within the chosen series with limited success. May lack sufficient examples from the text.	Student compares the theme, setting, and plot of multiple books within the chosen series. Provides examples from the text to support his or her thinking. Some components may be better developed than others.	Student consistently compares the theme, setting, and plot of books from within the chosen series and uses detailed and thoughtful examples from the text as the basis for his or her answers.	RL.3.1 RL.3.5 RL.3.9 RL.3.10 SL.3.1a–d SL.3.6 L.3.1 L.3.6
Craft a succinct summary of the series by focusing on story elements.	Student shows little or no evidence of successfully crafting a summary of the chosen series.	Student attempts to craft a summary of the series by focusing on the story elements. The summary may not be succinct or may have gaps.	Student crafts a succinct summary of the series by focusing on the story elements and including only the important information.	Student crafts a well-developed, succinct, and informative summary of the series by focusing on all the story elements.	RL.3.1 RL.3.5 RL.3.9 RL.3.10 W.3.4 W.3.8 W.3.10 SL.3.2 L.3.6
Collaborate with peers to create a visual and oral presentation that examines themes, settings, and plots across the chosen series.	Student struggles to create a visual and oral presentation that examines themes, settings, and plots across the chosen series. Presentation may lack visuals or be unclear or inaccurate.	Student creates, with limited success, a visual and oral presentation that examines themes, settings, and plots across the chosen series. Some components of the presentation may be more effective and well developed than others.	Student successfully creates a visual and oral presentation that examines themes, settings, and plots across the chosen series. Presentation is clear and accurate. Visuals are effective.	Student creates a thoughtful and well-organized visual and oral presentation that examines themes, settings, and plots across the chosen series. All aspects are thoroughly delivered and highly effective.	RL.3.1 RL.3.9 RL.3.10 SL.3.1a–d SL.3.3 SL.3.4 SL.3.6 L.3.1 L.3.6

Lesson Set Goal	Emerging	Approaching	Achieving	Exceeding	Standards Alignment
Ask and answer questions to demonstrate understanding of a text, referring explicitly to the text as the basis for the answers.	Student shows little or no evidence of actively and purposefully reading or searching the text for specific information and evidence. Student makes little or no attempt to ask or answer questions about the text.	Student attempts to actively and purposefully read or search the text for specific information and evidence. Student may be able to ask or answer some questions about the text, but may not provide explicit references to the text as a basis for the answer.	Student shows solid evidence of actively and purposefully reading or searching the text for specific information and evidence. Student consistently provides appropriate textual evidence to support his or her thinking.	Student demonstrates an exceptional ability to actively and purposefully read or search the text for specific information and evidence. Student provides accurate, explicit, and thoughtful textual references to support his or her thinking.	RL.3.1
By the end of the year, independently and proficiently read and comprehend literature, including stories, dramas, and poetry, at the high end of the grades 2–3 text complexity band.	Student shows little or no evidence of reading and comprehending a complex text appropriate for the grade 3 text complexity band at this point in the school year.	Student shows inconsistent evidence of independently and proficiently reading and comprehending complex texts appropriate for the grade 3 text complexity band at this point in the school year.	Student shows solid evidence of independently and proficiently reading and comprehending complex texts appropriate for the grade 3 text complexity band at this point of the school year.	Student shows solid evidence of independently and proficiently reading and comprehending complex texts above the grade 3 text complexity band at this point of the school year.	RL.3.10
Write routinely over extended time frames (time for research, reflection, and revision) and shorter time frames (a single sitting or a day or two) for a range of discipline-specific tasks, purposes, and audiences.	Student shows little or no evidence of writing routinely for short or long time frames for a range of discipline-specific tasks, purposes, and audiences.	Student shows some evidence of engaging routinely in writing for short and long time frames for a range of discipline-specific tasks, purposes, and audiences.	Student shows some evidence of writing routinely for short and long time frames for a range of discipline-specific tasks, purposes, and audiences.	Student shows exceptional evidence of consistently and accurately writing for short and long time frames for a range of discipline-specific tasks, purposes, and audiences.	W.3.10
In collaborative discussions, demonstrate evidence of preparation for discussion and exhibit responsibility to the rules and roles of conversation.	In collaborative discussions, student comes unprepared and often disregards the rules and roles of conversation.	In collaborative discussions, student's preparation may be evident but ineffective or inconsistent. May occasionally disregard the rules and roles of conversation.	In collaborative discussions, student prepares adequately and draws on the preparation and other information about the topic to explore ideas under discussion. Usually observes the rules and roles of conversation.	In collaborative discussions, student arrives extremely well prepared for discussions and draws on the preparation and other information about the topic to explore ideas under discussion. Always observes the rules and roles of conversation.	SL.3.1a SL.3.1b
In collaborative discussions, share and develop ideas in a manner that enhances understanding of the topic. Contribute and respond to the content of the conversation in a productive and focused manner.	Student shows little or no evidence of engaging in collaborative discussions and makes little or no attempt to ask and answer questions, stay on topic, link comments to the remarks of others, or explain his or her own ideas and understanding in light of the discussion.	Student shows some evidence of engaging in collaborative discussions and, with marginal success, attempts to ask questions to check understanding of information presented, stay on topic, link comments to the remarks of others, and explain his or her own ideas and understanding in light of the discussion.	Student engages in a range of collaborative discussions and asks questions to check understanding of information presented. Stays on topic most of the time and frequently links his or her own ideas and understanding in light of the discussion.	Student effectively and consistently engages in a range of collaborative discussions and asks high-level questions to check understanding of information presented. Always stays on topic and, with great insight and attention to the comments of others, links his or her own ideas and understanding in light of the discussion.	SL.3.1c SL.3.1d
Speak in complete sentences when appropriate and demonstrate a command of standard English grammar and usage.	Student shows little or no evidence of attempting to speak in complete sentences. Student demonstrates little or no command of standard English grammar and usage.	Student attempts to speak in complete sentences when appropriate and demonstrates some command of standard English grammar and usage.	Student speaks in complete sentences when appropriate and demonstrates a command of standard English grammar and usage.	Student always speaks in complete sentences when appropriate and demonstrates an extraordinary command of the conventions of standard English grammar and usage.	SL.3.6 L.3.1
Acquire and accurately use grade-appropriate conversational, general academic, and domain-specific vocabulary and phrases.	Student shows little or no evidence of the acquisition and use of grade-appropriate conversational and academic language.	Student shows some evidence of the acquisition and use of grade-appropriate conversational and academic language.	Student shows solid evidence of the acquisition and use of grade-appropriate conversational and academic language.	Student shows a high level of sophistication and precision when using grade-appropriate conversational and academic language.	L.3.6

Note: See the Core Ready Rubrics chart in the Welcome at the beginning of the book for descriptions of category headers.

Reading Lesson 1 . . . .

▼ Teaching Objective

Collaborative groups have rules and behaviors that help them run smoothly and be productive.

▼ Standards Alignment

SL.3.1a–d, SL.3.6, L.3.1, L.3.6

▼ Materials

- Collections of series books organized to match the independent reading levels or needs of each Core Crew
- Chart paper or interactive whiteboard

▼ To the Teacher

Today you will set the stage for your readers to work collaboratively to study a series of books that interests them and is at their appropriate reading level. Students will be working in groups, referred to here as *Core Crews*, each of which will be studying a series of their choice. However, I recommend dividing your class into Core Crews before beginning this lesson set, grouping children by similar reading levels. The crew does not have to be limited to students at a single reading level; rather, you can create groups of students in a similar *band* (for example, students reading independently at Fountas and Pinnell's levels M and N might be grouped together) to help ensure that all students will be able to successfully engage with a text (Fountas & Pinnell, 1997). Although students are not able to choose their groups, choice is still an important aspect of this lesson set. Provide Core Crews with several choices for book series at their appropriate level. See the table in the Practice segment of the lesson plan for high- and low-tech options for this.

In addition to focusing on the skills necessary to read across a series of books by the same author, this lesson set is driven by the productive conversations of your students. However, as we all know, engaging in effective conversation can be difficult and takes practice—especially in third grade! Concepts such as staying on topic, listening with care, speaking one at a time, and communicating clearly may be new ideas that present challenges to some of our students, regardless of their reading levels. This lesson provides the perfect opportunity to explicitly highlight and practice these essential speaking and listening skills that are a hallmark of a true Core Ready classroom.

▼ Procedure

Warm Up Gather the class to set the stage for today's learning Begin by sharing a favorite author with the class.

> Have you ever loved an author so much that you couldn't wait for his or her newest book to come out? I have a favorite author named _____. Whenever she comes out with a new book, I run to the library to pick it up. Anytime a friend asks me for a suggestion for a good book to read she is always one of the first authors I think about.

Now take a moment to set a purpose for students' work. Here is one way your introduction could unfold, but you will want to make sure to be more specific about the final product (the choices for which are described previously in the "To the Teacher" section of this lesson) you've chosen for your class to pursue:

> Third graders, today we are going to start an exciting study of our favorite authors and series! We're going to divide up into groups, called Core Crews, and do all our reading and thinking together for the next few weeks. Sharing what we read makes reading feel more powerful. Each crew is going to study a different series. At the end of our series study, each Core Crew will present their thinking and try to convince the rest of the class to run out and read their series. Are you ready to think deeply about your series and use your powers of argument to encourage others to get into your series too?

Teach Model what students need to learn and do

> You all are going to be working together for the next few weeks, so I want to make sure you stay excited and work together respectfully. Let's put our heads together and come up with some rules and behaviors that might help your crews run more smoothly.

As the class watches, title your chart "Core Crew Rules and Behaviors." Strategically creating a chart *with* students helps to ensure that students will own, understand, and use what you record.

> Okay. Let me take a second to imagine the last lovely conversation I had to help me think of what might go on this chart. I've got it. What often makes conversations feel strong for me is when my partner sits attentively and calmly with me. We are not busy doing other things. We can concentrate on each other. Let me add these things to our chart.

Add "sitting calmly and attentively" to the chart. Ask children to discuss and model what sitting calmly looks like. If you would like to take your chart one step further, photograph students as they model these behaviors and add the photos to the chart as visuals. **ELL** Provide Comprehensible Input—Models and Visuals. Visuals offer a pathway to understanding the chart without relying only on the words. If you are not able to take pictures, include hand-drawn pictures or clip art to illustrate the chart.

Some behaviors to include on your chart as the lesson set unfolds include:

- Sit calmly and attentively (show you care).
- Face your partner, knee to knee if sitting on the floor, or if you are side by side at a computer, elbow to elbow . . .
- Listen actively.
- Avoid interrupting where possible.
- Stay on topic.
- Respond to what others say before shifting the conversation.
- Affirm what others say with a thumbs up if you appreciate what they said.
- Come prepared to all discussions.
- If you have prepared written notes, use them to help the conversation.

Try Guide students to quickly rehearse what they need to learn and do in preparation for practice

Now solicit some help from the class. Ask students to picture the last great conversation they had with someone. Was it with their parent? A friend? Another teacher? Students can signal with a quiet thumbs up when they've got that conversation in their head. Once everyone is ready, direct the

group to think about what made that conversation so great: "Does that give anyone an idea about something you need to add to your chart to help your crews have productive conversations?" "What was one thing your listening partner did that helped you have the desire to continue?"

As students share their thinking, add relevant rules or behaviors to your chart in language that is clear and simple for your students to understand. Continue to have students model behaviors for the group and, if you choose, photograph their examples. (SL.3.1b, SL.3.1c)

Clarify Briefly restate today's teaching objective and explain the practice task(s)

Review the rules and behaviors you have charted today.

> We've listed a group of rules and behaviors that are going to help your Core Crews run smoothly and get a lot of exciting work done. These rules and behaviors will be something we continue to think about as our series study unfolds. Today, you are going to choose a series to study together. As you look at your options and begin to make your decision, practice the rules and behaviors we discussed today. At the end of your group time, I'll want to know what series you chose to study and I'll also want each group to reflect on how the conversation went.

Practice Students work independently or in small groups to apply today's teaching objective

Groups preview series options to study. (Note: In advance, select two or three series that represent appropriate reading levels and a range of genres for each group to select from. Place these series in a basket or tub for ease of student use.)

Goal	Low-Tech	High-Tech
Students preview book series.	Students flip through books in the series from which they can choose. The groups use prior knowledge, covers, titles, and jacket blurbs to get a sense of the series and make their decision.	Students view book trailers for various books within a variety of series. Students spend time looking through reviews of the series posted online as well as visit author websites.

As Core Crews are discussing their decision, circulate and listen for groups that are and are not following the rules and behaviors you discussed at the beginning of this lesson. Jot down a few key moments to share and discuss with the larger group. You will want to listen for moments in which Core Crews were following the charted behaviors beautifully, moments in which members of the group reminded one another of a particular rule or behavior. You can interrupt the groups briefly by saying: "I just want to call your attention to this Core Crew. I am noticing how kindly they are listening to one another, and how thoughtfully they are participating." It will be a boost for all to hear you say what you think is working well. These positive affirmations will go a long way.

Wrap Up Check understanding as you guide students to briefly share what they have learned and produced today

At the end of your reading block, bring students back together to share some of the highlights of the conversations you overheard. Restate the importance of effective speaking and listening during this lesson set. Have students reflect on their conversations by asking questions such as: What went well during your conversation? What rules did you find easy to follow? What rules felt harder to follow? Why do you think that is? You may choose to conclude your work by asking students to sign the Core Crews Rules and Behaviors chart, turning it into more of a contract than a simple chart. Working with your class (giving you another chance to model these behaviors), discuss and choose a location to display this chart so that students can easily refer to it during their reading work.

Reading Lesson 2

▼ Teaching Objective

Productive conversations use a series of strategies to stay focused.

Close Reading
Opportunity

▼ Standards Alignment

RL.3.1, RL.3.10, SL.3.1a–d, SL.3.3, SL.3.6, L.3.1, L.3.6

▼ Materials

- Core Crews Rules and Behaviors chart (created in Reading Lesson 1)
- Chart paper or interactive whiteboard
- Conversation Helpers (see the following section)

▼ To the Teacher

Before this lesson, generate a list of conversation stems or questions that students can rely on when their discussion gets stuck. Some ideas to include are:

- What did you mean by that?
- Can you say more about . . . ?

- What do you think about . . . ?
- Let's take a look at this part. . . .
- I have something to add to what you just said. . . .

When brainstorming other ideas for stems and questions, think about what will help students in *any* conversation, not just this particular conversation about a series. **ELL** Identify and Communicate Content and Language Objectives—Academic Vocabulary, Provide Comprehensible Input—Audiovisual Aids. These supports will be necessary for your beginning to intermediate English language learners to aid them in their group discussions. When you are forming the groups, consider members who may speak an ELL's home language so that, if needed, the group discussion could be in English and the home language. This lesson is an opportunity to highlight several essential speaking and listening skills that are critical to holding a productive conversation. These skills include, but are certainly not limited to, asking questions to check for understanding, linking comments, and explaining ideas clearly. (SL.3.1c, SL.3.1d)

Print your stems or questions neatly in word bubbles or print them out on heavy paper. Glue them to Popsicle sticks to create Conversation Helpers. Make one set of Conversation Helpers for each of your Core Crews. You may also choose to list Conversation Helpers as items on a small reference chart for Core Crews to take back to their meeting area.

Finally, think back to the conversations you overheard during Reading Lesson 1. Were there any moments of discord? Any moments when the conversation went off track? While you won't want to embarrass a group, you will want to bring up these examples anonymously as fodder for class discussion in today's lesson.

> " *There is zero correlation between having the gift of gab and having the best ideas.*
>
> —Susan Cain "

▼ Procedure

Warm Up Gather the class to set the stage for today's learning

It's normal for conversations to get stuck every once in awhile. The trick is noticing when your conversation is stuck and knowing what to do about it.

Yesterday, we thought about some rules and behaviors to help our conversations run smoothly. But even if you follow all the rules perfectly, your conversation can still get stuck. Today, I want to share with you some Conversation Helpers that can help you get unstuck when you are working with your group.

Teach Model what students need to learn and do

Introduce the Conversation Helpers. Take time to read each one to the class and talk about how it might be used. Following is one way your conversation could unfold.

This Conversation Helper says, "What did you mean by that?" Let's think about when we might need to use this helper. Have you ever been talking to someone who is super excited about an idea? They're so excited that they start talking really fast and sometimes their words sound jumbled up? Then, when they finish talking, they look at you to say something back and you realize that you have no idea what they were talking about? Maybe they were talking too fast, or maybe they weren't very clear. It doesn't matter. But their idea does matter. That's the perfect time to ask them: "What did you mean by that?" or "Can you say more about a specific part of that point?" to see if they can better explain their idea to you and how you can help them clarify it.

Explain that one of the tricks for using these Conversation Helpers well is knowing which Helper to use and when. Practice choosing the right Conversation Helper. List a few ways that your conversations might get stuck. Begin a basic T-chart like the following. Use the left side of the chart to record the ways a conversation might get stuck. Use the right side of the chart to record the Conversation Helper the class decides will be the most helpful. **ELL** Provide Comprehensible Input—Organizers. The sentence structures offered are a strong support for your ELLs. You can practice how to say the prompts beforehand so that ELLs feel comfortable taking part in the conversation.

Ways Conversations Can Get Stuck

Ways a conversation might get stuck:	Conversation Helper:

Following are some situations you will want to describe to your class, and the related Conversation Helpers:

- When someone shares an idea that you don't understand: "Can you say more about that?" and "What did you mean by that?"

- When the conversation just stops: "What did you think about . . . ?" and "Let's take a closer look at . . ."

- When the conversation goes off topic: "Let's stick to talking about . . ." or "How can what you are saying help us discover a new idea about our big topic?"

- Someone shares something that gives you a great idea: "I want to add to that . . . " and "What you said makes me think about . . . "

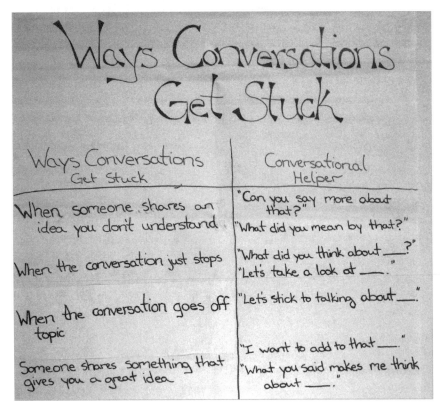

Ways Conversations Get Stuck

Ways Conversations Get Stuck	Conversational Helper
When someone shares an idea you don't understand	"Can you say more about that?" "What did you mean by that?"
When the conversation just stops	"What did you think about ____?" "Let's take a look at ____."
When the conversation goes off topic	"Let's stick to talking about ____."
Someone shares something that gives you a great idea	"I want to add to that ____." "What you said makes me think about ____."

reminded you of, and now it's hard to get the conversation back on track. Ask your students to do the same in pairs. Have one try to talk about a text, and have the other take it off track with a more personal connection. Then ask: "What's going to be hard in this conversation? Which Conversation Helper would be the most helpful?" This "Try" can be just two or three minutes in length, but it will feel powerful to have your students try a Helper and see how empowering it is to use language to redirect conversation when necessary.

Clarify Briefly restate today's teaching objective and explain the practice task(s)

Briefly review the conversation strategies and rationale for using them. Send your Core Crews to continue reading texts within the series they have chosen to study. Remind them to use the Conversation Helpers when they are discussing their reading as a group (and to add new ones if they create them.)

Practice Students work independently or in small groups to apply today's teaching objective

Allow students solid time to read. Capitalize on students' enthusiasm and give them ample opportunities to read for extensive periods of time, thereby building their reading stamina. Then, ask your Core Crews to discuss their thinking about the series thus far. Remind them to use their Conversation Helpers if any conversations get stuck.

Wrap Up Check understanding as you guide students to briefly share what they have learned and produced today

Gather students together and encourage them to reflect on their conversations and share examples of how the strategy Helpers supported them today.

Try Guide students to quickly rehearse what they need to learn and do in preparation for practice

Now it is time for students to try using Conversation Helpers. Have one student model this with you. Demonstrate how your student is trying to talk about the text, but you start talking about something personal the text

Reading Lesson 3

▼ Teaching Objective

Collaborative groups set clear goals for their work.

▼ Standards Alignment

RL.3.1, RL.3.10, SL.3.1a–d, SL.3.6, L.3.1, L.3.6

Close Reading Opportunity

▼ Materials

- Blank calendar pages for the month in which the study will take place

▼ Procedure

Warm Up Gather the class to set the stage for today's learning

Students, I am excited about the series you've chosen. I loved some of the conversations I overheard you having yesterday. I want to share some positive things I noticed as I saw you practice using the Conversation Helpers.

Remind students of the chart contents and its placement within the classroom.

Teach Model what students need to learn and do

Today you are going to teach your students how to create a reading plan. It is not necessary for each student in the group to read every book within the series. However, it is beneficial for the group to read as many books as they reasonably can complete and for some of the books to be read by multiple members of the group to enhance the conversation.

Today we are going to set goals for our reading. Make sure that you all read more than one book in the series. You will also want to make sure that some books are read by more than one member of the group. We're going to use these blank calendars to make our reading goals public. Watch me as I use the blank calendar page to set some goals for our reading of the Clementine series.

Using a blank calendar page, model how to calculate the number of pages you can read each day. Consider the amount of time you have to read each day, as well as how many pages you are usually able to read during that amount of time, making goals that push your stamina forward.

This is tricky work! I don't want to put down too many pages and fall short of my goals, but I also don't want to put down too few pages and not challenge myself. I need to come up with a number that is just right for me.

Once you've established a number of pages that is reasonable to read each day, model figuring out how many days it will take you to finish one book. Will you have time to read another book? The accompanying photo shows an example of what your calendar page might look like.

Try Guide students to quickly rehearse what they need to learn and do in preparation for practice

Ask your students to consider how many pages they can read each day. Remind them that they both need to do what feels comfortable but also push forward and build their stamina.

When students feel that they are ready with a number of goals, make sure they check in with you before beginning to work on setting individual goals for their reading work in this lesson set. Students should set their own goals independently before sharing their plans with their Core Crew.

Clarify Briefly restate today's teaching objective and explain the practice task(s)

As you set your goals today, remember to think about how many pages you think you can read each day, giving yourself a push to go even further where you can. Choose the specific books you'll want to read in the series. When you're done, share your plan with the rest of your crew.

Practice Students work independently or in small groups to apply today's teaching objective

Students set reading goals independently using a calendar page. Students will share their goals with their Core Crew. Students should then continue reading independently within their series.

 As students work to set their personal reading goals, circulate and confer with individual students. Guide them toward making smart choices about these goals; we don't want students to set the bar too high or too low. With the strongest possible positive encouragement, they can go a long way. **ELL** Enable Language Production—Reading and Writing. Goal setting with your Beginner and Intermediate ELLs will be important so that they can have a plan, and you can ensure that they are reading successfully. Offering them choices for check-in and time to clarify reading in their plan will help them work independently and understand how to advocate for help.

Wrap Up Check understanding as you guide students to briefly share what they have learned and produced today

Walk around and check in with each Core Crew individually to determine the status of their goal setting. Some questions to consider: Did the group encounter any problems? Are individual and group goals reasonable yet rigorous? Is the group set to read enough books within the series?

> " *What would you attempt to do if you knew you would not fail?*
>
> —Robert Schuller "

Reading Lesson 4 ·

▼ Teaching Objective

Readers can craft succinct summaries of their reading by focusing on story elements.

🔍 **Close Reading Opportunity**

▼ Standards Alignment

RL.3.1, RL.3.5, RL.3.9, RL.3.10, W.3.4, W.3.10, SL.3.1a–d, SL.3.2, SL.3.6, L.3.1, L.3.6

▼ Materials

- Story Elements graphic organizer (see Appendix 3.2)
- *Clementine* by Sara Pennypacker

▼ To the Teacher

In this lesson, students learn the difference between writing a sharp and short summary and simply retelling a chapter from their reading. Students will create summaries of at least one chapter they have read. Moving forward, students should continue to create a summary after reading each chapter as a way to process their reading and share it with the other members of their Core Crew. Provide a method for organizing these summaries, such as a reading notebook or online folder.

▼ Procedure

Warm Up Gather the class to set the stage for today's learning

Explain to your students the critical role that summaries will play in their work as a team.

It's important that your Core Crew works together as a team. Yesterday, you set some goals for your reading. You're each to read as much as you can, but you may not get to read every book in the series, which means you'll need to rely on one another. As our work continues, you may have to summarize what happens in a book that another member on your team didn't get a chance to read. You may also need to listen to another team member summarize a book for you.

Teach | Model what students need to learn and do

Today we're going to practice creating summaries that give the most important information while not giving too much information. We're going to do this by relying on the story elements and how they change across each book.

Before you continue, check to be certain that your students are comfortable naming and defining the elements of a story (character, setting, problem, solution, plot). Quickly review the terms.

Consider creating a quick chart that lists each element of story with a brief definition provided by the students.

We are going to use the important story elements we've gathered here to help us create a summary packed with information. Summaries are all about balance—you don't want to make them too long, but they can't be too short either. They have to pack a punch. When summaries are too long, they become a retelling of the story. When summaries are too short, they don't give enough information to be helpful. They have to have just enough information in them to compel the reader and not so much that the reader could read the text himself. The summary has to do its own kind of special work.

Model for your class how to use the Story Elements graphic organizer to help craft a succinct summary of a chapter from their reading.

ELL Provide Comprehensible Input—Organizers and Models. Charts offer a visual support for ELLs to refer back to when they are working independently. Consider visualizing the headers with pictures from the book you are using (e.g., picture of a character next to the header) for a visual tie instead of just the header. For the purposes of this lesson, we use Chapter 1 from the first book in the Clementine series; however, you can certainly use a chapter from any other series you have read with your class. To do this, first list the elements of this chapter on the Story Elements graphic organizer. Then model

transferring the information on the graphic organizer into four or five succinct sentences.

Here is what your Story Elements graphic organizer could look like.

Story Elements
TITLE: *Clementine*, Chapter 1
AUTHOR: Sara Pennypacker
CHARACTER(S): Clementine, Margaret, the art teacher, Principal Rice
SETTING(S): the art room, the girl's bathroom, the principal's office
PROBLEM: Clementine cut off all of Margaret's hair in the girl's bathroom.
SOLUTION: Clementine was sent to the principal's office.
PLOT (KEY EVENTS): Clementine and Margaret were working in the art room. When Margaret was gone in the bathroom too long, Clementine went to check on her and found Margaret crying. Margaret was upset because she had cut out a large chunk of her hair trying to get rid of some glue. Clementine offered to help her and ended up cutting off all of Margaret's hair. The art teacher walked in and caught the girls, sending Clementine to the principal.

Here is an example of a summary created using these Story Elements.

> In Chapter 1, Clementine gets caught cutting off all of Margaret's hair in the girl's bathroom. Clementine and Margaret were working in the art room. When Margaret was gone in the bathroom too long, Clementine went to check on her and found Margaret crying. Margaret was upset because she had cut out a large chunk of her hair trying to get rid of some glue. Clementine offered to help her and ended up cutting off all of Margaret's hair. The art teacher walked in and caught the girls, sending Clementine to the principal.

Try | Guide students to quickly rehearse what they need to learn and do in preparation for practice

Take out a fresh Story Elements graphic organizer (see Appendix 3.2) to display for the class. Ask the class to help you in identifying the key story elements from Chapter 2 of *Clementine*. Then, as a class, draft a shared writing that transfers the information on the graphic organizer into a four- or five-sentence summary of that chapter.

© pressmaster / Fotolia

Check understanding as you guide students to briefly share what they have learned and produced today

When students have had a chance to complete summaries, review their summaries to monitor their level of understanding and to guide your future teaching. Gather your students to discuss their work from today. What was difficult? What went well? If you feel as though your class needs additional modeling, read another chapter from your shared series, use the graphic organizer to list the story elements, and write a shared summary of your reading.

Milestone Performance Assessment

Creating Summaries

 Use this checklist to assess student summaries.

Standards Alignment: RL.3.2, RL.3.5, RL.3.9, W.3.4, SL.3.2

	Achieved	Notes
Summary includes key characters.		
Summary includes setting.		
Summary includes problem.		
Summary includes solution.		
Summary includes key events in plot in sequence.		
Summary is succinct (not a retelling).		

Clarify Briefly restate today's teaching objective and explain the practice task(s)

Today we are using the story elements from each chapter to create short summaries of our reading. These summaries are going to be very important as you continue reading in your series and are asked to remember what happened in a previous book. At the end of our reading time today, I'm going to tell you to draft a summary of your reading from today. Moving forward, we'll create a summary of our reading every day in order to solidify our reading in our minds.

Practice Students work independently or in small groups to apply today's teaching objective

Students continue working in their Core Crews. Each student continues reading to meet his or her reading goal for the day. Once students have had a significant amount of time to read independently, each student will summarize his or her reading using the Story Elements graphic organizer.

Reading Lesson 5

▼ Teaching Objective

Readers can identify the themes of their reading by using a variety of clues.

Close Reading Opportunity

▼ Standards Alignment

RL.3.1, RL.3.5, RL.3.9, RL.3.10, SL.3.1a–d, SL.3.2, SL.3.4, SL.3.6, L.3.1, L.3.6

▼ Materials

- Clues We Can Use to Infer Theme chart
- *Clementine* by Sara Pennypacker

▼ To the Teacher

Before today's lesson, prepare a chart that lists the clues readers can use to infer the theme of their reading

As this lesson unfolds, be sure to return continuously to the importance of supporting your thinking about theme with explicit examples from the text. We want students to use the text itself as a basis for their answers. Think of this as having your students to craft a thesis statement about their reading and then support it with concrete and specific examples from the text.

Finally, today's teaching also reminds students of the importance of conversation to enhance understanding of their reading. Moving forward, you want to make sure to provide your students with ample time to read independently *and* time to discuss their reading with their Core Crew. A fun idea is to find simple ways to turn your classroom into a coffee shop during this time of day. Play light instrumental music in the background, have a small snack available at the front of the room, or rearrange seating to promote intimate conversation.

▼ Procedure

Warm Up Gather the class to set the stage for today's learning

Explain the plan for students to have time for reading and talking with others about their reading.

Now that you've all really dug into your books, I want to make sure that you and your crew do two things every day. I want you to have time to read independently, and I want you to have time to discuss your reading with your group. Remember to use the Conversation Helpers we worked on a couple of days ago and to follow the rules and behaviors for having a strong conversation.

Teach Model what students need to learn and do

Tell the class that one thing you would like your Core Crew to discuss is the theme of the book or series they are reading. Explain that the theme is usually one or two words that tell the big idea or overall feeling of the book or series. Alert students that sometimes they might hear the theme called the central message, the big idea, or the "so what" of the book.

Today I'm going to teach you how readers figure out the theme of a text. You see, the author hardly ever comes right out and tells us what the theme is—we have to figure it out for ourselves. So we have to be good detectives and look for certain clues that help to reveal the theme. Here are some clues you can use in trying to uncover the theme of your books.

Show the class your pre-made chart titled "Clues We Can Use to Infer Theme." It should include the following:

- Title
- What characters say and do
- How the characters change
- What the characters learn

Choose a book from your class shared series study that you have finished (or almost finished) reading. For the purposes of this lesson, we will be using *Clementine,* the first book in the Clementine series by Sara Pennypacker.

As you model your thinking about the themes, be sure to name the clues on the list that you are using along with examples from the text. Point to the clues on the chart as you use them to make this abstract skill as concrete as possible for your students. Work your way through the first few items on the list, saving the remainder to think about collaboratively with your students.

When I think about the things that Clementine says and does, right away I think about how she's always thinking about how hard it is to feel different from everyone else. Now let me think if there is anything she does about feeling different. Remember the part of the story where she cut off her own hair so that Margaret wouldn't be the only one without hair? Or she drew on her own head so Margaret wouldn't be the only one? With all these examples from the story, I determine that one theme of *Clementine* is about being different or not fitting in and how people work through that.

Reiterate for students your thought process, being sure to emphasize how you turned to the text to find an explicit example to support your thinking about theme.

Try Guide students to quickly rehearse what they need to learn and do in preparation for practice

Divide your class in half. Ask half of the class to think in pairs about any themes in *Clementine* using the "how characters change" clue. The remaining half of the class will discuss in pairs "what the characters learn" to infer theme in this text.

Listen in to student conversations, coaching them to stay on topic, name the clues they are using to infer the theme of this text, and reference explicit examples from the text to support their thinking. **ELL** Enable Language Production—Increasing Interaction. ELLs are able to clarify and learn from their peers during this time in an informal forum. This is an opportunity to whisper in when needed or listen in to understand how to best support their language needs.

Following is an idea of the themes and related moments from the book students may discuss or notice:

- How characters change
  - Clementine takes care of her brother instead of making fun of him when she makes bologna eyes to get him to laugh. (Possible theme = family, siblings take care of each other)
- What characters learn
  - Clementine learns it's okay to be different at the end of the story when her family and friends throw her a party to celebrate her creative solution to The Pigeon Wars. (Possible theme = being different, not fitting in is ok)

- Clementine learns that friendships have their ups and downs. There are multiple examples of her ups and downs with Margaret throughout the book. (Possible theme = friendship has ups and downs)
- Clementine learns that her family loves her just the way she is, even though her brother is considered "the easy one." (Possible theme = family members care about each other in similar and different ways)

Clarify Briefly restate today's teaching objective and explain the practice task(s)

Today we used a list of clues to help us figure out the themes explored in *Clementine* by Sara Pennypacker. From now on, as you're reading, keep these clues in the back of your mind. Keep thinking about the theme of your book and series.

Tell the class that at the end of their reading time they will have some time to practice using these clues to uncover the themes explored in their books. After jotting their ideas down, they should be ready to discuss their thinking with their Core Crew.

Practice Students work independently or in small groups to apply today's teaching objective

After allowing students sufficient time to meet their reading goals for the day, ask students to use the clues you discussed today to infer the theme of the text they are currently reading. Instruct them to jot down their thinking to discuss later. Before concluding their reading work for the day, students should share their thinking with the members of their group, name the specific clues that led them to their interpretation of the theme, and give explicit examples from the text to support their thinking. (SL.3.1a, SL.3.1b, SL.3.4)

Wrap Up Check understanding as you guide students to briefly share what they have learned and produced today

Have a few groups share their thinking about theme and the evidence they found to support it. Briefly remind students that the work they did on theme today is useful and important whenever they read fiction text.

Reading Lesson 6

▼ Teaching Objective

Readers use explicit examples from the text as evidence to support their thinking about the theme of their books.

Close Reading Opportunity

▼ Standards Alignment

RL.3.1, RL.3.2, RL.3.5, RL.3.9, RL.3.10, W.3.4, W.3.10, SL.3.1a–d, SL.3.6, L.3.1, L.3.6

▼ Materials

- Thinking about Theme graphic organizer (see Appendix 3.3)

▼ To the Teacher

Navigating a chapter book to find text to use as evidence can be a difficult task for many third graders. While they are apt to understand the concept, many may struggle to find the perfect example and, therefore, spend an overwhelming amount of time flipping through pages with increasing frustration. Scaffold this process for students through heavy class modeling, small-group instruction, and one-on-one conferencing.

▼ Procedure

Warm Up Gather the class to set the stage for today's learning

Third graders, we've worked hard to uncover the themes hidden in our series books using the clues we discussed yesterday. I've been very impressed with the conversations you've been having with one another. Not only are you using the Conversation Helpers and following our rules and behaviors for productive conversations beautifully, but you've also done some good thinking.

Teach Model what students need to learn and do

Today I want to teach you how to support your thinking about the theme of your book by using evidence from the text. Identifying the theme of your reading is wonderful, but you must make your thinking one step smarter by finding text evidence as well.

Demonstrate finding explicit moments in the text as evidence to support a theme from the book. During Reading Lesson 4, students began to create a summary of each chapter they read. Now, model using these chapter summaries to help you locate the correct page or moment from the book.

We know that one of the most important themes in *Clementine* is the theme of friendship and how friendships have ups and downs.

At the top of your Thinking about Theme graphic organizer, jot "friendships have ups and downs" for the theme.

It would be really great if I could make my thinking one step smarter by coming up with a specific example of when Clementine and Margaret's friendship felt wonderful or difficult. Let me think about some of the moments from the book that come to my mind. What about when Clementine yells about Margaret in the principal's office? Remember that? I couldn't believe she yelled at the principal, but she did it because she was so angry with Margaret. Let me look at my summaries to help me narrow down what page that was on.

Flip through your chapter summaries, skimming their contents as you go. Clementine yells at the principal in Chapter 6.

Here it is! Chapter 6. Now let me go to the book and find the exact page.

Find the correct page and read aloud to the class. Add the page number and a sentence or two about your example to the graphic organizer. **ELL** Provide Comprehensible Input—Models. Modeling offers a time for ELLs to hear you use language and demonstrate the thought process of thinking about text evidence. This model may be the structure they refer to when thinking through this on their own. Recap your process for students.

First, I chose one of the themes we found in the book: friendship. Then I thought about all the moments from Clementine and Margaret's friendship that stood out in my head until I found a good example of when their friendship felt difficult. I used my summaries to remind me what each chapter was about and to help me focus my search of the book. Once I identified the correct chapter using my summaries, then I flipped through the pages in that chapter until I found my piece of evidence.

Try Guide students to quickly rehearse what they need to learn and do in preparation for practice

It is excellent to have more than one piece of evidence to support your thinking, so let's keep going with the same theme—friendships have ups and downs. I want you to spend a moment thinking back on Clementine and Margaret's friendship. Is there a moment that stands out in your mind that would be a good example of a time when their friendship felt wonderful?

Allow students to think independently for a moment, then prompt them to share their thinking with a partner. Listen in to several partnerships. Choose an example shared by a partnership to share with the class. Work together to use the chapter summaries to locate a chapter and a page number. Add your example and the corresponding page number to the Thinking about Theme graphic organizer.

Clarify Briefly restate today's teaching objective and explain the practice task(s)

Today we talked about finding evidence from the book to help support your thinking about the theme of your reading. I want you to choose a theme of your own about your story. Write it at the top of your graphic organizer. Then, spend a few minutes finding evidence from your book to support your thinking. Don't forget to write down the page number and jot a sentence or two about the moment you've chosen as an example.

Practice Students work independently or in small groups to apply today's teaching objective

Students read independently. They choose a theme from their reading and use the Thinking about Theme graphic organizer to collect evidence from the text to support their thinking.

Wrap Up Check understanding as you guide students to briefly share what they have learned and produced today

Have Core Crews share their thinking and textual evidence around a theme with the other members of the group. Circulate the room to help facilitate conversations and determine whether students were successful with this lesson.

Collect student work to analyze and determine whether your students need more support with this work through additional whole-class teaching, small groups, or individual conferences.

Milestone Performance Assessment

Determining Theme with Text Evidence

 Use this checklist to assess student work on the Thinking about Theme graphic organizer.

Standards Alignment: RL.3.1, RL.3.2, RL.3.5, RL.3.9

	Achieved	Notes
Identify a theme present in the text.		
Provide text evidence of the theme (connected to what characters say, do, and learn, and how they change).		

Reading Lesson 7

Close Reading Opportunity

▼ **Teaching Objective**

Readers think deeply about an author's work by comparing the setting, plot, and theme across several books.

▼ **Standards Alignment**

RL.3.1, RL.3.5, RL.3.9, RL.3.10, W.3.4, W.3.10, SL.3.1a–d, SL.3.6, L.3.1, L.3.6

▼ Materials

- Large Venn diagram—you can use two hula hoops, chart paper, or an interactive whiteboard
- Large Venn diagrams for Core Crew collaborative use
- Copies of Venn diagram page for student use
- *Clementine* by Sara Pennypacker
- *Clementine and the Family Meeting* by Sara Pennypacker

▼ To the Teacher

This lesson focuses on the idea of making connections across a number of texts. In second grade, students are asked to compare two versions of the same story by different authors or cultures. This year, we are asking students to make deeper text-to-text connections that increase their understanding of an author or series. Using key elements discussed throughout this lesson set (setting, plot, and theme) gives students a jumping-off point for this sort of thinking. Students may need to develop this ability to make *meaningful* connections that truly augment their understanding of an author or series across several sessions. For example, you may want to model this and then allow Core Crews time to practice these skills collaboratively (Teach, Try) on one day and ask students to complete this work independently (Clarify, Practice, Wrap Up) on another day.

▼ Procedure

Warm Up Gather the class to set the stage for today's learning

By now you're deep into reading a series of books by the same author. I know that when I've read more than one book by the same author, I start to compare them. Authors have trends. And these trends are actually comforting to us as readers. They help us read faster, even. Because the more we know about how an author writes a series, the more quickly we can dig right in. We know the flow. For example, I begin to notice similarities in the setting. Does the author have a particular place where he or she likes to make things happen ? I notice similarities in the types of characters the author creates. Or even that the characters re-emerge in every book. I think about how the characters stay the same and how and if they change. These observations are some of the important work that we're going to practice today with our Core Crews.

Teach Model what students need to learn and do

Have a large blank Venn diagram prepared for your teaching today. **ELL** Provide Comprehensible Input—Organizers. During your description of the Venn diagram, you may need to provide a visual description for "same and different," such as two apples for same and an apple and orange for different. You may also want to provide visuals for key concepts, such as setting. Explain to students that comparing and contrasting two books from the same series can help readers understand more about the series as a whole. Tell the class you will use the Venn diagram to compare the setting, plot, and themes of *Clementine* and *Clementine and the Family Meeting* (or any other two books from the series you've chosen to share with your class). Does the Clementine series usually deal with the same sort of themes in every book? If so, what does that teach us about the series as a whole? Are there similarities in the plots or settings of Clementine books that can help us predict what may happen in the next Clementine book we encounter?

Begin by thinking aloud about the settings from the two books you are going to compare. Demonstrate a strategy for getting started, such as retelling one of the books you are comparing with a focus on the setting. Once you have named a setting, discuss: "Was this setting used in both books, or just this one?"

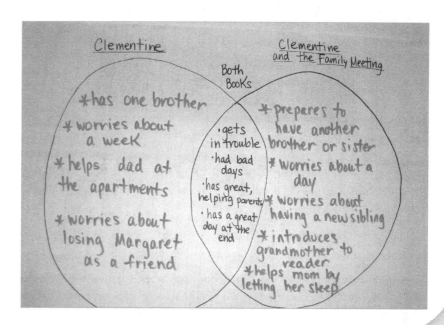

Next, model thinking about explicit examples from the plot in both books. **ELL** **Provide Comprehensible Input—Models** Demonstrate including only the most important events rather than considering each and every small moment. Our goal is for students to get a broad understanding of the series as a whole and not get bogged down in too many details.

Recap your process for the students thus far.

Did you notice how I got started by thinking about the different settings? Then I moved on to thinking about the most important events from the plot. Now it's time to think about the different themes from the two books.

Continue to model plotting your thinking about theme in the Venn diagram. Briefly remind the class of the strategies you discussed in Lesson 5 for determining the theme of a text. Refer back to the chart you created during this lesson as needed. Begin by recalling a theme from *Clementine* you identified in Lessons 5 and 6. As you recall individual themes, think aloud.

Is this a theme that both books share? Do we see this theme in *Clementine and the Family Meeting*?

Try Guide students to quickly rehearse what they need to learn and do in preparation for practice

Tell Core Crews to select two books from the series they have been studying. Then, Core Crews will collaboratively use a large Venn diagram to compare and contrast the settings, plots, and themes of these books. Each crew should be prepared to share their Venn diagram with the class. **ELL** **Enable Language Production—Increasing Interaction.** The time to speak with peers using their graphic organizers offers ELLs time to clarify their thinking and vocabulary about ideas that they wrote, as well as expand their thinking through the peer conversation.

Clarify Briefly restate today's teaching objective and explain the practice task(s)

Remind the students that today you are comparing the settings, plots, and themes of two books from the same series so that you can begin to see patterns across the texts. Briefly recap your process for the class.

First, we thought about the settings from each book. Then, we moved on to focusing on the most important events from the plot of each book. Last, we determined and considered the themes of each book.

Practice Students work independently or in small groups to apply today's teaching objective

Students work individually to create one Venn diagram that represents their thinking about setting, plot, and theme across two books from the series they have been studying during this lesson set.

Wrap Up Check understanding as you guide students to briefly share what they have learned and produced today

Take another look at the Venn diagram you created as a group during this lesson. Focus on the middle of the diagram—the elements that the two books have in common. Model using this information to make a broad statement about the series. For example, you might say, "The Clementine series deals with issues of growing up and the struggles kids may have with their families and friends and at school."

Have students consider the shared elements of the books they compared. What broad statement can they make about this series? Collect students' individual Venn diagrams for your review. Do students need additional support and practice with this work?

Milestone Performance Assessment

Comparing Multiple Texts in a Series

 Use this checklist to assess student work comparing texts with a Venn diagram.

Standards Alignment: RL.3.1, RL.3.5, RL.3.9, W.3.4, W.3.10

	Achieved	Notes
Venn diagram includes setting, plot, and theme for each book.		
Venn diagram indicates items both texts have in common.		
Make a broad statement about the series that connects to what is common across multiple texts.		

Reading Lesson 8 . . . .

▼ Teaching Objective

Readers find out more about the author to make deeper connections to their books.

Close Reading Opportunity

▼ Standards Alignment

RL.3.1, RL.3.9, RL.3.10, W.3.4, W.3.8, W.3.10, SL.3.1a–d, SL.3.6, L.3.1, L.3.6

▼ Materials

- Author websites or nonfiction texts about the authors being studied by Core Crews
- Method for brief student note taking

▼ Procedure

Warm Up Gather the class to set the stage for today's learning

Today we're going to pause to find out more about the authors of our series to see if there is information that will help us understand some of the decisions they made in their writing.

Teach Model what students need to learn and do

Today you will model for students how to find out more information about the author who wrote their series and make connections back to their text. Please see the following options for this lesson.

Goal	Low-Tech	High-Tech
Students research the author who wrote the series their crew has been studying.	• Students visit the library to find informational texts about the author of their series. • Students do a close reading of the About the Author section of their books.	• Students navigate author websites that have been bookmarked for them in advance. • Students conduct a Google search for their author and visit relevant sites.

Model reading more about the author of the series you have chosen to study as a class and taking a few brief notes. Think aloud about any connections you can make between the life of the author and the series he or she has brought to life in the books you're reading. For example, Sara Pennypacker, the author of the Clementine series, is enormously passionate about reading. She also struggled with fitting in when she was a child, just like Clementine struggles with being different from her friends and classmates.

Try Guide students to quickly rehearse what they need to learn and do in preparation for practice

Ask students to talk with a classmate about any connections they can make between the information the class has found about the author of the series the class has studied together and any of the themes or ideas addressed in that author's writing. **ELL** Enable Language Production—Increasing Interaction, Listening and Speaking. This is a time for ELLs to practice their thinking out loud in English and clarify any language issues they may be struggling with. If you have chosen to study the Clementine series, here are some connections students might make:

- Sara Pennypacker loves to paint and draw. Clementine also loves art and her mother is an artist.
- Sara Pennypacker talks about having a funny hairstyle as a child and Clementine cuts off her hair in the first book from the series.
- Sara Pennypacker grew up in Massachusetts and Clementine lives in Massachusetts with her family.

Clarify Briefly restate today's teaching objective and explain the practice task(s)

Today we researched the author of our series to see if we could make connections between the author's life and the books she has created. We found many connections between Sara Pennypacker's own life and the life she creates for Clementine in her books. I learn from this that authors often take a lot from their own lives when they're writing stories to share with all of us. I wonder what you will find out about each of the authors you are studying. Each Core

Crew will spend time researching the author of their series to make connections to their reading.

Practice Students work independently or in small groups to apply today's teaching objective

Core Crews work collaboratively to find out more about the author who wrote the series they have chosen to study. Core Crews should jot notes as they research, looking for connections between the author's life and the books in their series.

Wrap Up Check understanding as you guide students to briefly share what they have learned and produced today

Check in with each group as their work draws to a close. What connections were they able to make? What information did they uncover about the author?

Reading Lesson 9

▼ Teaching Objective

Readers share their ideas with others.

Close Reading Opportunity

▼ Standards Alignment

RL.3.1, RL.3.5, RL.3.9, RL.3.10, W.3.4, W.3.8, W.3.10, SL.3.1a–d, SL.3.3, SL.3.4, SL.3.6, L.3.1, L.3.6

▼ Materials

• Artifacts related to series study (See table for low- and high-tech options.)

Goal	Low-Tech	High-Tech
Core Crews share their thinking about a series.	Core Crews collect a variety of artifacts (drawings, summaries, quotes, etc.) to represent their learning and thinking about the series. These artifacts can be displayed • On a poster • On a tri-fold presentation board • As a museum exhibit	Core Crews create a PowerPoint or Prezi presentation that includes both images and text.

▼ To the Teacher

You may need to give Core Crews several days to create engaging presentations. You may also need to set aside an additional day for crews to present their work to the remainder of the class.

▼ Procedure

Warm Up Gather the class to set the stage for today's learning

Now it's time to get ready to share what you think. Remember, being able to talk about your reading and present your ideas to others is something you're going to have to do a lot while you are in school, and it's an important skill to have as an adult too. Always be sure to have a thoughtful reason for what you are saying, based on some evidence you can point to.

Teach Model what students need to learn and do

Explain to the class that each final presentation must include the following:

• Summaries for each of the texts read by the members of the group

• A list of themes represented across the series with relevant examples from the text

• Any broad statements about the settings, plots, or themes included in the series

• Relevant information about the author's life and any possible connections to the books within the series

Model the process of creating the final product you have chosen for your Core Crews. Guide the groups as they

• Divide the necessary work up into various jobs for each member

• Set deadlines for one another

• Make decisions about the text and images to include

• Lay out their final product

Try Guide students to quickly rehearse what they need to learn and do in preparation for practice

Turn to the class to help you create a final presentation of your collective thinking about the Clementine series (or any other series you have chosen to study together throughout this lesson set). Present them with a variety of texts and images you have gathered. You should include any writing you have generated through your teaching (summaries, lists of themes, etc.) as well as several images you have collected (illustrations of particular key scenes, printed copies of book jackets, the author's picture, images of the main characters, etc.). Prompt students to turn and talk—ask them to think about the guidelines for what should be included in the final presentation and make decisions about what should and should not be included. Then, lead the class in a discussion regarding *how* to lay out the text and images you have decided to include.

Clarify Briefly restate today's teaching objective and explain the practice task(s)

Remind Core Crews of what their presentations should include (see list in Teach segment). Chart this information for the class to refer back to or provide each group with a list to help focus their work.

Practice Students work independently or in small groups to apply today's teaching objective

 Core Crews work collaboratively to create a final presentation of the group's thinking around their chosen series. Each group member must take on an appropriate amount of responsibility and contribute to the group work. **ELL** Enable Language Production—Listening and Speaking. This is a good time to check in with beginner ELLs to evaluate their comfort level with presenting in English or to help them clarify and practice their part in order for them to feel comfortable with speaking in front of the groups.

Wrap Up Check understanding as you guide students to briefly share what they have learned and produced today

 Provide time for Core Crews to present their final products to the class. Class presentations are an excellent opportunity to review and practice key speaking and listening skills for third graders. Skills you may wish to highlight at this time related to speaking include coming to the discussion prepared, staying focused and using relevant details, speaking clearly at an understandable pace, and speaking in complete sentences. Skills you may wish to highlight related to listening include sitting respectfully, listening with care, and asking relevant questions of the speaker. (SL.3.1a–b, SL.3.3, SL.3.4, SL.3.6)

> " *Education's purpose is to replace an empty mind with an open one.*
>
> —Malcolm Forbes "

Milestone Performance Assessment

Comparing Elements across Texts

 Use this checklist to assess student presentations on their study of a series.

Standards Alignment: RL.3.1, RL.3.2, RL.3.5, RL.3.9, W.3.4, W.3.8, SL.3.1a–b, SL.3.3, SL.3.4, SL.3.6, L.3.1, L.3.6

	Achieved	Notes
Include an accurate summary of each text.		
Articulate themes suggested across the series with relevant examples from the text.		
Make a broad statement about the series that connects to what is common across multiple texts.		
Include relevant information about the author and how this information connects to the content of the series.		
Collaborate effectively with group in preparing and presenting the material.		

Reading Lesson 10

▼ Teaching Objective

Readers reflect on the Core Questions and make plans for their future reading.

▼ Standards Alignment

RL.3.9, W.3.4, W.3.10

▼ Materials

- Future Reading Plans sheet (see Appendix 3.4)

▼ Procedure

Warm Up Gather the class to set the stage for today's learning

Briefly recap some of the highlights from each Core Crew's presentation. Ask students to share some of their favorite moments or presentations.

Teach Model what students need to learn and do

Explain to the class the importance of knowing oneself as a reader and making plans for oneself as a reader. Think aloud about your own reading tastes and preferences, making sure to mention the various genres or text types you usually avoid as well. Demonstrate choosing two new books or series to read—one book should match your identified tastes as a reader and the other should represent a book or series outside your usual comfort zone.

> It's important that we know what we like to read and that we sometimes push ourselves to read books we might not normally choose. You never know when you'll discover a book or author that you will love! Let's use a Core Question to help us with this reflective work. Today we're going to answer the question, "What types of genres, settings, plots, and themes appeal to you as a reader? Why?"

As you are modeling and thinking aloud, be sure to write down your choices (including the title and author) on a Future Reading Plans sheet (see Appendix 3.4). On this sheet, students will indicate the following:

- I usually enjoy books and series in the following genres (mystery, adventure, fantasy, realistic fiction, etc.):
- I usually enjoy books and series with the following types of settings (school, magical worlds, sporting events, etc.):
- I usually enjoy books and series with plots and themes about (friendship, seeking adventure, overcoming hardships, fighting evil, etc.):
- Even though I don't normally choose this type of book or series, I plan to expand my reading and try (describe a different type of book or series to try):
- List specific books, authors, or series for your future reading list:

Try Guide students to quickly rehearse what they need to learn and do in preparation for practice

Ask your class to reflect on the books that you have shared together this year. Is there a particular type of genre, setting, plot, or theme that your class enjoys the most? Is there a type of book or genre that you do not usually share or have not shared yet?

Have students turn and talk about two choices for class read-alouds—one that represents the type of book you love to share together and one that represents a new kind of choice for your class.

Clarify Briefly restate today's teaching objective and explain the practice task(s)

> Today we are reflecting on ourselves as readers using one of our Core Questions: "What types of genres, settings, plots, and themes appeal to you as a reader, and why? Give thoughtful reasons for why these appeal to you."

Remind the students that they might wish to pick a book or series that was presented by one of their fellow Core Crews. One book choice should match their current identity as a reader and the other should push them to try something new.

Practice Students work independently or in small groups to apply today's teaching objective

Students reflect independently, writing their responses on their Future Reading Plans sheet.

Wrap Up Check understanding as you guide students to briefly share what they have learned and produced today

Gather the class to share some of their choices. Be sure that students explain their choices by making clear why they have chosen each of these titles.

Writing Lessons

The Core I.D.E.A. / Daily Writing Instruction at a Glance table highlights the teaching objectives and standards alignment for all 10 lessons across the four stages of the lesson set (Introduce, Define, Extend, and Assess). It also indicates which lessons contain special features to support ELLs, technology, speaking and listening, and formative (Milestone) assessments.

The following Core Ready Writing Rubric is designed to help you record each student's overall understanding across four levels of achievement as it relates to the lesson set goals. I recommend that you use this rubric at the end of the lesson set as a performance-based assessment tool. Use the Milestone Performance Assessments and checklists as tools to help you gauge student progress toward these goals, reteach, and differentiate as needed. See the foundational book, *Be Core Ready: Powerful, Effective Steps to Implementing and Achieving Common Core State Standards,* for more information about the Core Ready Reading and Writing Rubrics.

The Core I.D.E.A. / Daily Writing Instruction at a Glance

Grade 3 The Reader and Writer's Opinion: A Collaborative Author Study

Instructional Stage	Lesson	Teaching Objective	Core Standards	Special Features
Introduce: notice, explore, collect, note, immerse, surround, record, share	1	Writers write for different purposes.	RL.3.1 • RL.3.10 • SL.3.1a • SL.3.1b L.3.1 • L.3.6	Close Reading ELL
Define: name, identify, outline, clarify, select, plan	2	Book reviews use strong and precise language to persuade.	RL.3.1 • RL.3.4 • RL.3.10 • W.3.1a • W.3.4 W.3.10 • SL.3.1a–d • SL.3.6 • L.3.1 • L.3.6	Close Reading ELL Milestone Assessment
	3	Writers organize their writing to suit their task and purpose.	RL.3.1 • RL.3.9 • RL.3.10 • W.3.1a–d • W.3.4 W.3.10 • SL.3.1a–d • SL.3.6 • L.3.1 • L.3.6	Close Reading ELL
Extend: try, experiment, attempt, approximate, practice, explain, revise, refine	4	Writers capture the reader's attention by crafting strong introductions.	W.3.1a • W.3.1b • W.3.4 • W.3.10 • SL.3.1a–d SL.3.6 • L.3.1 • L.3.6	ELL Milestone Assessment
	5	Writers use relevant text as evidence to strengthen their opinions.	RL.3.1 • RL.3.9 • RL.3.10 • W.3.1a • W.3.4 SL.3.1a–d • SL.3.6 • L.3.1 • L.3.6	Close Reading ELL S&L
	6	Writers use linking words and phrases to connect their opinions and reasons.	W.3.1c • W.3.4 • W.3.10 • SL.3.1a • SL.3.1b SL.3.6 • L.3.6	ELL
	7	Writers craft strong conclusions that leave the audience thinking.	W.3.1d • W.3.4 • W.3.10 • SL.3.1a • SL.3.1b SL.3.6 • L.3.6	ELL
	8	Writers revisit their writing with a partner and make choices about how to strengthen their work, including following standard English conventions.	W.3.1a–d • W.3.4 • W.3.5 • W.3.10 • SL.3.1a–d SL.3.6 • L.3.1 • L.3.2 • L.3.3 • L.3.6	ELL S&L
	9	Writers prepare their reviews for publication.	W.3.1a–d • W.3.6 • W.3.10 • SL.3.1a–d • SL.3.6 L.3.1 • L.3.2 • L.3.3 • L.3.6	ELL Tech
Assess: reflect, conclude, connect, share, recognize, respond	10	Writers use their persuasive writing skills in a variety of contexts.	W.3.1a–d • W.3.4 • W.3.10 • SL.3.1a • SL.3.1b SL.3.6 • L.3.1 • L.3.6	ELL Milestone Assessment Tech

Core Ready Writing Rubric

Lesson Set Goal	Emerging	Approaching	Achieving	Exceeding	Standards Alignment
Take notes on relevant information to use for gathering supporting details.	Student shows little or no evidence of taking notes on relevant information to use for gathering supporting details.	Student attempts to take notes but some notes may be unclear, incomplete, or irrelevant.	Student takes useful, sufficiently organized notes on relevant information to use for gathering supporting details. Some areas may be better developed than others.	Student takes exemplary notes on relevant information to use for gathering supporting details. Student's notes are well organized and clear.	RL.3.1 RL.3.10 W.3.4 W.3.8 W.3.10
Use textual evidence and details to support opinion statements.	Student shows little or no evidence of using textual evidence and details to support opinion statements.	Student uses some textual evidence and details to support opinion statements.	Student uses several examples of textual evidence and details to support opinion statements.	Student uses many examples of textual evidence and details to support opinion statements.	RL.3.1 RL.3.10 SL3.1a–d SL.3.6 L.3.1 L.3.6
Craft a well-organized persuasive piece of writing (book review) about a book series that includes a strong introduction and concluding statement and linking words or phrases.	Student produces little or no evidence of a successful review. Lacks organization, introduction, concluding statement, and linking words or phrases.	Student attempts to craft a well-organized book review about a book series that includes an introduction, concluding statement, and linking words or phrases. Some components may be better developed than others.	Student crafts an effective, organized book review about a book series that includes a clear introduction, concluding statement, and linking words or phrases.	Student crafts a well-organized and thoughtful book review. Introduction, concluding statement, and linking words or phrases are particularly engaging and effective.	RL.3.1 RL.3.9 RL.3.10 W.3.1a–d W.3.4 W.3.5 W.3.10 L.3.6
With guidance and support from peers and adults, plan, revise, and edit book review, paying close attention to the conventions of standard English and clarity of the story's development.	Student makes little or no attempt to develop and strengthen writing through planning, revising, and editing, even with the support and guidance of peers and adults.	Student attempts to develop and strengthen writing as needed by planning, revising, and editing. Writing may still contain significant errors or lack clarity.	Student develops and strengthens writing as needed by planning, revising, and editing. Some areas of the planning, revision, and editing may be better developed than others.	Student extensively develops and strengthens writing by planning, revising, and editing as needed. Few or no errors or lapses of clarity evident.	W.3.5
Prepare and publish final book review.	Student shows little or no evidence of success preparing and publishing a final book review.	Student attempts to prepare and publish a final book review with some success. Some criteria may be better developed than others.	Student prepares and publishes a final book review. All established criteria are met.	Student prepares and publishes an exemplary final book review. Established criteria are exceeded in some ways.	W.3.6 W.3.10 SL.3.6 L.3.1 L.3.2 L.3.3

Lesson Set Goal	Emerging	Approaching	Achieving	Exceeding	Standards Alignment
Ask and answer questions to demonstrate understanding of a text, referring explicitly to the text as the basis for the answers.	Student shows little or no evidence of active, purposeful reading or searching the text for specific information and evidence. Student makes little or no attempt to ask or answer questions about the text. Text evidence is minimal or nonexistent.	Student shows some evidence of active, purposeful reading and searching the text for specific information and evidence. Student may be able to ask or answer some questions about the text accurately, but may not provide sufficient textual evidence to support thinking.	Student shows solid evidence of active, purposeful reading and searching the text for specific information and evidence. Student usually asks and answers questions accurately and provides appropriate textual evidence to support thinking.	Student demonstrates exceptional evidence of active, purposeful reading and searching the text for specific information and evidence. Student asks and answers questions with accuracy and provides appropriate, detailed, and thoughtful textual evidence to support thinking.	RL.3.1
Write an organized opinion piece that includes a clear introduction, point of view, supporting reasons, linking words and phrases, and concluding statement.	Student writes an opinion piece with little or no evidence of an introduction or concluding statement. Does not articulate a clear point of view and supporting reasons are missing or insufficient. Omits linking words and phrases or uses inappropriately.	Student writes an opinion piece and attempts to include an introduction and concluding statement. Attempts to identify a point of view but supporting reasons may be weak or irrelevant. May lack needed linking words and phrases.	Student writes an opinion piece with a solid introduction and concluding statement. Articulates a point of view and supports with relevant supporting reasons. Uses linking words and phrases when appropriate.	Student writes a highly effective opinion piece with a strong introduction and concluding statement. Point of view is apparent and supported with clear and relevant reasons. May use advanced linking words and phrases selectively.	W.3.1
By the end of the year, independently and proficiently read and comprehend literature, including stories, dramas, and poetry, at the high end of the grades 2–3 text complexity band.	Student shows little or no evidence of reading and comprehending a complex text appropriate for the grade 3 text complexity band at this point in the school year.	Student shows inconsistent evidence of independently and proficiently reading and comprehending complex texts appropriate for the grade 3 text complexity band at this point in the school year.	Student shows solid evidence of independently and proficiently reading and comprehending complex texts appropriate for the grade 3 text complexity band at this point in the school year.	Student shows solid evidence of independently and proficiently reading and comprehending complex texts above the grade 3 text complexity band at this point in the school year.	RL.3.10
Write routinely over extended time frames (time for research, reflection, and revision) and shorter time frames (a single sitting or a day or two) for a range of discipline-specific tasks, purposes, and audiences.	Student shows little or no evidence of engaging routinely in writing for short or long time frames for a range of discipline-specific tasks, purposes, and audiences.	Student shows some evidence of engaging routinely in writing for short and long time frames for a range of discipline-specific tasks, purposes, and audiences.	Student shows solid evidence of engaging routinely in writing for short and long time frames for a range of discipline-specific tasks, purposes, and audiences.	Student shows exceptional evidence of consistently and accurately writing for short and long time frames for a range of discipline-specific tasks, purposes, and audiences.	W.3.10
In collaborative discussions, demonstrate evidence of preparation for discussion and exhibit responsibility to the rules and roles of conversation.	In collaborative discussions, student comes unprepared and often disregards the rules and roles of conversation.	In collaborative discussions, student's preparation may be evident but ineffective or inconsistent. May occasionally disregard the rules and roles of conversation.	In collaborative discussions, student prepares adequately and draws on the preparation and other information about the topic to explore ideas under discussion. Usually observes the rules and roles of conversation.	In collaborative discussions, student arrives extremely well prepared for discussions and draws on the preparation and other information about the topic to explore ideas under discussion. Always observes the rules and roles of conversation.	SL.3.1a SL.3.1b

Core Ready Writing Rubric, Grade 3, *continued*

Lesson Set Goal	Emerging	Approaching	Achieving	Exceeding	Standards Alignment
In collaborative discussions, share and develop ideas in a manner that enhances understanding of a topic. Contribute and respond to the content of the conversation in a productive and focused manner.	Student shows little or no evidence of engaging in collaborative discussions and makes little or no attempt to ask and answer questions, stay on topic, link comments to the remarks of others, or explain his or her own ideas and understanding in light of the discussion.	Student shows some evidence of engaging in collaborative discussions and, with marginal success, attempts to ask questions to check understanding of information presented, stay on topic, link comments to the remarks of others, and explain his or her own ideas and understanding in light of the discussion.	Student engages in a range of collaborative discussions and asks questions to check understanding of information presented. Stays on topic most of the time and frequently links his or her own ideas and understanding in light of the discussion.	Student effectively and consistently engages in a range of collaborative discussions and asks high-level questions to check understanding of information presented. Always stays on topic and, with great insight and attention to the comments of others, links his or her own ideas and understanding in light of the discussion.	SL.3.1c SL.3.1d
Speak in complete sentences when appropriate and demonstrate a command of standard English grammar and usage.	Student shows little or no evidence of attempting to speak in complete sentences. Student demonstrates little or no command of standard English grammar and usage.	Student attempts to speak in complete sentences when appropriate and demonstrates some command of standard English grammar and usage.	Student speaks in complete sentences when appropriate and demonstrates a command of standard English grammar and usage.	Student always speaks in complete sentences when appropriate and demonstrates an extraordinary command of the conventions of standard English grammar and usage.	SL.3.6 L.3.1
Demonstrate knowledge of standard English and its conventions.	Student demonstrates little or no knowledge of standard English and its conventions.	Student demonstrates some evidence of knowledge of standard English and its conventions.	Student consistently demonstrates knowledge of standard English and its conventions.	Student demonstrates an exceptional understanding of standard English and its conventions.	L.3.1 L.3.2 L.3.3
Acquire and accurately use grade-appropriate conversational, general academic, and domain-specific vocabulary and phrases.	Student shows little or no evidence of the acquisition and use of grade-appropriate conversational and academic language.	Student shows some evidence of the acquisition and use of grade-appropriate conversational and academic language.	Student shows solid evidence of the acquisition and use of grade-appropriate conversational and academic language.	Student shows a high level of sophistication when using grade-appropriate conversational and academic language.	L.3.6

Note: See the Core Ready Rubrics chart in the Welcome at the beginning of the book for descriptions of category headers.

Writing Lesson 1

▼ Teaching Objective

Writers write for different purposes.

▼ Standards Alignment

RL.3.1, RL.3.10, SL.3.1a, SL.3.1b, L.3.1, L.3.6

▼ Materials

- Three signs—with a large *P*, a large *I*, and a large *E*, respectively
- A variety of texts including:
  - Poems
  - Picture books
  - Chapter books
  - Informational books
  - Informational articles
- Copies of a variety of persuasive texts for students to read; think about including book reviews, restaurant reviews, and opinion pieces written for children (*Time for Kids* has several free pieces that are easy to find by searching "debate" on their site: www.timeforkids.com.)

▼ To the Teacher

Your students should have had the opportunity to write persuasive pieces in previous grades, but it is likely that they have had limited exposure to *reading* persuasive texts. Today, you will launch this lesson set with a discussion of the author's purpose and then allow students to spend some time reading pieces of persuasive text.

▼ Procedure

Warm Up Gather the class to set the stage for today's learning

Show the class a newspaper article, a nonfiction text, a poem, and a picture book.

Close Reading
Opportunity

Each author wrote his or her text for a different reason. What do you think are some of the reasons authors write?

Record student responses.

Teach Model what students need to learn and do

Today I want to give you an easy way to remember the three different reasons authors write: PIE! P-I-E is an acronym that stands for persuade, inform, and entertain.

Make sure students know the meaning of all three words by giving examples of all three. Use the demonstration texts as appropriate to provide examples of these definitions. **ELL** Identify and Communicate Content and Language Objectives—Academic Vocabulary. If needed, you may choose to visualize these three words, put them in context, or translate them into the home language of beginner ELLs to provide support and transfer of vocabulary between languages.

It is important to know the author's purpose because it makes us think differently as we read. For example, I know this nonfiction text is trying to inform, so I will learn facts. I know that I'm reading this fiction text or silly poem just for fun. I also know that this newspaper editorial is trying to persuade me and may not give me all the facts. I know I'll need to read more to make up my own mind about the topic.

Model sorting several of your previously shared texts into the appropriate categories under the most appropriate sign.

Try Guide students to quickly rehearse what they need to learn and do in preparation for practice

Allow the class the opportunity to identify the purpose of several previously shared texts. Guide them in realizing that you have read many examples of texts intended to entertain and inform but have read fewer examples of texts intended to persuade. Tell them that today they will spend time reading examples of mentor texts intended to persuade, in preparation for writing their own persuasive pieces.

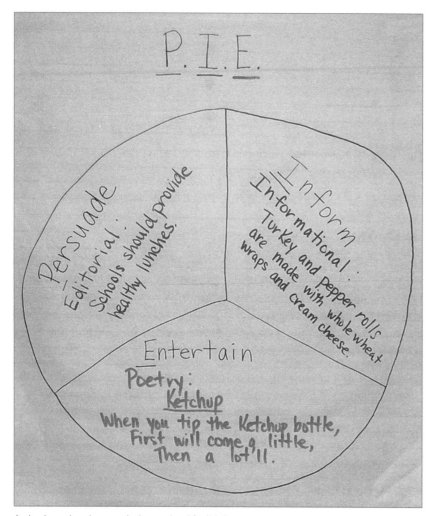

P. I. E.

Persuade
Editorial:
Schools should provide healthy lunches.

Inform
Informational:
Turkey and pepper rolls are made with whole wheat wraps and cream cheese.

Entertain
Poetry:
Ketchup
When you tip the Ketchup bottle,
First will come a little,
Then a lot'll.

A chart one teacher created as a visual for this lesson.

Clarify Briefly restate today's teaching objective and explain the practice task(s)

Today we talked about author's purpose. When an author sets out to write, he or she always has a specific purpose in mind—to persuade, inform, or entertain. We noticed that we have many mentors to turn to if our purpose as writers is to inform or entertain; however, we have fewer mentors to consider when our purpose is to persuade.

Set students up to immerse themselves in the genre of persuasive writing by independently reading a variety of mentor texts.

Practice Students work independently or in small groups to apply today's teaching objective

Students independently read persuasive mentor texts. Students should be prepared to share what they noticed about the content and structure of persuasive writing pieces.

Wrap Up Check understanding as you guide students to briefly share what they have learned and produced today

Gather the class to share what they noticed about the genre of persuasive writing. Record their notes for later use. Some things they might notice include the following:

- The authors try to convince us to do or believe something.
- The authors try to change our opinion.
- The topics usually have to do with current issues.
- The authors seem to feel strongly about the topic.
- The authors use a lot of facts and statistics to convince the reader.
- The authors try to show how those who disagree are incorrect.

Writing Lesson 2

▼ Teaching Objective

Book reviews use strong and precise language to express an opinion.

Close Reading
Opportunity

▼ Standards Alignment

RL.3.1, RL.3.4, RL.3.10, W.3.1a, W.3.4, W.3.10, SL.3.1a–d, SL.3.6, L.3.1, L.3.6

▼ Materials

- Sample book review of *Judy Moody Gets Famous* (see Appendix 3.5)
- Strong Opinions T-chart (included later in this lesson)
- Chart paper or interactive whiteboard
- Two or three sample book reviews of the same book from the Spaghetti Book Club website: www.spaghettibookclub.org (Note: Choose a book that your class is familiar with, such as a read-aloud from earlier in the year.)

▼ Procedure

Warm Up Gather the class to set the stage for today's learning

Tell the students that they will be writing reviews of the books they are reading, including the series books they are reading for their work in Core Crews. Select a model book review to use as a mentor text throughout this lesson set. You can use the one provided in Appendix 3.5, or you may substitute another.

> Yesterday we looked to experts to give us an idea of what our writing should eventually look like or sound like. Here's a book review I found that I think can serve as a great model for our writing in this lesson set.

Share the model book review for *Judy Moody Gets Famous* with your class.

Teach Model what students need to learn and do

Take a moment to read through several short book reviews posted about the same book on the Spaghetti Book Club website. Focus on the different opinions represented in each review. Think aloud about how these reviews are similar and how they are different. What point of view does each review represent?

Now, turn back to the model review of *Judy Moody Gets Famous* in Appendix 3.5. Highlight the strong opinion statement. Explain to your students that a strong third-grade opinion says more than just "I liked the book" or "I didn't like the book." A strong opinion should be connected directly to important

elements or observations about the book such as the characters, setting, plot, theme, book structure, or author's writing. Return to the mentor text, as well as some of the texts you shared with the class yesterday, and look closely at the language used by the authors, focusing on the opinion statement.

> Notice in the review of *Judy Moody Gets Famous* that the author is very specific when stating her opinion. She could have just written that she enjoys Judy Moody because Judy is funny. Instead, the author used strong language and gave us a very clear picture of exactly what she liked about the book. The review says, "I enjoyed this book because it was really witty and Judy is a lovable character. The author, Megan McDonald, has a sharp sense of humor that makes this book very entertaining."

Highlight the use of precise language—the words *witty, lovable,* and *sharp sense of humor.* Also, call attention to the clarity of this opinion—we know that this reviewer found the author's writing style to be funny and really enjoyed Judy as a character.

Demonstrate crafting a strong opinion about a shared class read-aloud such as *Clementine* (the series used as an example throughout the reading lesson set), using some of the language you highlighted earlier in this lesson. Your opinion might be something like this:

> *Clementine* is a book readers will appreciate, especially third graders who are thinking about groups and fitting in.

Reiterate for the class the importance of not simply stating "I liked the book" or "I didn't like the book."

Try Guide students to quickly rehearse what they need to learn and do in preparation for practice

Now give your students a chance to practice crafting their own opinion statement. Ask partners to craft a strong opinion about another recent read-aloud you have shared with your class. **ELL** Enable Language Production—Increasing Interaction. Both increasing interaction and offering opportunities to talk give ELLs time to practice their learning in English or their native language. Triad partnerships (one English speaker, one ELL, and one bilingual student) are often powerful for sharing and modeling language. Any easily accessible book will do. Remind students to work together to use strong language and to say more than simply whether they liked or didn't like the book.

Circulate to various partnerships, noting solid examples to share with the class.

Clarify Briefly restate today's teaching objective and explain the practice task(s)

We are going to be writing book reviews. Today we focused on crafting a strong third-grade opinion that goes beyond whether you liked or didn't like the book. Practice writing an opinion for some of the books you're reading independently. Record your opinions and the titles of the books on a T-chart to keep your thinking organized.

Book Title	Strong Opinions *Opinion may be about the character, setting, plot, theme, author's writing, text structure, and more.*

Practice Students work independently or in small groups to apply today's teaching objective

Students work independently to write strong opinions about their independent reading books, recording their thinking on the Strong Opinions T-chart. Set a quota of at least three strong opinions about the text.

Wrap Up Check understanding as you guide students to briefly share what they have learned and produced today

Gather the class, asking students to have their Strong Opinions T-charts handy. Have several students share the opinions they wrote today. Ask students, "What are your opinions about?" As the class discusses this question, collect their responses on a chart titled "Book Reviews—Our Opinions Can Be About . . ."

Some topics you might collect on your chart include:

- The characters
- The setting
- The theme(s) addressed in the book

- The plot (problem, solution, action, ending, etc.)
- The structure of the book
- The language used by the author

At the end of today's lesson, collect students' T-charts and analyze their opinions. Are students successfully crafting more nuanced opinions or do they need additional support and practice? **ELL** Assess for Content and Language Understanding—Formative Assessment. This is an opportunity to assess your ELLs' language needs and then use this information to inform upcoming work and to determine how you may need to scaffold language in upcoming lessons.

Book Title	Strong Opinions (Opinion may be about the character, setting, plot, theme, author's writing, text structure +more)
A Jigsaw Jones Mystery- The Case of Hermie the Missing Hamster	This book keeps us interested because we can't wait for each clue the author gives so we can try and figure out the mystery.
A to Z Mystery The Canary Caper	We think Josh is an interesting character because he tells jokes and treats his friends well.
The Boxcar Children #1	We think this book has a good theme: work hard, even when life is hard.
Geronimo Stilton #1 Lost Treasure of the Emerald Eye	We think the author's writing is unique. The use of different fonts, colors and pictures makes us not want to put the book down.

Milestone Performance Assessment

Articulating Strong Opinions of a Text

 Use this checklist to assess student Strong Opinion T-charts.

Standards Alignment: RL.3.1, RL.3.4, W.3.1a, W.3.10, SL.3.1a

	Achieved	Notes
Articulate three or more strong opinions of the text.		
Mention specific text elements, structure, or author's writing.		

We cannot live only for ourselves. A thousand fibers connect us with our fellow men.

—Henri Melvill

Writing Lesson 3

▼ Teaching Objective

Writers organize their writing to suit their task and purpose.

▼ Standards Alignment

RL.3.1, RL.3.9, RL.3.10, W.3.1a–d, W.3.4, W.3.10, SL.3.1a–d, SL.3.6, L.3.1, L.3.6

▼ Materials

- Persuasive Book Review graphic organizer (see Appendix 3.6)
- Mentor book review of *Judy Moody Gets Famous* (see Appendix 3.5)
- Strong Opinion T-charts students filled out in Writing Lesson 2
- Chart from Writing Lesson 2, "Book Reviews—Our Opinions Can Be About . . ."

Close Reading Opportunity

▼ Procedure

Warm Up Gather the class to set the stage for today's learning

Remind the class of the important work you did crafting strong opinions about your books yesterday. Quickly review your "Book Reviews—Our Opinions Can Be About . . ." chart to reinforce the idea that third-grade opinions are more than whether a student cared for the book.

Teach Model what students need to learn and do

Focus the class's attention on the mentor book review you began using in Writing Lesson 2. Explain that book reviews often have a predictable structure so that they are easy for people to read and understand. Starting at the beginning of the review, highlight the different elements of the mentor book review, labeling and explaining each element as you make your way through the text. Following are the elements to highlight and explain:

- Introduction
- Mention of important characters
- Mention of setting
- Opinion statement(s)
- Reasons to support the opinion
- Conclusion/recommendation

Introduce your students to the Persuasive Book Review graphic organizer included in Appendix 3.6. Demonstrate using the graphic organizer to record your thinking about the book you have chosen to review as a model for the class. **ELL** Provide Comprehensible Input—Organizers.

Try Guide students to quickly rehearse what they need to learn and do in preparation for practice

Distribute students' Strong Opinions T-charts from yesterday along with a Persuasive Book Review graphic organizer.

> Let's review the opinions you wrote yesterday. Choose one, maybe the one you feel is the most interesting or persuasive, and use it to begin filling in your graphic organizer right now.

Once students have their graphic organizers started with an opinion, have them turn and talk with a partner.

> How do you plan to complete the graphic organizer? What do you plan to include? **ELL** Enable Language Production—Increasing Interaction. This is an informal opportunity for you to support ELLs' language acquisition in "real time." You may find it helpful to carry Post-it notes for quick support and modeling. This is also an opportunity for ELLs to ask for support or clarification in a smaller-scale setting.

Clarify Briefly restate today's teaching objective and explain the practice task(s)

> Today we focused on the structure of our book reviews—the elements they need to include and the order in which they appear—using our mentor text as a guide. We discovered that a powerful book review includes an introduction,

an opinion statement, reasons to support the opinion, and a concluding statement or section. I want you to use this graphic organizer to help you prepare your thoughts for writing a truly persuasive book review.

Practice Students work independently or in small groups to apply today's teaching objective

Students work to complete the Persuasive Book Review graphic organizer. If they complete their original graphic organizer, they can move on to a fresh one and collect their thinking about another book.

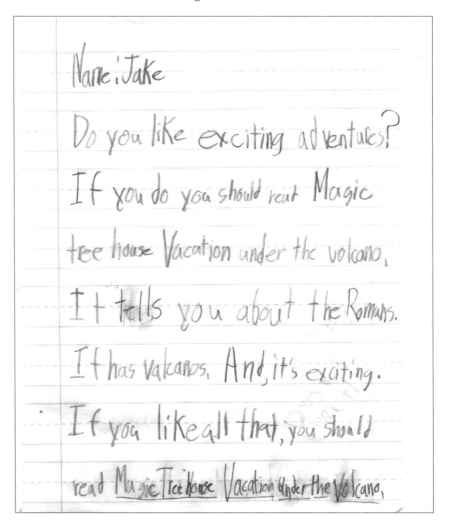

Sample book review draft.

Gather your class, asking students to bring one completed Persuasive Book Review graphic organizer. Students should share their work with a partner, using this time as an oral rehearsal for their writing.

Writing Lesson 4

▼ Teaching Objective

Writers capture the reader's attention by crafting strong introductions.

▼ Standards Alignment

W.3.1a, W.3.1b, W.3.4, W.3.10, SL.3.1a–d, SL.3.6, L.3.1, L.3.6

▼ Materials

- Two model book reviews, such as those included in Appendixes 3.5 and 3.7
- Chart paper or interactive whiteboard

▼ Procedure

Warm Up Gather the class to set the stage for today's learning

Yesterday, we began thinking about how persuasive book reviews are structured. We discovered that strong reviews include an introduction, an opinion statement, reasons to support the opinion, and a conclusion.

Teach Model what students need to learn and do

Today we're going to learn about different kinds of introductions that capture the reader's attention and set the stage for the review.

Begin a chart titled "Strong Introductions." **ELL** Provide Comprehensible Input—Organizers. This modeling will offer support as ELLs navigate how to use different kinds of introductions; consider taking a photo

of the chart and printing a smaller version so that students have a quick reference when writing. Tell your class that strong book reviews can start in a variety of ways. Explain and give examples of each of the following types of introductions, adding them to the chart as you go:

- A question
- An intriguing quote from the text
- An image from the text
- A summary

Model trying each of these introductions for your review of *Clementine.* Following is an idea of how each type of introduction might sound:

- Question: Have you ever felt like you didn't fit in?
- Intriguing quote from the text:
  - "Thursday morning I woke up with a spectacularful idea. I am lucky that way—spectacularful ideas are always sproinging up in my brain. The secret thing I know about ideas is that once they sproing into your head you have to grab them fast, or else they get bored and bounce away." (p. 65)
  - "I have had not so good of a week." (p. 1)
- Image from the text: Imagine a little girl surrounded by a pile of hair with her best friend, standing right next to her, holding the scissors.
- Summary: *Clementine* is about a third grader who is having a rough week. She tries to help out her friend Margaret, but ends up getting into a lot of trouble. The week just gets worse from there, and Clementine worries that her parents may be plotting to send her away and keep her brother since he is "the easy one."

Reiterate the idea of trying a number of introductions before choosing the one that best fits your book review.

> Did you notice how I tried all four introductions for one book review of *Clementine*? Now that I have all four introductions drafted, I can choose the one that best fits my review.

Tell students that the introduction to a book review is not composed of a lead and an opinion alone. Authors of strong book reviews also include the title and author of the book, as well as basic story elements (characters, setting, and main problem).

Try Guide students to quickly rehearse what they need to learn and do in preparation for practice

Ask students to take out their completed Persuasive Book Review graphic organizers. On a separate piece of paper or on the back of their graphic organizer, have students draft one type of lead. When students are finished, they can share their lead with a partner. As students are writing, circulate and collect examples to share with the entire group.

Once students have tried at least one lead, tell them that a *full* introduction to a book review should include one of these leads, the title and author, as well as basic story elements (main characters, setting, and the main problem). The author should hold back the solution (the spoiler) so that readers can discover it on their own.

Clarify Briefly restate today's teaching objective and explain the practice task(s)

> Today we're focusing on creating strong introductions to our book reviews. We've discovered there are many interesting ways to begin. Let's quickly review our chart.

Review the chart and remind students that they should try a variety of leads before choosing the strongest one for their review. Then, reiterate for students the other elements of a strong book review introduction (strong lead, title and author, basic story elements, opinion), jotting each element on a quick chart for student reference.

Practice Students work independently or in small groups to apply today's teaching objective

Students draft several interesting introductions for their book reviews before choosing the strongest one to use. If students finish drafting a variety of introductions for the review of one book, they can move on to draft introductions for other reviews they have started planning.

Wrap Up Check understanding as you guide students to briefly share what they have learned and produced today

 Ask two or three students to share an example of each of the types of leads you discussed today. Then, lead the class in a discussion of which introduction they believe would be the strongest start to your review of *Clementine.* Be sure that students state *why* they believe one introduction is stronger than the others. Facilitating a large-group discussion focused on making a collaborative decision is a great opportunity to reinforce and practice speaking and listening skills such as sitting respectfully, listening to others with care, speaking one at a time, staying on topic, and linking comments to those made by others. (SL.3.1b, SL.3.1d)

Once students have selected the type of lead they wish to use, they will compose their full introduction, which should include the lead, the title and author, and basic story elements (main character[s], setting, and main problem).

Writing Lesson 5 ·

▼ Teaching Objective
Writers use relevant text as evidence to strengthen their opinions.

Close Reading
Opportunity

▼ Standards Alignment
RL.3.1, RL.3.9, RL.3.10, W.3.1a, W.3.4, W.3.10, SL.3.1a–d, SL.3.6, L.3.1, L.3.6

▼ Materials

- Persuasive Book Review graphic organizers
- A copy of *Clementine* or any other book you have chosen to model reviewing for the class
- Two model book reviews, such as those included in Appendixes 3.5 and 3.7

▼ To the Teacher

In grade 2, students were asked to state reasons that support their opinion. Therefore, as third graders, they can and should be expected to elevate their reasoning. This might mean making more specific choices, discarding irrelevant or unrelated evidence, or citing directly from the text. We want to move students away from reasoning such as "I know the book is funny because the characters do a lot of funny things" or "I laughed a lot."

▼ Procedure

Warm Up Gather the class to set the stage for today's learning

Book reviews really help readers decide what to read and why. Your reviews will be helpful to other readers, and we will be sure to post them and share them in ways that will influence others.

Remind your class of the various elements you listed as part of a strong persuasive book review during Lesson 2.

Teach Model what students need to learn and do

Today we're going to focus on the evidence that supports our opinions. We want to give reasons that show that our opinions are well thought out and something that people should consider seriously. Let's turn to our mentors.

Return to your two mentor book reviews. Reread and think aloud about what you notice about the reasons provided for the authors' opinions. Be sure to highlight that these mentor texts provide two or three reasons for each opinion. Also emphasize that the reasons are specific and tightly related to the opinion stated.

© micromonkey / Fotolia

Now turn to the review of *Clementine* you have been crafting as a model for the class. Reread your opinion statement. Then demonstrate finding specific evidence to support your opinion. Here is how your modeling could unfold:

> Let me read my opinion statement again. "*Clementine* is an important book for all third graders to read, especially for those third graders who are having a hard time feeling like they fit in." Let me list my reasoning across my fingers. First, I think this book is a good example of not fitting in because Clementine struggles with fitting in throughout the whole book, so there are a lot of examples. Second, I think this is an important book to read because it might make other children who feel like they don't fit in feel better. Third, Clementine realizes that not fitting in can be a good thing too.

Demonstrate turning your thinking into sentences with examples for your review. **ELL** Provide Comprehensible Input—Models. These models offer support for your ELLs as they are crafting responses. They will refer to these models when they need help using language to express their thinking. Be sure to include specific examples from the text, modeling for students how to summarize rather than copy directly from the book. Recap your process for students.

Did you notice how I started by rereading my opinion statement? Then I listed the reasons I have this opinion across my fingers. Next, I turned my reasons into sentences. Look at what I've written. Do you see how specific my reasons are?

Try Guide students to quickly rehearse what they need to learn and do in preparation for practice

Take a look at your opinion statement. Think for a moment—what are some reasons behind your opinion? Do you have examples from the text? Be sure that your reasons are specific enough to really support your opinion.

Give students a moment to think quietly. Then ask them to share their thinking with a partner.

Clarify Briefly restate today's teaching objective and explain the practice task(s)

Today we are focusing on giving reasons to support our opinions. We need to be careful that our reasons aren't too general and that they are closely related to our opinions.

Remind students to begin by clearly stating the reasons for their opinions. Then students should adjust their thinking on their graphic organizers and develop their reasons into several sentences for their book review.

Practice Students work independently or in small groups to apply today's teaching objective

Students independently review their opinions and provide reasons to support their opinions. Students should adjust their notes on their graphic organizers accordingly and begin to draft sentences to express these reasons in their book review.

Wrap Up Check understanding as you guide students to briefly share what they have learned and produced today

Choose one or two students to share their work with the class today. Then collect one sample review from each member of the class for review. Ask students to submit a review that includes an introduction, opinion, and reasons to support their opinion. Use this work to determine whether your students need additional guidance or practice with crafting strong opinions and supporting those opinions with relevant and specific reasons from the text. **ELL** Assess for Content and Language Understanding—Formative Assessment. This is the time to think about how ELLs are progressing with the language demands of the work that you have been doing. Use this as an opportunity to jot some notes on how to scaffold and support upcoming language demands.

Milestone Performance Assessment

Writing Persuasive Book Reviews

 Use this checklist to assess student book review drafts at this point.

Standards Alignment: W.3.1a, W.3.1b, W.3.4, W.3.10

	Achieved	Notes
Draft includes a strong lead.		
Draft includes an introduction with a succinct summary (without solution).		
Draft includes at least one opinion statement with specific support from text.		

Writing Lesson 6 •

▼ **Teaching Objective**

Writers use linking words and phrases to connect their opinions and reasons.

▼ **Standards Alignment**

W.3.1c, W.3.4, W.3.10, SL.3.1 a, SL.3.1b, SL.3.6, L.3.6

▼ Materials

- Students' working drafts of one book review and a writing tool
- Chart paper or interactive whiteboard
- Mentor book reviews (see Appendixes 3.5 and 3.7)

▼ Procedure

Warm Up Gather the class to set the stage for today's learning

You have been using examples from the text to support your opinions in your reviews. Let me share a few.

Read aloud several student examples of strong opinions supported by relevant reasoning.

Teach Model what students need to learn and do

Today we're going to polish up this part of our writing by adding in linking words or phrases. A linking word or phrase helps you to connect ideas and sentences so that people can better follow your reasoning. When you are trying to persuade someone to agree with your argument, being clear in your thinking is very important.

Introduce several linking words and phrases such as *because, therefore, since, for example,* and *in addition to.* Add these words and phrases to a small chart titled "Linking Words and Phrases." Be sure that students understand the meanings of these words and phrases and are able to use them correctly in a sentence. **ELL** Identify and Communicate Content and Language Objectives—Academic Vocabulary. You can pull small groups of your newer ELLs to practice using these words and phrases in the context of their own work, as well as translate if you are able so that they can transfer between languages.

Now, refer back to your mentor texts (included in Appendixes 3.5 and 3.7) and highlight examples of linking words and phrases in action.

Now it is time to demonstrate how to revise your writing to include these words and phrases. Model rereading the draft of the review you have created for *Clementine* throughout this lesson set. **ELL** Provide Comprehensible Input—Models.

Think aloud about how you decide where to put these words and phrases. Be sure to model rereading your writing with these new additions to ensure that your writing is still clear and makes sense.

Try Guide students to quickly rehearse what they need to learn and do in preparation for practice

Ask students to reread their drafts and find one place to revise their work to add in a linking word or phrase. As students work, circulate through the room, coaching students as necessary and looking to collect examples of successful revisions to share with the rest of the class.

Clarify Briefly restate today's teaching objective and explain the practice task(s)

Today we are going to revise our book reviews to add in linking words and phrases in order to make sure our writing is as clear as possible. We are trying to convince people, and clarity will guide them toward our point of view. Remember, begin by rereading your draft, then find places to connect your thoughts with linking words or phrases. Reread your work to make sure it sounds right and still makes sense and even read it aloud to yourself or to a partner to be sure your clarity is there.

Practice Students work independently or in small groups to apply today's teaching objective

Students reread the drafts of their reviews, revising them to add in linking words as appropriate. When students are finished, they should continue drafting additional reviews of their independent reading books or their Core Crew series books.

Wrap Up Check understanding as you guide students to briefly share what they have learned and produced today

Return to the Linking Words and Phrases chart you created earlier in the lesson. Ask students to share examples of each linking word or phrase from their own revised writing. Add one or two of these examples for each word or phrase to the chart.

Writing Lesson 7

▼ Teaching Objective

Writers craft strong conclusions that leave the audience thinking.

▼ Standards Alignment

W.3.1d, W.3.4, W.3.10, SL.3.1 a, SL.3.1b, SL.3.6, L.3.6

▼ Materials

- Mentor book reviews (from Appendixes 3.5 and 3.7)
- Students' draft of one book review and a writing tool

▼ Procedure

Warm Up Gather the class to set the stage for today's learning

For the last few days, our writing work has been all about choosing strong opinions, words, and reasons so that we can create the best piece of persuasive writing possible. We started with a strong introduction that captured the reader's attention, continued to craft a strong opinion with strong reasons to support it, and now it's time to draft a strong conclusion that will leave our readers thinking.

Teach Model what students need to learn and do

Today I want to teach you how to craft a strong conclusion by trying a variety of different endings to your writing before making the best choice.

Remind students how, earlier in this lesson set, you tried a variety of introductions before choosing the best one. Drafting your options first resulted in stronger choices. Begin a chart titled "Strong Conclusions." **ELL** Provide Comprehensible Input—Organizers. Just as you provided this reference for introductions, consider offering your ELLs a smaller version of the chart focused on conclusions for reference to promote independent work habits. Tell your class that strong book reviews can end in a variety of ways. Explain and give examples of each of the following types of conclusions, adding them to the chart as you go:

- Question
- Rating
- Recommendation

Model trying each of these conclusions for your review of *Clementine*. Following is an idea of how each type of conclusion might sound:

- Question: "Who doesn't want a friend like Clementine?"
- Rating: "I give *Clementine* two thumbs up for making me laugh and for sharing her third-grade struggles with all of us."
- Recommendation: "If you have ever felt left out or like you're having the worst week ever, then *Clementine* is just the book to pick your spirits up!"

Reiterate the idea of trying a number of conclusions before choosing the one that best fits your book review.

Try Guide students to quickly rehearse what they need to learn and do in preparation for practice

Ask students to take out a draft of a review they have been working on. On a separate piece of paper (or on a screen), have students draft one type of conclusion. When students are finished, they can share their work with a partner. As students are writing, circulate and collect examples to share with the entire group, or use an online system such as Google docs to confer remotely with individual students.

Clarify Briefly restate today's teaching objective and explain the practice task(s)

Today we are focusing on creating strong conclusions for our persuasive writing. Over the last few days, we realized how important it is to make strong editorial choices throughout this process. Let's quickly review our chart.

Review the chart and remind students that they should try a variety of conclusions before choosing the strongest one for their review.

Practice Students work independently or in small groups to apply today's teaching objective

Students draft several interesting conclusions for their book reviews before choosing the strongest one to use. If students finish drafting a variety of conclusions for the review of one book, they can move on to drafting conclusions for other reviews they are working on.

Wrap Up Check understanding as you guide students to briefly share what they have learned and produced today

Ask two or three students to share an example of each of the types of conclusions you discussed today. Then lead the class in a discussion of which conclusion they believe would be the strongest for the review of *Clementine*. Be sure that students state *why* they believe one conclusion is stronger than the others.

Writing Lesson 8

▼ Teaching Objective

Writers revisit their writing with a partner and make choices about how to strengthen their work.

▼ Standards Alignment

W.3.1a–d, W.3.4, W.3.5, W.3.10, SL.3.1a–d, SL.3.6, L.3.1, L.3.2, L.3.3, L.3.6

▼ Materials

- Copies of Finalizing Book Review Checklist (see Appendix 3.8)
- An unedited version of your shared book review or another unedited book review

▼ To the Teacher

This lesson may benefit from being divided over two days—one day for revision and one day for implementing editing conventions. *Revision* means to "see again," and you will want your students to focus on how they have addressed the key elements of a book review (strong introduction, clearly stated opinions with relevant reasons to support them, a thought-provoking ending, and transitional words and phrases). Editing is about conventions. Do all of the sentences end with appropriate punctuation? Are book titles underlined and are characters' names capitalized? Since this piece of writing requires a particular focus for revision, the Finalizing Book Review Checklist (see Appendix 3.8) will serve as an important tool for students to independently account for the elements of a strong piece of persuasive writing as well as the conventions that are most critical to this genre and are consistent with the Common Core State Standards for third grade. **ELL** Provide Comprehensible Input—Graphic Organizers/Outlines.

▼ Procedure

Warm Up Gather the class to set the stage for today's learning

Your strong reading/writing voices impact each other and you bring a new perspective on the books you've read and reviewed. You've spent a lot of time choosing the strongest words, phrases, and sentences so that you can be sure to persuade your audience to share your opinion. Now we are ready to reread our reviews with a partner, checking to make sure our writing is as strong as possible and also understandable to our readers.

Teach Model what students need to learn and do

When writers go to publish their pieces, they have an editor read over their work to make sure it is clear for the reader. An editor is someone who rereads with a purpose in mind. Your partner will become your editor, and together you will read each other's work with the purpose of making it as strong and as easy to read as possible.

Before taking a look at our own writing, let's take a look at my review of *Clementine* and practice using the Finalizing Book Reviews Checklist to help strengthen our writing.

Model for students how to use the Finalizing Book Reviews Checklist with the first paragraph of the unedited version of your shared book review. **ELL** Provide Comprehensible Input—Organizers, Models. This checklist is a powerful resource for ELLs to edit their work independently. If you have beginner ELLs, consider modifying the checklist to meet their writing levels. Also model how to make revisions and edits as needed.

Try Guide students to quickly rehearse what they need to learn and do in preparation for practice

Have partners finish reading your review of *Clementine,* using the Finalizing Book Reviews Checklist and making revisions and edits as needed. Circulate throughout the room, supporting students' work and looking for examples to share with the rest of the class.

Clarify Briefly restate today's teaching objective and explain the practice task(s)

> Now that you've helped this writer make her book review even better, you are ready to read your partner's review with a new lens—that of an editor. Using the Finalizing Book Reviews Checklist, make sure your partner's review includes the key elements of a book review and that it follows the rules for proper capitalization, punctuation, and spelling to make the writing as clear as possible.

Practice Students work independently or in small groups to apply today's teaching objective

Students will work with a partner, using the Finalizing Book Reviews Checklist. **ELL** Enable Language Production—Increasing Interaction. Take this opportunity to showcase ways that ELLs are tackling the editing process in English. These strategies will aid other ELLs in the class. Some students

may need extra support with this stage of the writing process in order to know how to revise a piece when they see an element missing, such as if the review is missing a reason to support the opinion. Guide these students in revisiting the mentor texts you have shared with the class and refer back to the charts you have created as a group. Other students may need additional support with basic writing conventions such as capitalization and punctuation. The Finalizing Book Review Checklist is designed to help students revise for the content and conventions of persuasive book reviews as well as conventions of standard English.

Providing time for students to discuss their work collaboratively is a wonderful opportunity to reinforce key speaking and listening skills such as asking questions to check understanding of the information presented, staying on topic, and explaining ideas in light of the discussion. (SL.3.1c, SL.3.1d)

Wrap Up Check understanding as you guide students to briefly share what they have learned and produced today

Have students share one revision or edit they made today. Congratulate them on their promotion to editors!

> " To penetrate and dissipate these clouds of darkness, the general mind must be strengthened by education.
>
> — Thomas Jefferson "

Writing Lesson 9

▼ Teaching Objective

Writers prepare their reviews for publication.

▼ Standards Alignment

W.3.1a–d, W.3.6, W.3.10, SL.3.1a–d, SL.3.6, L.3.1, L.3.2, L.3.3, L.3.6

▼ Materials

- Students should choose their strongest review to publish (prior to this lesson)
- Chart paper or interactive whiteboard
- Materials relevant to your final product choice (see the To the Teacher section that follows)

▼ To the Teacher

You have a choice in how you have your students publish their book reviews. The ultimate goal is for students to put their work into the world in meaningful ways. Following is a chart of low-tech and high-tech options. Choose the option that best suits your level of comfort, the resources you have available to you, and the interests of your students. Regardless of the method you choose, preparing student work for publication may need to be spread across more than one day.

Goal	Low-Tech	High-Tech
Students publish their work in meaningful and real-world ways.	• Students recopy their work neatly onto a large index card to be affixed to the inside cover of the book reviewed. • Students fancy up their work with a colorful illustration and post their reviews in the school or public library for others to read. • Students type up their reviews using a word-processing program such as Word or Pages. Compile their reviews into a mock book review list or section of a newspaper.	• Students post their reviews on a book review website (such as Spaghetti Book Club or Amazon). • Students type up their reviews in plain text. Then students use a QR code generator (such as www.qrstuff.com) to generate a QR code to link to their review. Print the QR code and affix it to the back cover of the book being reviewed. Future readers can then scan the book (using an iPod, iPad, or smartphone) and read the review.

▼ Procedure

Warm Up Gather the class to set the stage for today's learning

We're about ready to send your book reviews out into the world! Today we will prepare and finalize our reviews so they are suitable for publication. Our words really can inspire others to try a new book or to see a familiar character in a new way.

Teach Model what students need to learn and do

Explain your choice of final product to the class, elaborating on the steps students will need to take to prepare their work for publication. As you discuss these steps, add them to a chart for students to refer back to. **ELL** Provide Comprehensible Input—Organizers For example, if you choose to have your class create QR codes to link to their reviews, your chart might look like this:

Preparing Your Work for Publication

1. Type up your review using TextEdit. (Make sure you save your work as plain text!)

2. Generate a QR code for your work at www.qrstuff.com.

   Select "plain text."
   Cut and paste your book review into the text box.
   Choose a foreground color.
   Download the QR code generated for you.

3. Print your QR code.

4. Try your QR code to make sure it works!

5. Glue your QR code to the back of the book you reviewed.

Demonstrate the most difficult aspects of preparing a work for publication. For example, if you choose to generate QR codes, you may want to demonstrate navigating the QR code generator.

Try Guide students to quickly rehearse what they need to learn and do in preparation for practice

Have students discuss the process with a partner. Ask them, "What steps seem the most challenging or time consuming? What can you do if you get stuck or run into problems?"

Clarify Briefly restate today's teaching objective and explain the practice task(s)

Recap the process students must follow to prepare their work for publication. Draw their attention back to the chart you created, reminding them to use this as a reference point as they work.

> Today we are preparing our work for publication—it's an exciting day! Take care as you work through the steps we've outlined here and remember to problem-solve your way through any tricky spots.

Practice Students work independently or in small groups to apply today's teaching objective

Students independently prepare their work for publication.

Wrap Up Check understanding as you guide students to briefly share what they have learned and produced today

Ask students to interact with the work of their peers—take a gallery walk of reviews displayed in the library, use smartphones or iPads to scan one another's QR codes, or search for their peers' reviews on a book review website.

Preparing Our Work for Publication

1. Type up your review using TextEdit (Make sure you save your work as Plain Text!)
2. Generate a QR Code for your work at QRStuff.com
   - Select "Plain Text"
   - Cut and paste your book review in the text box.
   - Choose a foreground color
   - Download the QR code
3. Print your QR code
4. Glue your QR code to the back of the book you reviewed
5. Try your QR code and make sure it works!

Milestone Performance Assessment

Writing Persuasive Book Reviews

 Use this checklist to assess student book reviews.

Standards Alignment: W.3.1a–d, W.3.6, W.3.10, SL.3.6, L.3.1, L.3.2, L.3.3

Revising	Yes or No	Notes
Include a strong lead.		
Include an introduction with a succinct summary (without solution).		
Include at least one opinion statement with specific support from text.		

Revising	Yes or No	Notes
Include a strong conclusion.		
Use transitional phrases to connect ideas.		
Follow teacher-directed procedures to publish review.		

Revising	Yes or No	Notes
COPS Editing Checklist*		
Correct **c**apitalization.		
Correct **o**rder and usage of words.		
Correct **p**unctuation.		
Correct **s**pelling.		

*We recommend that you focus your assessment lens in these areas. Select and assess a few skills you have previously taught or that have emerged as areas of need in your ongoing assessment of student writing.

Writing Lesson 10

▼ Teaching Objective

Writers use their persuasive writing skills in a variety of contexts.

▼ Standards Alignment

W.3.1a–d, W.3.4, W.3.10, SL.3.1a, SL.3.1b, SL.3.6, L.3.1, L.3.6

▼ Materials

- Chart paper or an interactive whiteboard

▼ To the Teacher

Reflection is a crucial element of this work. It provides students with the necessary time to think about and articulate their own learning as well as develop and express their identities as readers and writers.

▼ Procedure

Warm Up Gather the class to set the stage for today's learning

We have learned a lot about how to state our opinions using strong language and how to support our opinions with relevant reasons and evidence. These are skills we will use for a lifetime.

Teach Model what students need to learn and do

Today I want us to take some time to reflect on everything we've learned about persuasive writing and book reviews in particular. One thing we worked very hard on as a group was crafting a strong third-grade opinion that said more than "I liked the book" or "I didn't like the book" and supporting our opinions with reasons or evidence from the text. We thought a lot about how to make our ideas clear and strong. Now that we've finished this work with book reviews, I want us to think a bit about where else we think we can use this skill. In what other situations will it be important for us to craft strong opinions and support them with relevant reasons?

Name another context in which this type of thinking and writing will be useful, such as making a change to a rule at school.

Try   Guide students to quickly rehearse what they need to learn and do in preparation for practice

Lead the class in a discussion around this question. As the discussion unfolds, begin to craft a shared response to other situations in which we can use persuasive writing skills. **ELL** Provide Comprehensible Input—Models. This model offers an opportunity for ELLs to hear you use English and discuss class thinking while turning that thinking into a response. This activity will aid ELLs when they are doing this work on their own. Ideally, your class response should name other contexts to which students can transfer this skill, such as student government speeches, online reviews, and letters to editors or community leaders.

Clarify   Briefly restate today's teaching objective and explain the practice task(s)

It's important to take some time to reflect on your learning every once in a while. This helps make what you learn stay in your brain so you can use it later! I want to know what you have learned about persuasive writing through this process. Today, you are going to write a response to the following question: "What rule or routine at school do you think should be changed? Why?"

Post this question in a central location for students to refer back to as they work.

Goal	Low-Tech	High-Tech
Students craft a written response to a given question.	Students answer the questions using pencil and paper and then share their responses orally. You could choose key snippets of conversations to write up and create a reflection bulletin board.	Students draft a response in a Word document, practicing their keyboarding skills. They can share this document with you by dragging it into a shared folder, using Dropbox, or sending it via email. In addition, students can post their reflections to a class blog to share with their peers. As homework, students could comment thoughtfully on the reflections of two (or more) of their classmates.

Remember to state your opinion using strong language and provide reasons for your opinion!

Practice   Students work independently or in small groups to apply today's teaching objective

Students individually craft responses to the question posed. **ELL** Enable Language Production—Reading and Writing. You can take this time to confer with your ELLs to see how they may need support in crafting their responses.

Wrap Up   Check understanding as you guide students to briefly share what they have learned and produced today

After students have had sufficient time to complete their responses, call the class together to share their ideas. Lead a discussion centered on this question. Encourage students to use details to support their thinking.

Milestone Performance Assessment
Writing to Persuade

 Use this checklist to assess student persuasive writing pieces.

Standards Alignment: W.3.1a–d, W.3.4, W.3.10

	Achieved	Notes
Include an engaging lead.		
Introduction answers question.		
Provide strong and precise reasons to support thinking.		
Use transitional words and phrases to connect ideas.		
Include a strong conclusion.		

Language Companion Lesson

This lesson is best implemented early in the lesson set so that students can apply the new words they discover to their discussions and writing about authors and books.

▼ Teaching Objective

When writers choose powerful adjectives, the message is clearer and stronger.

▼ Standards Alignment

L.3.1a, L.3.3a

▼ Materials

- Student thesauruses (print or digital)
- Charting materials (chart paper, whiteboard, interactive whiteboard, etc.)
- Student writing materials
- Poster-making supplies

▼ To the Teacher

This lesson encourages students to expand their vocabulary and strengthen their message by choosing powerful words to convey their opinions about books and authors.

▼ Procedure

Warm Up Gather the class to set the stage for today's learning

Create a two-column chart. Title one column "So-so" and one column "Super!" Ask students to think of their favorite book. Direct them to write down three sentences that explain why they like this book. As students write, take a look at what they are creating. You should be on the lookout for students who have used adjectives to describe the books.

Teach Model what students need to learn and do

When students are done, ask volunteers to share some of their sentences. As students use adjectives in their sentences, point them out. If providing background on adjectives is necessary, briefly explain that adjectives are words that describe people, places, or things.

Ask the class to evaluate whether the adjectives they share are "So-so" or "Super!" Explain that so-so adjectives are basic, vague words that students frequently use when expressing an opinion.

- ▶ Cynthia Rylant is a good author.
- ▶ Matt Christopher's books are always interesting to me.
- ▶ Jon Scieszka has funny characters in every book.

In contrast, super adjectives are more specific or feel stronger than so-so adjectives. They help make our opinions clearer and more convincing to others.

- ▶ Cynthia Rylant is an outstanding author.
- ▶ Matt Christopher's books are always compelling to me.
- ▶ Jon Scieszka has hilarious characters in every book.

Try Guide students to quickly rehearse what they need to learn and do in preparation for practice

Use the two-column chart to record some of the adjectives students suggest within the two categories. It is OK if students do not have many super adjectives yet.

Clarify Briefly restate today's teaching objective and explain the practice task(s)

Tell the students that they will be working in groups to go on a hunt for super adjectives they can use when they share their opinions of authors and books. Assign a so-so adjective to a small group of students. Some common so-so words you might select:

- Good
- Bad

- Interesting
- Funny
- Nice
- Exciting
- Fun
- Boring

Practice Students work independently or in small groups to apply today's teaching objective

Each group will use a thesaurus and their own ideas to create a poster with the heading "Why Use _____ When You Can Use . . ." Fill in the blank with the group's assigned so-so word. In the space beneath the heading, students fill in super words with the same meaning from their hunt.

Check in with groups to guide their work. Expect to have to help students understand that not every word listed in the thesaurus will work. They may have to consider the form, part of speech, and meaning of their original word when selecting words from a thesaurus.

Wrap Up Check understanding as you guide students to briefly share what they have learned and produced today

Have students share their posters. Hang them in the classroom or create a handout students can use as a reference when they write and talk about their reading opinions. Discuss the impact of using super words when expressing opinions.

GLOSSARY

author's purpose: the reason an author decides to write about a specific topic

chapter: one of the main sections of a book, usually marked with a number or title

evidence: something that provides proof or a reason to believe

opinion: what one thinks about a character or action, especially a judgment, not necessarily based on fact

persuade: to cause someone to do something or believe in something through reasoning or arguing

plot: the story line or order of events in a book, play, or movie

point of view: the position or place from which an author or character may view, consider, or appraise something; viewpoint; standpoint

series: a group of related events, works, or objects that come one after another in sequence or are arranged in a particular order on the basis of a common characteristic

setting: the time and place in which something happens; surroundings; context; environment

summary: a short and usually comprehensive statement of what has been previously stated

theme: the main subject or topic of a literary work

Accompanying *Core Ready for Grades 3–5*, there is an online resource site with media tools that, together with the text, provides you with the tools you need to implement the lesson sets.

The PDToolkit for Pam Allyn's *Core Ready* Series is available free for 12 months after you use the password that comes with the box set for each grade band. After that, you can purchase access for an additional 12 months. If you did not purchase the box set, you can purchase a 12-month subscription at **http://pdtoolkit.pearson.com.** Be sure to explore and download the resources available at the website. Currently the following resources are available:

- Pearson Children's and Young Adult Literature Database
- Videos
- PowerPoint Presentations
- Student Artifacts
- Photos and Visual Media
- Handouts, Forms, and Posters to supplement your Core-aligned lesson plans
- Lessons and Homework Assignments
- Close Reading Guides and Samples
- Children's Core Literature Recommendations

In the future, we will continue to add additional resources. To learn more, please visit **http://pdtoolkit.pearson.com.**

Grade 4

Poetry Wars: Reading, Interpreting, and Debating Meaning in Poetry

Introduction

The Common Core State Standards require students in grade 4 to engage with grade-appropriate complex literature. This lesson set emphasizes the close reading of poetry to consider and debate the meaning of poems. Students will look closely at poetry, both at the word level and at the poem as a whole, to understand what meaning the poet may have intended and to establish their own interpretation of the poem's meaning using text evidence to support their thinking. This lesson set culminates with a poetry debate in which students will craft arguments to persuade an audience that their interpretation is accurate.

Helping students not only understand but also interpret what they read is a hallmark of grade 4. In this lesson set, the short texts poetry provides offer a great opportunity for students to think deeply about what they are reading. In support of the reading standards, students are taught in this lesson

Why This Lesson Set?

In this lesson set, students will:

- Read closely to determine the meaning of words and phrases and the significance of structural elements in poems

- Read closely to examine details in poetry to form interpretations, citing textual and experiential evidence to support their thinking in order to persuade others of their view

- Build speaking and listening skills through the oral presentation of poems

- Compose original poems incorporating techniques to strengthen meaning

- Write organized opinion pieces that defend their interpretations of poems

set to ask questions of one another, to deepen understanding of the meaning of poetry, and to consider how poets carefully choose their words to convey particular messages. Students will have many opportunities to read aloud and offer appropriate elaboration on the ideas of classmates by building on what has been said before. By focusing on what poems mean, students will develop a deeper understanding of the genre and what strategies they can employ to more deeply understand a poem's message.

Through writing their interpretations of poems and then debating those interpretations with textual evidence, students will become stronger readers of poetry and stronger advocates for their own ideas about their reading. Through the writing process, students will practice using the language of poetry and persuasion to explain their stance on the poet's intended meaning.

Common Core State Standards Alignment

Reading Standards

RL.4.1 Refer to details and examples in a text when explaining what the text says explicitly and when drawing inferences from the text.

RL.4.2 Determine a theme of a story, drama, or poem from details in the text; summarize the text.

RL.4.4 Determine the meaning of words and phrases as they are used in a text, including those that allude to significant characters found in mythology (e.g., Herculean).

RL.4.5 Explain major differences between poems, drama, and prose, and refer to the structural elements of poems (e.g., verse, rhythm, meter) and drama (e.g., casts of characters, settings descriptions, dialogue, stage directions) when writing or speaking about a text.

RL.4.7 Make connections between the text of a story or drama and a visual or oral presentation of the text, identifying where each version reflects specific descriptions and directions in the text.

RL.4.10 By the end of the year, read and comprehend literature, including stories, dramas, and poetry, in the grades 4–5 text complexity band proficiently with scaffolding as needed at the high end of the range.

Writing Standards

W.4.1 Write opinion pieces on topics or texts, supporting a point of view with reasons and information.

a. Introduce a topic or text clearly, state an opinion, and create an organizational structure in which ideas are logically grouped to support the writer's purpose.

b. Provide logically ordered reasons that are supported by facts and details.

c. Link opinion and reasons using words, phrases, and clauses (e.g., *consequently, specifically*).

d. Provide a concluding statement or section related to the opinion presented.

W.4.4 Provide clear and coherent writing in which the development and organization are appropriate to the task, purpose, and audience.

W.4.5 With guidance and support from peers and adults, develop and strengthen writing as needed by planning, revising, and editing.

W.4.6 With some guidance and support from adults, use technology, including the Internet, to produce and publish writing, as well as to interact and collaborate with others; demonstrate sufficient command of keyboarding skills to type a minimum of one page in a single sitting.

W.4.10 Write routinely over extended time frames (time for research, reflection, and revision) and shorter time frames (a single sitting or a day or two) for a range of discipline-specific tasks, purposes, and audiences.

Speaking and Listening Standards

SL.4.1 Engage effectively in a range of collaborative discussions (one-on-one, in groups, and teacher-led) with diverse partners on grade 4 topics and texts, building on others' ideas and expressing their own clearly.

a. Come to discussions prepared, having read or studied required material; explicitly draw on that preparation and other information known about the topic to explore ideas under discussion.

b. Follow agreed-upon rules for discussions and carry out assigned roles.

c. Pose and respond to specific questions to clarify or follow up on information, and make comments that contribute to the discussion and link to the remarks of others.

d. Review the key ideas expressed and explain their own ideas and understanding in light of the discussion.

SL.4.2 Paraphrase portions of a text read aloud or information presented in diverse media and formats, including visually, quantitatively, and orally.

SL.4.3 Identify the reasons and evidence a speaker provides to support particular points.

SL.4.5 Add audio recordings and visual displays to presentations when appropriate to enhance the development of main ideas or themes.

SL.4.6 Differentiate between contexts that call for formal English (e.g., presenting ideas) and situations where informal discourse is appropriate (e.g., small-group discussion); use formal English when appropriate to task and situation.

Language Standards

L.4.1 Demonstrate command of the conventions of standard English grammar and usage when writing or speaking.

a. Use relative pronouns (who, whose, whom, which, that) and relative adverbs (where, when, why).

b. Form and use the progressive (e.g., I was walking; I am walking; I will be walking) verb tenses.

c. Use modal auxiliaries (e.g., *can, may, must*) to convey various conditions.

d. Order adjectives within sentences according to conventional patterns (e.g., a small red bag rather than a red small bag).

e. Form and use prepositional phrases.

f. Produce complete sentences, recognizing and correcting inappropriate fragments and run-ons.

g. Correctly use frequently confused words (e.g., *to, too, two; there, their*).

L.4.2 Demonstrate command of the conventions of standard English capitalization, punctuation, and spelling when writing.

a. Use correct capitalization.

b. Use commas and quotation marks to mark direct speech and quotations from a text.

c. Use a comma before a coordinating conjunction in a compound sentence.

d. Spell grade-appropriate words correctly consulting references as needed.

L.4.3 Use knowledge of language and its conventions when writing, speaking, reading, or listening.

a. Choose words and phrases to convey ideas precisely.

b. Choose punctuation for effect.

c. Differentiate between contexts that call for formal English (e.g., presenting ideas) and situations where informal discourse is appropriate (e.g., small-group discussion).

L.4.6 Acquire and use accurately grade-appropriate general academic and domain-specific words and phrases, including those that signal precise actions, emotions, or states of being (e.g., quizzed, whined, stammered) and that are basic to a particular topic (e.g., wildlife, conservation, and endangered when discussing animal preservation).

Essential Skill Lenses (PARCC Framework)

As part of its proposal to the U.S. Department of Education, the multi-state Partnership for Assessment of Readiness for College and Careers (PARCC) developed model content frameworks for English Language Arts to serve as a bridge between the Common Core State Standards and the PARCC assessments in development at the time of this publication. In the grade 3 to 5 lesson sets, we expect students to engage in reading and writing through eight PARCC specified skill lenses that are rooted in the standards. The following table details how each skill lens is addressed across the lesson set (PARCC, 2011).

	Reading	Writing
Cite Evidence	Students will be asked to cite the text as evidence throughout this lesson set. In particular, students will be using text as evidence to support their ideas about the meaning of poetry and persuade others of their views.	Students will be expected to cite specific textual evidence as reasoning to support their interpretation of poetry. Two to three pieces of textual evidence should be used in their work to support the main arguments.
Analyze Content	In this lesson set, students must carefully analyze poems to determine the meaning and author's purpose. In addition, students will be asked to make comparisons of poems by the same and different poets.	Students will analyze a poem and write an interpretation that they will defend at the end of the lesson set.
Study and Apply Grammar and Usage	Students must demonstrate the ability to convey their ideas clearly, using language that is appropriate to the situation and audience.	Students will analyze their own writing to improve its clarity, using a Literary Essay Checklist as a guide.
Study and Apply Vocabulary	Students will be asked to use key lines and language from poems as clues to identify the larger theme of the selected work. In addition, specific learning language is included with this lesson set. Students will be exposed to this terminology and will incorporate terms into their speaking and writing.	In this lesson set, students are expected to choose precise language to strengthen their writing. Students will brainstorm stronger word choices and make changes to their work accordingly.
Conduct Discussions	Students will engage in discussions of poems daily. They will discuss their interpretations of poetry with the goal of persuading others of their view. Rules and behaviors that foster productive conversation are crucial elements of this study.	Students will continuously engage in conversations to analyze and improve their own writing throughout this lesson set. In addition, students will use the language of opinion and disagreement to conduct debates about what poems mean.

	Reading	Writing
Report Findings	Students will be required to report on well-known works of poetry through book poster or book trailer presentations. Emphasis is placed on using specific examples from the text to support their thinking.	Students will craft and deliver oral presentations that express their opinions about poems. Presentations must be reported to the group in an organized manner and include an introduction, clear statement of opinion, two or three supporting reasons with textual evidence, and a strong conclusion. Students will respond to one another using the language of opinion and disagreement.
Phonics and Word Recognition	We recommend that teachers plan opportunities for students to build Reading Foundational Skills by exploring grade-level appropriate skills in the context of the core texts from each lesson set and applying this knowledge to their independent reading.	We recommend that teachers encourage students to apply Reading Foundational Skills in the context of their daily writing.
Fluency and Stamina	Through shared and repeated reading of poems, students will improve their fluency and stamina within a specific genre.	Throughout this study of poetry, students will be asked to write across short and long time frames, crafting their own poems as well as more lengthy persuasive reviews of poems. This combination will support students as they develop their skills to write fluently and with purpose in a variety of situations.

Core Questions

Learning to draw evidence from poems to support analysis and reflection is an essential skill set for fourth graders. These questions should remain at the core of your teaching. Refer back to them often, encouraging your students to share their thinking as it evolves.

- What clues can we use to interpret poetry? (In other words, how do we figure out what poems mean?)
- What are the structures found in poetry?
- What techniques do poets use that I can use in my writing?
- What poetry mentors can I model my writing after?
- What language can I use to define and support my opinion?
- What is the purpose and structure of a debate?
- What is the best approach to persuade others to accept my ideas and interpretations of poetry?

Ready to Get Started?

Let's explore the power of poetry and persuasion . . .

Fourth graders are learning to more clearly define what they like and don't like about texts and why they feel the way they do. This lesson set is inspired by Sharon Creech's *Love That Dog*, which is a core text in this lesson set. In this book, the main character, Jack, is learning about poetry in school. At first Jack hates poetry, yet he finds that poems start to inspire him. This book is the story of Jack, his dog, his teacher, and how he found a way to talk about something important to him through his words and his poetry. The story develops through Jack's responses to poems they are learning in class. Jack's teacher, Miss Stretchberry, helps Jack realize that he has a lot to say and that poetry might be the way to say it. Jack is like many fourth graders we know. He is stubborn, kind, warmhearted, funny, curious, and serious. Poetry gives our fourth graders an outlet—a confined space to express what they love, what they hate, what they find funny, and what they find deeply serious. The book is told through Jack's journal entries and his poetry. As Jack studies particular poems in school, we learn his response to these classic works and how they inspire his own poetry. We are confident your students will find their poetic voice through this lesson set, both as readers with interpretations to share with others and writers with ideas to express through their own poetry.

Lesson Set Goals

Within this lesson set, there are many goals we want to help our students reach.

Reading Goals

- Read and interpret poetry using details and examples from the text when drawing inferences. (RL.4.1, RL.4.2, RL.4.10, SL.4.1a-d, L.4.1, L.4.6)

- Determine the meaning of words and phrases in poems. (RL.4.1, RL.4.4, RL.4.10, L.4.6)

- Refer to the structural elements of a poem in discussion. (RL.4.1, RL.4.5, RL.4.10, SL.4.1a-d, SL.4.2, L.4.1, L.4.6)

- Identify the reasons and evidence a speaker provides when discussing the meaning of a poem, and agree or disagree with the interpretation. (RL.4.1, RL.4.2, RL.4.10, SL.4.1a-d, SL.4.3, SL.4.6, L.4.6)

- Compare and contrast poems focusing on meaning and structural elements. (RL.4.1, RL.4.2, RL.4.4, RL.4.5, RL.4.10, W.4.1, W.4.4, W.4.10, SL.4.1a-d, L.4.6)

- Read poems aloud to further convey the meaning. (RL.4.1, RL.4.7, RL.4.10, SL.4.5, L.4.1, L.4.6)

- Refer to details and examples in a text when explaining what the text explicitly says and when drawing inferences from the text. (RL.4.1)

- Write an organized opinion piece that includes a clear introduction, point of view, supporting reasons, linking words and phrases, and a concluding statement. (W.4.1)

- By the end of the year, proficiently read and comprehend a variety of literature in the grades 4–5 text complexity band, with scaffolding as needed at the high end of the range. (RL.4.10)

- Write routinely over extended time frames (time for research, reflection, and revision) and shorter time frames (a single sitting or a day or two) for a range of discipline-specific tasks, purposes, and audiences. (W.4.10)

- In collaborative discussions, demonstrate evidence of preparation for discussion and exhibit responsibility to the rules and roles of conversation. (SL.4.1a, SL.4.1b)

- In collaborative discussions, share and develop ideas in a manner that enhances understanding of topic. Contribute and respond to the content of the conversation in a productive and focused manner. (SL.4.1c, SL.4.1d)

- Demonstrate knowledge of standard English and its conventions. (L.4.1, L.4.2, L.4.3)

- Acquire and accurately use grade-appropriate conversational, general academic, and domain-specific vocabulary and phrases. (L.4.6)

Writing Goals

- Write poems in tribute to well-known works. (RL.4.1, RL.4.10, W.4.4, W.4.10)

- Use strong word choice to convey strong images. (RL.4.4, W.4.4, W.4.6, W.4.10)

- Use line breaks and white space for impact. (W.4.4, W.4.6, W.4.10, L.4.3)

- Write an interpretation of a poem, supporting one's point of view with evidence from the poem (RL.4.1, RL.4.2, RL.4.4, RL.4.5, RL.4.10, W.4.1a, W.4.4, W.4.10)

- Express and develop ideas in conversations with others. (SL.4.1a-d, SL.4.3, SL.4.6, L.4.1, L.4.6)

- With guidance and support from peers and adults, develop and strengthen writing as needed by planning, revising, and editing. (W.4.5)

- Refer to details and examples in a text when explaining what the text explicitly says and when drawing inferences from the text. (RL.4.1)

- Write an organized opinion piece that includes a clear introduction, point of view, supporting reasons, linking words and phrases, and a concluding statement. (W.4.1)

- By the end of the year, proficiently read and comprehend a variety of literature in the grades 4–5 text complexity band, with scaffolding as needed at the high end of the range. (RL.4.10)

- Write routinely over extended time frames (time for research, reflection, and revision) and shorter time frames (a single sitting or a day or two) for a range of discipline-specific tasks, purposes, and audiences. (W.4.10)

- In collaborative discussions, demonstrate evidence of preparation for discussion and exhibit responsibility to the rules and roles of conversation. (SL.4.1a, SL.4.1b)

- In collaborative discussions, share and develop ideas in a manner that enhances understanding of topic. Contribute and respond to the content of the conversation in a productive and focused manner. (SL.4.1c, SL.4.1d)

- Demonstrate knowledge of standard English and its conventions. (L.4.1, L.4.2, L.4.3)

- Acquire and accurately use grade-appropriate conversational, general academic, and domain-specific vocabulary and phrases. (L.4.6)

Choosing Core Texts

For this lesson set, we recommend using poetry that has been suggested by the Common Core State Standards Committee in addition to poetry that will tap into your students' particular interests. For independent reading, we recommend creating a packet of poems for your students so that they can choose which poems speak to them on a given day. This will also allow students to reread poetry, which will not only help build fluency but will also help students read more closely as they read the same poems with a new lens.

Fletcher, Ralph. *A Writing Kind of Day*.
Poems in this text that work well with this lesson set:

"A Writing Kind of Day"
"A Writing Kind of Night"
"Frost in the Woods"
"Hungry for Poetry"
"Metaphor"

"Poetry Recipe"
"Writer's Block"
"Writer's Notebook"

Collins, Billy. *Introduction to Poetry*.
Creech, Sharon. *Love That Dog*.
Poems in this text:

Adoff, Arnold. "Street Music."
Blake, William. "The Tiger."
Frost, Robert. "Stopping by Woods on a Snowy Evening."
Frost, Robert. "The Pasture."
Rigg, S. C. "The Apple."
Williams, William Carlos. "The Red Wheelbarrow."
Worth, Valerie. "dog."

Poems Recommended by Common Core State Standards Committee in Appendix B to the standards:

Blake, William. "The Echoing Green."
Dahl, Roald. "Little Red Riding Hood and the Wolf."
Dickinson, Emily. "In the Garden."
Frost, Robert. "Dust of Snow."
Lazarus, Emma. "The New Colossus."
Mora, Pat. "Words Free as Confetti."
Nichols, Grace. "They Were My People."
Sandburg, Carl. "Fog."
Thayer, Ernest Lawrence. "Casey at the Bat."

A Note *about* Addressing Reading Standard 10: Range of Reading and Level of Text Complexity

This lesson set provides all students with opportunities to work with texts deemed appropriate for their grade level as well as texts at their specific reading level. Through shared experiences and focused instruction, all students engage with and comprehend a wide range of texts within their grade-level complexity band.

We suggest a variety of high-quality complex texts to use within the whole-group lessons and recommend a variety of additional titles under Choosing Core Texts to extend and enrich instruction. During independent practice and in small group collaborations, however, research strongly suggests that all students need to work with texts they can read with a high level of accuracy and comprehension (i.e., at their developmentally appropriate reading level) in order to significantly improve their reading (Allington, 2012; Ehri, Dreyer, Flugman, & Gross, 2007). Depending on individual needs and skills, a student's reading level may be above, within, or below the grade-level band.

Teacher's Notes

Some of us may have loved learning about poetry and creating our own poems in school. Others of us may remember feeling overwhelmed when given the instruction, "Write a poem," or "What does this poem mean?" We need to fill our classrooms with the joy and love of poetry. Fostering our students as readers and writers of poetry means inviting them into this genre with enthusiasm and lots of encouragement. This lesson set is designed to set students up for success with poetry. This lesson set introduces complex poems that contain strong imagery and show the power of a few words to tell a compelling story. It gives students, however, the scaffolding and tools to interpret these poems through different lenses. As they develop ideas and interpretations, students will share their thinking in a variety of ways with the goal of persuading others that their views are justified. Writing poetry is often a powerful means for our fourth graders to express themselves, their questions, their worries, and their wonderings. The boundaries created by writing poetry in the style of a well-known work gives students at this level the scaffolding needed to begin, keep going, and hopefully, want to write some more. We recommend kicking off the lesson set with an opportunity for students to read and reflect on a variety of poems. Our core texts give you some suggestions, but you should also feel free to include your favorites. Your enthusiasm for poetry will be contagious, and your students will look forward to see what poem of the day you are going to focus on next. If you are not a natural lover of poetry, be alert to students who will gravitate to this genre, and invite them to assist you in making selections and "leading" this lesson set with their passion.

Core Message to Students
(See Appendix 4.1)

Did you ever find you had something to say but you weren't sure how to say it? Did you ever find you were full of ideas and weren't sure how to share them? Did you ever find you were inspired by something and wanted to make your own version? Poetry is the perfect small package for our messages to the world. In this lesson set, we're going to read poems and think about what we like about them, what we don't, what we can learn from them, and how we can find poems to honor through our own writing. This lesson set is about reading poems closely and carefully to consider all the things the writer is trying to tell us in such a small space. This lesson set is also about writing our own poems, and modeling them after poems that speak to us. Finally, this lesson set is about discussing, debating, and persuading others to agree with what you think poems *really* mean.

Questions for Close Reading

The Core Ready lessons include many rich opportunities to engage students in close reading of text that require them to ask and answer questions, draw conclusions, and use specific text evidence to support their thinking (Reading Anchor Standard 1). These opportunities are marked with a close reading icon. You may wish to extend these experiences using our recommended Core Texts or with texts of your choosing. Use the following questions as a resource to guide students through close reading experiences of poetry.

- Are there any lines and words seem especially important to this poem? Why do you think so?
- What parts of the poem convey the strongest emotions or mood? Why?
- Can you tell who is narrating the poem? What do you discover about the narrator?
- What is the setting of the poem (location and time)?
- What are the strongest images in the poem? How do they connect to the overall meaning?

- What literary devices does the poet use? How do they connect to the overall meaning?
- Do you have any background information on the poet? How does it connect to his or her poetry?
- Why do you think the poet wrote this poem?
- What themes or message comes through to you? Why?

Building Academic Language

Following is a list of academic language to build your students' comprehension of the focus of this lesson set and facilitate their ability to talk and write about what they learn. Rather than introduce all the words at once, slowly add them to a learning wall as your teaching unfolds. See the glossary at the end of this chapter for definitions of the words. Also listed are sentence frames that may be included on a sentence wall (Carrier & Tatum, 2006), a research-proven strategy for English language learners (Lewis, 1993; Nattinger, 1980), or on a handout to scaffold student use of the content words. Some students, especially English language learners, may need explicit practice in using the sentence frames. Encourage all students to regularly use these words and phrases in their conversations and writing.

Opinion Phrases:
I think . . . , In my opinion . . . , The way I see it . . . , As far as I'm concerned . . . , I suppose . . . , I suspect that . . . , I'm pretty sure that . . . , I'm convinced that . . . , I honestly feel that . . . , I strongly believe that . . . ,

Agreement Phrases:
I agree because . . . , I also feel that . . . .

Disagreement Phrases:
I don't think that . . . , I don't agree that . . . , Shouldn't we consider . . . , But what about . . . .

Recognition

At the end of the lesson set, it is important to recognize the hard work your students have put into their learning and the way they've thought about them-

Core Words

poem	mood
alliteration	imagery
assonance	onomatopoeia
simile	personification
metaphor	repetition
hyperbole	white space	theme
idiom	rhyme	author's purpose

Core Phrases:

- This poem reminds me of when (personal connection) . . .
- This poem reminds me of (another poem, book, etc.) _____.
- I think the poet's message is _____.
- This poem makes me feel _____ because _____.
- _____ is a metaphor for _____.
- The big idea or theme of this poem is _____.
- This poem appeals to my senses (with examples). . . .
- This poem paints a picture of _____.
- I like how the poet _____.
- I noticed a technique this poet uses is _____.
- I have noticed something in many of this poet's poems. . . .
- This poem is important to me because _____.
- The main idea of this poem is _____.
- My favorite part of the poem is _____ because _____.

- This poem reminds me of another poem we've read called _____ because _____.

- I think this because _____ (textual evidence to support your thinking).

selves and others. At the end of the reading lesson set, students will be reading aloud a well-known poem of their choosing and listening to the voices of each other. At the end of the writing lesson set, students will be writing their own poems, reading the poems of their classmates, and debating what they think each other's poems really mean. Consider creating your own version of a coffee house or poetry slam for students as they read the words of well-known poets or their own poems. Discuss with students how poets share their poems aloud in collective spaces and that these performances move audiences not only because of the power of the words but also through the power of the performance. Consider inviting families or another class in for a poetry celebration to honor the hard work your students have done throughout the lesson set. Other engaging celebrations of learning include:

- Posting your students' poems around the school for others to stop and enjoy

- Having students post famous poems around the school for others to stop and enjoy

- Creating a poetry anthology with your students' poems alongside the poem that inspired their writing

- Creating a poetry corner in the classroom where students can read, reflect, and comment on poems

- Creating a poet of the day sign-up sheet for students to read aloud their own poems or poems they've found in their reading

Assessment

 Assessment in this lesson set is both ongoing and culminating, meaning that as teachers we are constantly watching and observing how

students are making meaning and how they are interpreting new material. Throughout this lesson set, look for performance-based assessments, called Milestone Performance Assessments, each marked with an assessment icon. Milestone Performance Assessments are opportunities to notice and record data on Core standards-aligned indicators during the course of the lesson set. Use the results of these assessments to determine how well students are progressing toward the goals of the lesson set. Adjust the pace of your teaching and plan instructional support as needed.

We also encourage you to use the Reading and Writing Rubrics, also marked with assessment icons, with each lesson set to evaluate overall student performance on the Core standards-aligned lesson set goals. In this lesson set, the finalized poems and interpretations are an important piece of summative assessment that can be analyzed and then placed in a portfolio of student work. See the foundational book, *Be Core Ready: Powerful, Effective Steps to Implementing and Achieving the Common Core State Standards,* for more information about the Core Ready Reading and Writing Rubrics.

In addition, we have provided a Universal Speaking and Listening Assessment Checklist (see Appendix 4.10) that provides observable Core Standards–aligned indicators to assess student performance as speakers and listeners. There are multiple opportunities in every Core Ready lesson set to make such observations. Use the checklist in its entirety to gather performance data over time or choose appropriate indicators to create a customized checklist to match a specific learning experience.

Core Support for Diverse Learners

This lesson set was created with the needs of a wide variety of learners in mind. Throughout the day-by-day lessons, you'll find examples of visual supports, graphic organizers, highlighted speaking and listening opportunities, and research-driven English language learner supports aimed at scaffolding instruction for all learners. Also, we urge you to consider the following areas of challenge with which your students may need guided support. The following sections are written to spotlight important considerations as you move through the lesson sets.

Reading

Choosing texts that are at students' reading levels is essential for their reading success and reading identity. When finding texts make sure you have various levels represented in your classroom reading collection. Your students (or some of your students) may benefit from repeated exposure to a lesson's teaching point over several days. This can be accomplished with the whole class or in small group settings.

Closely monitor your students who are reading below grade level to determine if they are reading with accuracy and fluency to support comprehension. Encourage students to use context to confirm or self-correct word recognition and understanding and to reread when necessary. Refer to the Common Core Foundational Skills Standards both at the grade 4 level as well as earlier grade level standards for direct, explicit foundational skills support that your students reading below grade level may need.

Poems are layered with multisyllabic words that will require teacher support to decode. In addition, the figurative language within poems can be particularly challenging. Diverse learners may need a great deal of help with interpreting poetry. You may want to pair students with a poem partner to foster discussion and meaning-making. Refer to our Core Words guide for vocabulary that you may want to frontload with small groups of students. Be cognizant of unfamiliar language embedded within the selections of poems you choose for both whole class teaching as well as independent reading and preview the texts you provide to students reading below grade level to provide additional support with decoding and comprehension.

As you continue your work with students, use observational notes and reading assessment data to create two to three specific short term goals for your students with diverse needs. For example, as stated above, these goals may be related to increasing word accuracy, building vocabulary, improving fluency, or enhancing comprehension. Throughout this lesson set, tailor your individualized and small group instruction set so that it addresses and evaluates student progress toward these goals.

Writing

Inspired writers are motivated writers. Allowing students to choose the topic of their writing is critical for their ultimate success and their positive development of identity as a writer. When immersing your students in a new genre, form, or purpose for writing, be sure to emphasize the meaning and function this particular type of writing may have in their own lives. Many of your students will also benefit from exposure to strong mentor texts, examples of your own writing as well as the experience of sharing their own work—both the final product and in process.

Many of your students will significantly benefit from the opportunity to sketch their ideas about the themes of poems before adding text. This is especially helpful for visual learners and students who need to "sketch to stretch." Even your most proficient writers can benefit from this step, but many of your resistant writers will feel more comfortable with getting their ideas on paper through drawing first. Giving students some sentence starters can vastly help them focus on their ideas and have the stamina to get their thoughts on paper (refer to our Core Words and Core Phrases) such as:

- The theme of this poem is _____ as evidenced by _____.

- When the poet writes _____ I believe it means _____ because _____.

As your students move from determining their ideas for their poetic interpretations and begin putting their thoughts on paper, provide your students with a variety of paper choices that are fourth-grade appropriate. For students with fine motor control issues, providing students with a variety of paper choices that have handwriting lines with a dotted line in the middle can offer support as letter formation may require significant energy for some writers. Also consider having students type and electronically publish their poetic interpretations as well as original poems rather than handwrite them if that is a medium more conducive to their writing success.

We want our fourth graders to communicate their ideas to an audience and supporting them as developing writers is essential. In addition to providing students with topic choice and the opportunity to draw prior to writing, we can provide further scaffolding by having students orally rehearse their debate points to us or to a peer. For some students, the oral rehearsal will provide a springboard to writing. For others, they will have greater success dictating their ideas to you.

As with the reading lessons, your students may benefit from several days on a single lesson's teaching point. This can be done with the whole class or in small group settings.

English Language Learners

While it is always our goal as teachers to get to know all of our students deeply both in and out of the classroom setting, this work is perhaps more critical when considering our English language learners. Honoring families' cultural traditions and experiences is important to getting to know, understand, and work with your students in meaningful ways.

English language learners are learning about poetry alongside native English speakers in your classroom, but they are also simultaneously learning English. For our English language learners, it is essential to simultaneously develop their ability to easily hold conversations about their reading and writing and build their academic language base. Goldenberg (2008) defines "academic English" as the more abstract, complex, and challenging language that permits us to participate successfully in mainstream classroom instruction. English language learners will over time be responsible for understanding and producing academic English both orally and in writing. However, language acquisition is a process and our English language learners range in their development of English language acquisition. We urge you to consider your students along a spectrum of language acquisition from students new to this country to those who are proficient conversationally to those who have native-like proficiency.

Refer to the English language learners icons throughout this lesson set for ways to shelter instruction for English language learners. These elements will help English language learners participate successfully in the whole-group lesson and support the development of their language skills. Although these moments during instruction are designed to support English language learners, many schools are adding a separate English language development (ELD) block targeted at oral English language development to further support their students in language acquisition.

Students with growing English proficiency will benefit from a Poetry Word Wall to build vocabulary (refer to our Core Words and Phrases). A sentence word wall to give them sentence starters to help with conversation will also offer students another layer of support. Some students may benefit from having their own personalized copies of these words to keep in their reading or writing notebooks for quick reference. Visual aids will further support students and give them a reference to what words are important to this study and what they mean.

Consider forming small groups of students in poetry circles for those students who need more scaffolding. In addition, it will be important to include a variety of poem types in your poetry packet. Consider poems in other languages that are represented by the children in your classroom. Consider the length of poems, vocabulary, and strong imagery when creating your poetry packets for English language learners in your classroom.

Some students will benefit from several days on the same teaching point. You may consider gathering small groups of readers or writers for repeated instruction or using one-on-one conferences as an opportunity to revisit teaching points.

Complementary Core Methods

Read-Aloud

Take the opportunity to share a wide variety of poems during read-aloud. Make sure to include poems that vary in length, structure, and theme. Use your knowledge of students' interests to select poems that will inspire and excite your class. When appropriate, use your read-aloud as another chance for students to practice one or two of the following skills:

- Asking and answering questions about a text, using portions of the text as evidence in their responses
- Identifying and exploring the meaning of new vocabulary
- Identifying poetic structures
- Discussing the meanings of poems, particularly emphasizing lessons on mood, imagery, and poet's purpose

Shared Reading

Shared reading provides a wonderful opportunity to read poetry aloud together. Choose a variety of poems for this experience. Consider poems that rhyme and poems that don't. Consider poems that repeat lines, words, and phrases for emphasis. Consider poems that show varying structural elements, such as those with a variety of stanzas and those that use techniques like alliteration. Following are some prompts you may want to use in your conversations about these texts:

- What do you notice about this poem?
- What words stand out to you? Why?
- What are you picturing in your mind?
- What punctuation do you see this poet using? Is it the same as we use in prose?
- Does this poem rhyme? Do you see a pattern to the rhyming?

Shared Writing

Shared writing also provides an opportunity to write poems together. Use this time to:

- Determine themes from which to write
- Determine structural elements the class wants to try
- Determine patterns, such as rhyming at the end of a line or every other line

Core Connections at Home

Have students share their final writing projects with their families during a special recognition. Ask families to write a letter to their child sharing what they learned from their presentations. Display these letters alongside students' poems.

> A poet can survive everything
> but a misprint.
>
> —Oscar Wilde

Grade 4

Reading Lessons

The following table highlights the teaching objectives and standards alignment for all ten lessons across the four stages of the lesson set (introduce, define, extend, and assess). It also indicates which lessons contain special features to support ELLs, technology, speaking and listening, and formative ("Milestone") assessments.

The Core Ready Reading Rubric that follows is designed to help you record each student's overall understanding across four levels of achievement as it relates to the lesson set goals. We recommend that you use this rubric at the end of the lesson set as a performance-based assessment tool. Use the milestone performance assessments as tools to help you gauge student progress toward these goals, and reteach and differentiate as needed. See the foundational book, *Be Core Ready: Powerful, Effective Steps to Implementing and Achieving the Common Core State Standards,* for more information about the Core Ready Reading and Writing Rubrics.

The Core I.D.E.A. / Daily Reading Instruction at a Glance

Instructional Stage	Lesson	Teaching Objective	Core Standards	Special Feature
Introduce: notice, explore, collect, note, immerse, surround, record, share	1	Readers connect to poems for a variety of reasons.	RL.4.1 • RL.4.10 • SL.4.1a–d L.4.1 • L.4.6	Close Reading ELL S&L Tech
Define: name, identify, outline, clarify, select, plan	2	Readers answer the question, "What is this poem saying to me?"	RL.4.1 • RL.4.2 • RL.4.10 • SL.4.1a SL.4.1b • L.4.1 • L.4.6	Close Reading ELL S&L
Extend: try, experiment, attempt, approximate, practice, explain, revise, refine	3	Readers notice how a poet structures a poem.	RL.4.1 • RL.4.5 • RL.4.10 • SL.4.1a SL.4.1b • SL.4.2 • L.4.1 • L.4.6	Close Reading ELL Milestone Assessment Tech
	4	Readers interpret poems by focusing on strong feelings or the mood.	RL.4.1 • RL.4.4 • RL.4.10 • SL.4.1a–d L.4.1 • L.4.6	Close Reading ELL Tech
	5	Readers interpret poems by focusing on strong images.	RL.4.1 • RL.4.4 • RL.4.10 • SL.4.1a–d L.4.1 • L.4.6	Close Reading ELL Milestone Assessment
	6	Readers interpret poems by focusing on what the speaker or characters do and say.	RL.4.1 • RL.4.5 • RL.4.10 • SL.4.1a–d SL.4.2 • L.4.1 • L.4.6	Close Reading S&L
	7	Readers interpret poems by considering the author's purpose.	RL.4.1 • RL.4.10 • SL.4.1a–d L.4.1 • L.4.6	Close Reading ELL Milestone Assessment S&L
	8	Readers compare and contrast poems.	RL.4.1 • RL.4.2 • RL.4.4 • RL.4.5 RL.4.10 • SL.4.1a–d • L.4.1 • L.4.6	Close Reading ELL Milestone Assessment S&L
	9	Readers orally read poems with a strong voice to convey the author's message.	RL.4.1 • RL.4.7 • RL.4.10 • SL.4.5 L.4.1 • L.4.6	Close Reading ELL Tech
Assess: reflect, conclude, connect, share, recognize, respond	10	Readers reflect on core questions.	RL.4.1 • RL.4.10 • W.4.1a–d • W.4.4 W.4.10 • SL.4.1a–d • L.4.1 • L.4.6	Close Reading ELL Milestone Assessment Tech

Core Ready Reading Rubric

Lesson Set Goal	Emerging	Approaching	Achieving	Exceeding	Standards Alignment
Read and interpret poetry using details and examples from the text when drawing inferences.	Student struggles with reading and interpreting poetry. Interpretations may be far off track and/or lack text support.	Student reads and makes plausible interpretations of poetry. May lack detailed or relevant text support.	Student successfully reads and makes logical interpretations of poetry. Provides relevant details and examples from the text to support ideas.	Student successfully reads and interprets poetry with a great deal of independence. Provides thorough and thoughtful examples from the text to support ideas.	RL.4.1 RL.4.2 RL.4.10 SL.4.1a-d L.4.1 L.4.6
Determine the meaning of words and phrases in poems.	Student is able to determine the meaning of very few or no challenging words and phrases in poems without significant support.	Student has some success determining the meaning of challenging words and phrases in poems.	Student frequently and successfully determines the meaning of challenging words and phrases in poems.	Student consistently displays an advanced ability to determine the meaning of challenging words and phrases in poems.	RL.4.1 RL.4.4 RL.4.10 L.4.6
Refer to the structural elements of a poem in discussion.	Student rarely or never refers to the structural elements of a poem in discussion with accuracy.	Student attempts with moderate success to refer to the structural elements of a poem in discussion. Some inconsistency or inaccuracies present.	Student successfully refers to the structural elements of a poem in discussion with sufficient frequency and accuracy.	Student frequently and effectively refers to structural elements of a poem in discussion. Consistently accurate. Uses advanced terms.	RL.4.1 RL.4.5 RL.4.10 SL.4.1a-d SL.4.2 L.4.1 L.4.6
Identify the reasons and evidence a speaker provides when discussing the meaning of a poem and agree or disagree with the interpretation.	Student struggles to identify the reasons and evidence a speaker provides when discussing the meaning of a poem. Little or no attempt to agree or disagree with his/her interpretation.	Student attempts to identify the reasons and evidence a speaker provides when discussing the meaning of a poem. May be incomplete or inaccurate. Expresses opinion of interpretation but lacks sufficient support.	Student identifies reasons and evidence a speaker provides when discussing the meaning of a poem with adequate detail and accuracy. Expresses opinion of interpretation with sufficient support.	Student identifies reasons and evidence a speaker provides when discussing the meaning of a poem with thorough detail and accuracy. Expresses opinion of interpretation with detailed and insightful support.	RL.4.1 RL.4.2 RL.4.10 SL.4.1a-d SL.4.3 SL.4.6 L.4.6
Compare and contrast poems focusing on meaning and structural elements.	Student has little or no success comparing and contrasting poems by focusing on meaning and structural elements.	Student attempts with some evidence of success to compare and contrast poems by focusing on meaning and structural elements.	Student accurately compares and contrasts poems focusing on meaning and structural elements.	Student displays a noteworthy understanding of how to compare and contrast poems focusing on meaning and structural elements.	RL.4.1 RL.4.2 RL.4.4 RL.4.5 RL.4.10 W.4.1 W.4.4 W.4.10 SL.4.1a-d L.4.6

Core Ready Reading Rubric, Grade 4, *continued*

Lesson Set Goal	Emerging	Approaching	Achieving	Exceeding	Standards Alignment
Read poems aloud to further convey the meaning.	Student struggles to read poems in a way that conveys meaning.	Student has some success reading aloud poems in a way thay conveys meaning. The delivery at times may be flat or monotone.	Student successfully reads aloud poems in a way that conveys meaning. The delivery is varied and interesting without flatness or monotone.	Student has a strong ability to read aloud poems in a way that powerfully conveys meaning. The delivery is varied, interesting, and compelling, with variations in volume, pace, and emphasis.	RL.4.1 RL.4.7 RL.4.10 SL.4.5 L.4.1 L.4.6
Refer to details and examples in a text when explaining what the text explicitly says and when drawing inferences from the text.	Student shows little or no evidence of active, purposeful reading or searching the text for specific information and evidence. Student makes little or no attempt to provide details and examples when explaining what the text says explicitly and is unable to draw inferences from the text.	Student shows some evidence of active purposeful reading and searching the text for specific information and evidence. Student provides some details and examples, with marginal accuracy, when explaining what the text says explicitly and when drawing inferences from the text.	Student shows solid evidence of active, purposeful reading and searching the text for specific information and evidence. Student usually provides appropriate details and examples when explaining what the text says explicitly and when drawing inferences from the text.	Student demonstrates exceptional evidence of active, purposeful reading and searching the text for specific information and evidence. Student provides accurate, explicit, and thoughtful details and examples when explaining what the text says explicitly and when drawing inferences from the text.	RL.4.1
Write an organized opinion piece that includes a clear introduction, point of view, supporting reasons, linking words and phrases, and a concluding statement.	Student writes an opinion piece with little or no evidence of an introduction or concluding statement. Does not articulate a clear point of view and supporting reasons are missing or insufficient. Omits linking words and phrases or uses inappropriately.	Student writes an opinion piece with a weak introductory and concluding statement. Identifies a point of view but some supporting reasons are weak or irrelevant. Intermittently includes needed linking words and phrases.	Student writes an opinion piece with a solid introductory and concluding statement. Articulates a point of view and supports with relevant supporting reasons. Uses linking words and phrases when appropriate.	Student writes an effective opinion piece with a strong introductory and concluding statement. Point of view is apparent and supported with clear and relevant reasons. Uses advanced linking words and phrases effectively.	W.4.1
By the end of the year, proficiently read and comprehend literature, including stories, dramas, and poetry in the grades 4–5 text complexity band, with scaffolding as needed at the high end of the range.	Student shows little or no evidence of reading and comprehending texts appropriate for the grade 4 text complexity band.	Student shows inconsistent evidence of reading and comprehending texts appropriate for the grade 4 text complexity band with independence and proficiency.	Student shows solid evidence of reading and comprehending texts appropriate for the grade 4 text complexity band independently and proficiently. May need scaffolding at the grade 5 level.	Student shows solid evidence of reading and comprehending complex texts above the grade 4 text complexity band independently and proficiently.	RL.4.10
Write routinely over extended time frames (time for research, reflection, and revision) and shorter time frames (a single sitting or a day or two) for a range of discipline-specific tasks, purposes, and audiences.	Student shows little or no evidence of writing routinely for short or long time frames for a range of discipline-specific tasks, purposes, and audiences.	Student shows some evidence of writing routinely for short and long time frames for a range of discipline-specific tasks, purposes, and audiences. Student has trouble maintaining consistent focus while writing.	Student shows solid evidence of regularly writing routinely for short and long time frames for a range of discipline-specific tasks, purposes, and audiences.	Student shows exceptional evidence of consistently and accurately writing with excellent focus and stamina for short and long time frames for a range of discipline-specific tasks, purposes, and audiences.	W.4.10

Lesson Set Goal	Emerging	Approaching	Achieving	Exceeding	Standards Alignment
In collaborative discussions, demonstrate evidence of preparation for discussion and exhibit responsibility to the rules and roles of conversation.	In collaborative discussions, student comes unprepared and often disregards the rules and roles of conversation.	In collaborative discussions, student's preparation may be evident but ineffective or inconsistent. May occasionally disregard the rules and roles of conversation.	In collaborative discussions, student prepares adequately and draws on the preparation and other information about the topic to explore ideas under discussion. Usually observes the rules and roles of conversation.	In collaborative discussions, student arrives extremely well prepared for discussions and draws on the preparation and other information about the topic to explore ideas under discussion. Always observes the rules and roles of conversation.	SL.4.1a SL.4.1b
In collaborative discussions, share and develop ideas in a manner that enhances understanding of topic. Contribute and respond to the content of the conversation in a productive and focused manner.	Student shows little or no evidence of engaging in collaborative discussions and makes little or no attempt to ask and answer questions, stay on topic, link his/her comments to the remarks of others, or to explain his/her own ideas and understanding in light of the discussion.	Student shows some evidence of engaging in collaborative discussions and with marginal success attempts to ask questions to check understanding of information presented, to stay on topic, link his/her comments to the remarks of others, and explain his/her own ideas and understanding in light of the discussion.	Student engages in a range of collaborative discussions and asks questions to check understanding of information presented, stays on topic most of the time, and frequently links his/her own ideas and understanding in light of the discussion.	Student effectively and consistently engages in a range of collaborative discussions and asks high-level questions to check understanding of information presented, always stays on topic, and with great insight and attention to the comments of others links his/her own ideas and understanding in light of the discussion.	SL.4.1c SL.4.1d
Demonstrate knowledge of standard English and its conventions.	Student demonstrates little or no knowledge of standard English and its conventions.	Student demonstrates some evidence of knowledge of standard English and its conventions.	Student consistently demonstrates knowledge of standard English and its conventions.	Student demonstrates an exceptional understanding of standard English and its conventions.	L.4.1 L.4.2 L.4.3
Acquire and accurately use grade-appropriate conversational, general academic, and domain-specific vocabulary and phrases.	Student shows little or no evidence of the acquisition and use of grade-appropriate conversational and academic language.	Student shows some evidence of the acquisition and use of grade-appropriate conversational and academic language.	Student shows solid evidence of the acquisition and use of grade-appropriate conversational and academic language.	Student shows a high level of sophistication and precision when using grade-appropriate conversational and academic language.	L.4.6

Note: See the Core Ready Rubrics chart in the Welcome at the beginning of the book for descriptions of category headers.

Reading Lesson 1

▼ **Teaching Objective**

Readers connect to poems for a variety of reasons.

▼ **Standards Alignment**

RL.4.1, RL.4.10, SL.4.1a-d, L.4.1, L.4.6

▼ **Materials**

- A variety of poems (one per sheet) distributed around the classroom
- Reading Like a Poetry Scholar chart (shown later in lesson)
- Billy Collins's poem "Introduction to Poetry" (easily available online) or view the website Billy Collins Action Poetry at http://www.bcactionpoet.org/, to immerse students in how poetry is being taken up with diverse media

▼ **To the Teacher**

Poetry and fourth graders go together perfectly, though fourth graders initially can be hesitant about poetry. Today is all about getting your students comfortable with poetry by introducing them to a variety of poems and having them choose a poem that speaks personally to them for some reason. Choose from the poems we've listed in the Core Texts section of this lesson set, but also choose poems you love or that you think your students will love, such as the work of Shel Silverstein and Jack Prelustky. Today you will be launching your reading lesson set focused around the strategies good readers use to delve deeply into poetry. More specifically, over the next few weeks you will guide your students to critically analyze and interpret poems and persuade others to agree with their opinions by providing evidence to support their thinking.

Before beginning this lesson, display or distribute poems around the room on desks, tables, or any surfaces you have where students can easily move around and read the poems. Let your students know that they will be

Close Reading Opportunity

expected to read silently on their own for a few minutes as they make their way around the room. They may not read all of the poems today, but assure them that these are poems we'll come back to again and again in the next few weeks and that the poems will have a home somewhere in your classroom for their independent reading.

▼ **Procedure**

Warm Up Gather the class to set the stage for today's learning

Gather your students and announce that for the next few weeks you are going to be reading like poetry scholars and that today is all about reading poems and finding one that speaks to them.

> Students, today is about finding a poem that speaks to you. You'll notice that all around the room there are poems. Well, today you are going to read these well-known poems and look for one that speaks to you in some way.

Ask for some ways a reader knows when a poem speaks to him or her, such as:

- You strongly agree or disagree with the poem's message
- You have an emotional reaction (laughter, happiness, sadness, wonder, inspiration, etc.)
- There are lines or sections that make a strong impression on you
- You want to read the poem (or listen to it) over again for the enjoyment of it
- The poem changes your way of thinking about something
- The poem teaches you something new about the world
- The poem surprises you with a new way of looking at an object or topic
- The poem strongly reminds you of something you have experienced
- You feel the desire to share the poem with others

Teach Model what students need to learn and do

Create a chart titled "Reading Like a Poetry Scholar" to discuss strategies that encourage close reading of poetry. **ELL** Provide Comprehensible Input—Graphics. Organizers with descriptions, examples, and/or visuals can help ELLs to be independent learners. Making sure this chart is displayed in an accessible area or having a small copy for their own folder can further support their learning. Model for students what reading like a poetry scholar looks like and sounds like by reading one of your favorite poems. Then conduct a think-aloud in which you share what you're thinking about the poem. **ELL** Enable Language Production–Listening and Speaking. Modeling your thinking increases ELLs' listening skills while modeling fluent speaking skills.

When we're reading poems closely and carefully, we're really reading like poetry scholars. That means we need to read slowly and be aware of our own thinking. Listen and watch me as I read Billy Collins's "Introduction to Poetry."

This poem speaks to me because it reminds me to take my time when I'm reading poems. I like the line about the light switch because I can imagine myself struggling to find the switch in the dark. That's what it feels like for me as I try to understand what the poet is trying to tell me. I appreciate the line about water skiing on the surface of a poem. That makes me feel free, like I'm riding on a jet ski over the ocean's smooth surface. What is Billy Collins telling us about how to read poetry? He is defining what it means to be a "poetry scholar." It seems he's telling us that part of the fun is the hard work, the search for the light switch. He's telling us that part of the process is listening to the words of the poem like listening against the hive for the bees to tell their story. He's telling us that reading poetry can feel like you are skimming across the ocean's surface. Let's start a chart that we'll be adding on to in the next few weeks called "Reading Like a Poetry Scholar." We will discuss some strategies to help guide your reading of poetry. Then, you may have additional items to add to the chart.

Reading Like a Poetry Scholar

- Read slowly, taking care to really focus on each word
- Read again and again, each time slowly and carefully
- Read the poem out loud to yourself
- Think about what the poem is mainly about, and think about what words show that meaning
- See what the poem makes you feel, and find the words in the poem that make you feel that way
- See what words, phrases, and lines strike you
- Think about how the poet might have intended to affect the reader (mood, message, image, etc.)

Try Guide students to quickly rehearse what they need to learn and do in preparation for practice

Using Billy Collins's *Introduction to Poetry*, have students turn and tell a partner what they think of this poem and why.

> Share what you think of this poem. Does it speak to you? What do you think he's trying to tell us about reading poetry? What lines stand out to you? Do you agree or disagree? Why?

Clarify Briefly restate today's teaching objective and explain the practice tasks

Discuss with students how you want them to explore the poetry collection, reading and thinking about the poems you've chosen for today. Review the Reading Like A Poetry Scholar chart to orient students to how you want them to read poems slowly, carefully, and closely to connect to poems and form their own opinions.

> Today we are going to explore our poetry collection looking for poems that speak to us.

> You are going to start with one poem. Read it silently, think about it, and then move on to another poem. Remember from our Reading Like a Poetry Scholar chart that we want to read slowly and carefully, noticing words and phrases that grab our attention and images that form in our heads. At times, we want to reread poems for greater clarity. After a few minutes, you are going to think about one poem that struck you or that you like the most. When you've found a poem that speaks to you in some way you are going to select it and be prepared to justify why you've chosen that poem in particular.

Practice Students work independently or in small groups to apply today's teaching objective

Students will independently explore a variety of poems around the room to discover poems that speak to them. Emphasize the need for silent reading and concentration. Students will have a chance to share their choices and thinking at the end.

Wrap Up Check understanding as you guide students to briefly share what they have learned and produced today

Draw the class's attention back to the Reading Like a Poetry Scholar chart and then have them share why they find that a particular poem speaks to them.

> Today we've been digging into what it means to read like a poetry scholar. You've been reading slowly, closely, and carefully to choose a poem that speaks to you. Justify why you've chosen this particular poem. What about it resonated with you?

This conversation builds the foundation for helping students respond to specific questions and make comments that contribute to the discussion and link to the remarks of others. (SL.4.1c)

Goal	Low-Tech	High-Tech
Students will contribute to class ideas about what it means to read like a poetry scholar.	Students will read poetry around the room, either in books, on copies, or on charts that hang in different areas.	Students will view and listen to poetry on websites such as Billy Collins Action Poetry. Students will still consider what it means to read like a poetry scholar but may have additional considerations based on how technology is impacting the ways we experience poetry today.

Reading Lesson 2

▼ Teaching Objective

Readers answer the question, "What is this poem saying to me?"

Close Reading Opportunity

▼ Standards Alignment

RL.4.1, RL.4.2, RL.4.10, SL.4.1a, SL.4.1b, L.4.1, L.4.6

▼ Materials

- Copies of Pat Mora's "Words Free as Confetti" (see Appendix 4.2)
- Charting supplies or interactive whiteboard
- Reading Like a Poetry Scholar chart from yesterday
- Clues We Use Bookmarks (Appendix 4.3)
- Student poetry packets

▼ To the Teacher

Before this lesson, create Clues We Use Bookmarks (see Appendix 4.3, Clues We Use Bookmarks) for your students to help them in their investigation of poetry. Many of these clues will be emphasized in particular lessons in the coming days, and having the bookmark handy will help students as they read through poems in their packets and as they go off to read poetry from books in your classroom. As the lessons unfold, refer your students to their bookmarks and encourage them to think about poems through many different lenses. The bookmark also includes items that, while not specifically addressed in the coming lessons, are useful to readers of poetry and are worth exploring to extend the learning of your entire class or small groups.

Pat Mora's poem is wonderful for this lesson because it allows students to share what the poem is saying to them about words. You may have a favorite poem in mind that will work equally well for this lesson. We recommend a poem that serves as a vessel for a discussion of the power of words.

▼ Procedure

Warm Up Gather the class to set the stage for today's learning

Celebrate the work your students did yesterday as they searched for poems that spoke to them. Orient them to today's lesson, which will build on yesterday's work.

> Students, yesterday you spent time reading and thinking about why you certain poems speak to you. I thought a lot about your choices such as

_____ and _____, and the thoughtful ways you expressed what impressed you about these choices and why. Today's lesson is going to build on that important work.

Teach   Model what students need to learn and do

Explain to students that they will be reading poems and asking "what is this poem saying?" and citing examples in the text and their own experience to justify their thinking.

> As I watched you read and then listened to you share your thinking, I thought about how we enjoy poems when they speak to us personally. Today we are going to read poems and not only think about *whether* they speak to us, but also *what* poems *say* to us and find examples of what the poets *do* in their writing to convey the meaning of a poem and make us pause, reflect, and keep thinking long after we're done reading. **ELL** Frontload the Lesson—Set a Purpose for Reading. By setting a purpose for reading you are demystifying the upcoming activity through being explicit. This is helpful for ELLs because they are balancing comprehending the language and understanding the activity.

> I have a poem for us to read together today. We are looking for what we think the poem is saying and specific examples to support our thinking.

Read Mora's "Words Free as Confetti" aloud for your students. Share your thinking first. (What follows is an example of one teacher's response to the poem—modify it as needed to reflect your own response).

> As I read this poem I am asking myself, "What does this poem say to me?" This poem says to me that words have power, and variety, and the ability to do many things. They can make us feel many emotions, and they enable us to communicate in so many different ways. Now, I will provide some examples from the text that make me think this. I think this because the poet compares words to many things that are very different from each other: floating dandelion plumes compared to heavy black cement; dark tunnels and bright rainbows. Those are really strong images showing that words can be light or very heavy. They can be very dark or bright and joyful. What other contrasts do you see in the poem, students? This poem also says to me that words are to be cherished and enjoyed and used. One reason I think this is because of the repeated line about wanting to "say, say, say you." I think this shows how much the writer enjoys words, even just saying them is exciting to her. When I think about what a poem says to me,

> I'm focused on the many things that a poet does to express meaning—strong images, repeated lines, and the title are just some of the things I pay attention to. These are all clues to what the poem means. I notice words that I think are special like "say, say, say you." I notice the impact a poem has on me. I feel a sense of joy in reading this poem. I notice the images that stay in my mind like words falling from the ceiling and landing all around me like confetti. I know that I sometimes experience this kind of joy when I read.

> Refer to, and if applicable, add on to your Reading Like a Poetry Scholar chart from Reading Lesson 1. **ELL** Provide Comprehensible Input—Graphic Organizers. This chart will be a strong anchor chart that your ELLs refer to when reading poetry. Offer visuals to represent strategies when applicable (sketch a heart for feeling or a picture with a mind, etc. . . .)

Try   Guide students to quickly rehearse what they need to learn and do in preparation for practice

Have students discuss what the poem is saying to them. Remind them of the importance of examples from the text to support their thinking.

> Turn and talk to your partner. What do you think the poem is saying to you? What makes you think this?

> Encourage students to refer directly to relevant pieces of the poem and their own experience in order to justify their thinking. **ELL** Enable Language Production—Increasing Interaction. Triad partnerships aid in creating supporting language partnerships and models for ELLs. In a triad, you could partner the ELL with one student who mainly speaks English, and another student who is bilingual in both languages. This situation offers a chance for an exchange between the three students as well as an English discussion model. Remind students of agreed-on rules for partnership discussions. (SL.4.1b)

To help students focus their thinking, remind them of the Reading Like a Scholar chart. Here are some things that students might notice or cite as related to the message of the poem. Guide them toward these elements as needed:

- The many similes in the text—what the poet compares words to
- The references to the senses (taste, smell, sound, sight, touch)
- The ideas that suggest that words are always moving and active
- Other contrasting images in the text

POEM	WHAT DOES THE POEM SAY TO ME?	JUSTIFICATION
"If You Catch a Firefly" by Lillian Moore	The words remind me to be a giving person, not selfish.	Keeping the firefly makes the light go out. Letting it go makes it "star bright."
"Fireworks" by Valerie Worth	The poem makes me feel excited and energized. Reminds me of why I love fireworks	Strong, exciting images — cracking shells. Uses alliteration that sounds like firework "B" sounds & "S" sounds
"The Swing" by Robert Louis Stevenson	The poem is a clear description of what swinging on a swing is like and how much fun it is.	Swinging is the "pleasantest" thing. You get a great view like the one over the wall in the poem. The up and down, up down!
"The Reason I Like Chocolate" by Nikki Giovani	The poems tells me to be myself and do the things I like so I will be happy.	The narrator describes things she enjoys and why. Chocolate, scary movies, crying, books — all make her happy. "I really like to be happy" is the last line and most important.
"I Love the Look of Words" by Maya Angelou	We can all enjoy words as much as we enjoy buttered popcorn.	The poet compares eating popcorn to loving words. The words "leap" off the page like popcorn. The reader "gobbles" and "chomps" them. Yum

- The Spanish language lines
- The connection between words and being free

Have students share their ideas. It is important to honor differing interpretations as long as the student can justify their thinking with evidence from the text and/or their own experience.

Clarify Briefly restate today's teaching objective and explain the practice tasks

Today you are going to read poems that will be important to us in our learning over the next few weeks. Some of the poems you'll recognize from our poetry

study yesterday. Some are new. In your independent reading today, you are going to read the poems in the packet and think about the question "What does this poem say to me?" and "What parts of the poem can I use to justify my thinking?" Be prepared to share your thinking. Don't worry about reading all of the poems in the packet. Reading slowly and closely and thinking deeply are important qualities for readers and scholars of poetry to develop and to nourish.

Set a goal for how much students should accomplish by the end of practice.

Practice Students work independently or in small groups to apply today's teaching objective

Students will read independently from their packet of poems and choose a poem about which they will provide examples of what the poem is saying and why. Provide the Clues We Use Bookmarks to help them focus their examination. Consider meeting one-on-one with students who are not focusing on their reading or seem to be having difficulty choosing a poem. Have students write a response to the question "What does this poem say to me and why?" in preparation for their sharing, with the students instructed to cite specific words, phrases, or lines in the poem as part of their response. See the Core Phrases in the introduction for support in focusing students' responses.

Wrap Up Check understanding as you guide students to briefly share what they have learned and produced today

Have students share the poem they chose to spend time with today and what the poem said to them and why. Students should cite specific examples from the poem to justify their thinking. They should also listen carefully to one another so that they can successfully build on one another's ideas by sharing new thoughts or examples, rather than simply repeating the ideas already shared. (SL.4.1b, SL.4.1d)

> Thoughts that breathe,
> and words that burn.
>
> — Thomas Gray

Reading Lesson 3

▼ Teaching Objective

Readers notice how a poet structures a poem

Close Reading Opportunity

▼ Standards Alignment

RL.4.1, RL.4.5, RL.4.10, SL.4.1a, SL.4.1b, SL.4.2, L.4.1, L.4.6

▼ Materials

- Copies of "Dust of Snow" by Robert Frost
- Charting supplies or interactive whiteboard
- Poetic Structures chart (shown later in lesson)
- Student copies of Poetic Structures chart (see Appendix 4.4)
- Student poetry packets

▼ To the Teacher

So far your students have been immersed in a variety of poems that will guide this lesson set for you and your students. Each lesson moving forward will focus on the close reading of a particular poem. You may want to choose a poem that is one of your favorites or that you've noticed has quickly become a favorite in your class. For this lesson, we've chosen Robert Frost's "Dust of Snow" because it offers a few concrete structures for students to notice—namely the use of stanzas, white space, rhyme, and line breaks. There are many wonderful "Dust of Snow" interpretations available on YouTube that your class can view to extend their experience with this poem. Your students will be inspired by other students' work regarding this poem. Within the deceivingly simple text there lies great meaning that your students will identify with, particularly if they can think of a time when they were having a rough day and something unexpected, like the dust of snow falling from a tree, helped them see the day differently.

▼ Procedure

Warm Up Gather the class to set the stage for today's learning

Our reading of poetry so far has focused on what poems say to us and how—the meaning we make of the poem. We will continue to read poems in this way. Today, we are going to read with this question in mind: "What do you notice about the way the author structured the poem?"

Teach Model what students need to learn and do

To help us answer that question we're going to closely read another well-known poem, Robert Frost's "Dust of Snow."

Read the poem to the class and model for them what you notice about the way the poet structured the poem or invite them to share what they notice. **ELL** Enabling Language Production—Listening and Speaking. When you model your thinking, you are also modeling correct English language usage for your ELLs. Consider using varied sentence structures to describe your thinking to scaffold to meet the needs of the language proficiency levels of your students.

As I read this poem, I notice some important things about its structure. First, I notice that there are two stanzas. The white space between the stanzas creates a pause for me as a reader. I notice that the lines of this poem are short. There are only a few words on each line, and each line is about the same length. I also notice that some words rhyme and that these words come at the end of every other line. This is an important pattern Robert Frost set up for us as readers. Let's start a chart called "Poetic Structures" to help as we ask, "What do you notice about the way the author wrote the poem?" **ELL** Frontload the Lesson—Set a Purpose for Reading. When you set a purpose for reading you are offering a time that ELLs can clarify the purpose or ask any questions that they may have encountered.

Use the chart to collect class-discovered examples of various types of structures.

Poetic Structures

Structures	Poems In Which Structure Can Be Found
• Repetition • White space • Line breaks • Special font • Punctuation • Words that compose a shape	

Try Guide students to quickly rehearse what they need to learn and do in preparation for practice

Provide your students with another poem to read and discuss with a partner. Roald Dahl's "Little Red Riding Hood and the Wolf" works well because it is a storyline students are likely familiar with, and there are many structures Dahl uses that are important to the overall meaning. Guide students in seeing how Dahl uses line breaks, punctuation, and special fonts in the poem to create suspense, emotion, and energy. For instance, BIG TEETH emphasizes just how big the wolf's teeth really were. The end of the long second stanza with a flowing narrative of the wolf getting dressed up ends with some very short two-word sentences about Little Red Ridinghood stopping. And staring. The action is about to start, something is about to happen, the structure indicates. And one key line, a twist in the telling of this famous fairy tale, has Little Red Riding Hood asking the wolf about his furry coat rather than about his big teeth. That line is set off from the others. There is no line break in the long final stanza, where all the action just rolls off itself, with the wolf's quick demise transitioning immediately into the startling image of Little Red Riding Hood dressed in a warm wolf coat.

Clarify Briefly restate today's teaching objective and explain the practice tasks

In your independent reading today, read with this question in mind: "What do you notice about the way the author wrote the poem?" Choose a poem that has special structural features that you want to share with the class.

Practice Students work independently or in small groups to apply today's teaching objective

Students will read from their poetry packets and ask themselves, "What do I notice about the way the author wrote the poem?" Students will identify poems that have particular poetic structures and how the structure is important to the poem. Have students frame their findings with one or more poems as follows:

Poem	Structure Used	How the Structure Is Important to the Poem

Wrap Up Check understanding as you guide students to briefly share what they have learned and produced today

Have students share what poems they chose as examples for the discussion on structure and why. Encourage students to paraphrase the poem or parts of the poem and persuade others that their interpretation of how structure was important to the poem is accurate. (SL.4.2)

Goal	Low-Tech	High-Tech
Students will read and interpret "Dust of Snow" by Robert Frost noticing in particular the structure of the poem.	Students will read copies of the poem on paper.	Students will view and listen to multimedia interpretations of "Dust of Snow" through tools such as YouTube to first consider what the poem means. Use these to guide their reading, focusing on the structure of the poem and how that impacts the meaning.

Note which poems students selected; it will be interesting to see how many students chose the same one. Collect student copies of the Poetic Structures chart for the structures they've identified and which poems they've found those structures in. **ELL** Assess for Content and Language Understanding—Formative Assessment. This is the time you will understand the language supports and scaffolds needed for upcoming work.

Milestone Performance Assessment

Examining Poetic Structures

 Use this checklist to assess student work in identifying and explaining the importance of structures in poetry.

Standards Alignment: RL.4.5, SL.4.2

	Achieved	Notes
Accurately identify one or more structures in a poem.		
Provide logical explanations of how the structure is important to the poem.		

Reading Lesson 4

▼ Teaching Objective

Readers interpret poems by focusing on strong feelings or the mood.

Close Reading Opportunity

▼ Standards Alignment

RL.4.1, RL.4.4, RL.4.10, SL.4.1a-d, L.4.1, L.4.6

▼ Materials

- Large copy of "Casey at the Bat" (try the one illustrated by Christopher Bing)
- Charting supplies or interactive whiteboard
- Student poetry packets

▼ To the Teacher

There are wonderful picture book versions of "Casey at the Bat," such as the one illustrated by Christopher Bing. The pictures in this book will help students identify the mood of the poem and the strong feelings the poet intended. There is also a rendition read by James Earl Jones, whose voice helps students identify the mood and strong feelings of the poem. Disney also has an excellent film version from 1946 that will capture your students' imagination.

▼ Procedure

Warm Up Gather the class to set the stage for today's learning

As we read poems, we have been asking ourselves questions to help us think more deeply about what they mean and how we can interpret the meaning looking at the words and structures of the poems. Sometimes poems can fill us with a feeling that helps us understand the mood the poet was trying to create. Today we are going to read a poem that is well known for the feelings it evokes in its readers. We will examine the feeling the poem gives us and why—what is it in the words and structure of the poem makes us have this feeling.

 Engage students in a brief discussion of the emotions they feel when they watch a favorite sports team play a game. What is it

like when your team is winning? What about when it is losing? Or when it's a really close game? How do you feel about the star players on the team? How are these players important to the game and the fans? **ELL** Frontload the Lesson—Activate Prior Knowledge. When you activate prior knowledge you offer an opportunity for your ELLs to connect new vocabulary to native language. This is a time you can use pictures to help communicate, for example, a picture of different kinds of sports and players.

Teach Model what students need to learn and do

In the poem "Casey at the Bat," Ernest Lawrence Thayer did something that a lot of really good writers and poets do—he used words that evoke strong feelings and that create a mood. Listen as I read the first three stanzas and think about how it makes you feel and what mood Thayer was trying to create. **ELL** Enabling Language Production—Model Language.

Read the first three stanzas of the poem. Then go back and underline words that indicate the mood at the beginning of the poem ("Cooney died at first," "sickly silence," "deep despair," "grim melancholy sat"). After underlining these phrases, have students identify the mood created by these words—for example, uncertainty, nervousness, worry.

Continue to read the next two stanzas and have students help you identify the words that evoke a particular feeling. Possible phrases include "wonderment of all," "dust had lifted," "there rose a lusty yell," and "For Casey, mighty Casey, was advancing to the bat," which evoke emotions such as excitement, hope, and anticipation of something good.

Try Guide students to quickly rehearse what they need to learn and do in preparation for practice

Read the remaining stanzas and have students underline with a partner words and phrases that evoke feelings that indicate the mood of the poem. Discuss with students the words and phrases they chose.

With your reading partner I'd like you to read the rest of the poem and underline the words that helped you to understand the mood the poet was creating.

Have partners share one word or phrase they underlined and how it made them feel. Encourage students to use terms particular to poetry in their explanations, such as *stanza* and *line*. **ELL** Enabling Language Production—Increasing Interaction. This is a time for ELLs to practice their thinking and speaking around poetry. This is a time for them to clarify language structures with their partner.

Clarify Briefly restate today's teaching objective and explain the practice tasks

As you go off to read poetry today, pay attention to places where the poet creates a feeling in you and how that helps you understand the mood the poet was creating. Make a note on any parts in which the poet used words to evoke a feeling.

© micromonkey / Fotolia

Practice Students work independently or in small groups to apply today's teaching objective

Students will read independently from their poetry packets, identifying words and phrases that evoke an emotion in them and indicate a mood the poet intended to create. Have students frame their findings with one or more poems as follows:

Poem	Mood in Poem	Quote or Description of Section That Created This Mood	How the Mood Is Important to the Poem

Wrap Up Check understanding as you guide students to briefly share what they have learned and produced today

Have students share what they discovered about the moods of their poems providing the evidence from the text to persuade others that their interpretations are correct.

Goal	Low-Tech	High-Tech
Students will interpret "Casey at the Bat" by identifying words that evoke a feeling and the mood the poet was creating.	Read illustrated copies of the poem.	Listen to an audio recording or watch a film version of the poem and have students make connections between the text and the visual or oral presentation. (RL.4.7)

Reading Lesson 5

▼ Teaching Objective

Readers interpret poems by focusing on strong images.

Close Reading Opportunity

▼ Standards Alignment

RL.4.1, RL.4.4, RL.4.10, SL.4.1a-d, L.4.1, L.4.6

▼ Materials

- Large copy of "Fog" by Carl Sandburg (see Appendix 4.5)
- Copies of "Street Music" by Arnold Adoff (The book *Street Music: City Poems* is full of wonderful poetry possibilities.)
- Charting supplies or interactive whiteboard
- Student poetry packets

▼ To the Teacher

There are many great poems that create strong images in our minds. "Fog" by Carl Sandburg is a short poem with a powerful image coming from the personification of the fog. "Street Music" by Arnold Adoff is one of the poems Jack reads in *Love That Dog*, and it creates compelling images in the reader's mind of a bustling city.

▼ Procedure

Warm Up Gather the class to set the stage for today's learning

Remind your students to visualize, or picture in their minds, what an author is saying. Connect this to poetry reading and introduce Carl Sandburg's powerful short poem, "Fog."

As you know, strong readers visualize what is happening as if a movie is playing in their mind. The trick is to picture it so clearly in our mind we feel as if we were almost there. As we're learning to interpret poetry, let us read a poem by Carl Sandburg, a classic American poet who creates powerful images with words.

Teach   Model what students need to learn and do

This is a fun opportunity to have your students only listen to the poem at first. Encourage your students to close their eyes. Do a couple readings of the poem to help everyone imagine how Sandburg is painting a picture in our minds.

> Close your eyes and listen as I read Carl Sandburg's poem, "Fog."

> Carl Sandburg brings the fog to life. He personifies the fog. With his words, we are able to visualize the scene. The mental picture we see or visualize in our mind as we read is referred to in literary language as *imagery*.

> I'm going to read the poem again and underline all the places he gives life to the fog so that we can picture it clearly. (Underline the action and descriptive words like "comes on little cat feet," "sits looking," "on silent haunches," "moves on.") **ELL** Provide Comprehensible Input—Modeling. This modeling will help your ELLs see how words will bring the poem to life. This is a perfect time to sketch the visualization as well as acting out action verbs.

Try   Guide students to quickly rehearse what they need to learn and do in preparation for practice

> Now I'm going to read another poem that has great imagery in it. I'll read it through twice. Oftentimes with poetry I need to read it a few times to better understand it.

Read "Street Music" by Arnold Adoff. Your students will experience the difference in this poem from "Fog." While Sandburg created a sense of quietness by describing the fog, "Street Music" is all about movement, volume, and motion. Tap into that excitement with how you read the poem. Once you've read it twice, or more, if you feel students would benefit, direct students to work with a partner to underline words that helped them visualize the scene.

> With your reading partner I'd like you to read the poem again and underline the words that helped you visualize what was happening.

Have partners share their underlined words and how these words helped them better visualize what was happening.

Clarify   Briefly restate today's teaching objective and explain the practice tasks

Remind students of the powerful words poets use to help us picture the scene in our minds. Today's work is about close reading of those words and talking about the images they create for us as readers.

> As you read poetry today, pay attention to where you are most easily able to visualize what is happening. Mark places where the poet used imagery to assist you in creating these mental pictures in your minds.

Practice   Students work independently or in small groups to apply today's teaching objective

Students will read in their poetry packets, noting specific places that create strong pictures in their minds. They should think about and try to persuade others how the image is important to the overall meaning of the poem by referring to specific words and phrases from the text. Have students frame their findings with one or more poems as follows:

Poem	Quote or Section with Strong Image	How That Image Is Important to the Poem

Wrap Up   Check understanding as you guide students to briefly share what they have learned and produced today

Have students share one place they marked in their poetry packet. Emphasize questions such as:

> Why did you make this selection?

> What image did the poet create in your mind?

> How did the poet create this image (words, structure, etc.)?

> How is this image important to the poem?

Collect student poetry packets and look for places where students have marked strong visual images the poet creates as an informal assessment of your students' understanding. (Assess for Content and Language Understanding—Formative Assessment)

Milestone Performance Assessment

Examining Poetic Images

 Use this checklist to assess student work with identifying strong images in poetry.

Standards Alignment: RL.4.1, RL.4.4

	Achieved	Notes
Accurately identify a strong image in a poem.		
Provide logical explanation of how the image is important to the poem.		

Reading Lesson 6

▼ Teaching Objective

Readers interpret poems by focusing on what the speaker or characters do and say.

▼ Standards Alignment

RL.4.1, RL.4.5, RL.4.10, SL.4.1a-d, SL.4.2, L.4.1, L.4.6

▼ Materials

- Copies of "The New Colossus" by Emma Lazarus (see Appendix 4.6)
- Charting supplies or interactive whiteboard
- Student poetry packets

▼ Procedure

Warm Up Gather the class to set the stage for today's learning

Review your work so far in this lesson set. Then, introduce your students to the mystery image for today. Let them know that Emma Lazarus is writing

Close Reading Opportunity

about an important symbol for our country and challenge your students to work on picturing it for themselves.

> So far our work on poetry has focused on the structure of how poems are written and what we think they mean based on the words the poet chose. Yesterday, we pictured in our minds the fog sitting and moving as if it were a living, breathing thing. Today, we're going to read a poem that fills our minds with an important image and symbol of our country's strength and resilience. As I read the poem, see if you can identify what object Emma Lazarus is writing about.

Have students share what they think the mystery object is that Lazarus is writing about (the Statue of Liberty).

Teach Model what students need to learn and do

Focus your students' attention on what the statue is doing. They will notice things like she is standing, limbs astride, her eyes commanding attention. She holds her lamp aloft, next to the "golden door." How does this description better help us understand the meaning of the poem? Now focus your students' attention on the words the statue is expressing. These are famous words to our country's history and hold important meaning as a symbol of freedom.

You have identified the mystery object our poet of the day wrote about. Now, let's zoom in on something special this poet does. Emma Lazarus makes the statue come alive by giving her words. Let's look at what the statue is saying:

> Keep, ancient lands, your storied pomp! cries she
> With silent lips. Give me your tired, your poor,
> Your huddled masses yearning to breathe free,
> The wretched refuse of your teeming shore.
> Send these, the homeless, tempest-tossed to me,
> I lift my lamp beside the golden door!

Ask students about the last five lines of this poem, which represent the Statue calling out to immigrants coming by boat to New York Harbor. Ask students who these people are, of the "tired," the "poor," the "masses" of people coming over by sea "yearning to breathe free." What does the poet mean by "wretched refuse"? In some cases people looked down on them in their homelands and they were poor and hungry. What is your interpretation of "tempest-tossed"—how the immigrants were seeking a better, more dignified life crossing a dangerous ocean? Why would they leave their homelands to go to an unknown place?

Emphasize with students the importance of the statue's words as the most impactful part of the poem.

> Her words are the most powerful part of the poem. Without them we would only have her description. Her words make her come alive. But does the Statue actually speak? What do the poem's words actually say? One thing especially important to notice is that the Statue of Liberty speaks quoted words in the poem even though she has "silent lips." Poems are a place statues can speak through silent lips.

Try Guide students to quickly rehearse what they need to learn and do in preparation for practice

Give your students an opportunity to share their thinking, to build on the ideas of others, and to cite specific words and phrases in the text to support their thinking. **ELL** Enabling Language Production—Increasing Interaction. This collaborative time is an opportunity for students to learn and increase their vocabulary around their discussion.

What do you think the statue is saying to the immigrants? Why do you think her words are such an important part of the poem?

Continue leading the class in a discussion. As students talk, encourage them to listen thoughtfully to one another and to build on each other's ideas rather than simply repeating one another. (SL.4.1b, SL.4.1c) Also, this is a good opportunity to model for students how to use the text as evidence in their conversation. (SL.4.2)

Clarify Briefly restate today's teaching objective and explain the practice tasks

Poets who have speakers or characters who say and do things create poems that we are even better able to picture in our minds because we hear the speakers saying their words. These are important moments in the poem to which you should pay attention. In your independent reading today, I want you to look for other times poets have the speakers or characters say things. What impact do these words have on the poem?

© Monkey Business / Fotolia LLC

Practice Students work independently or in small groups to apply today's teaching objective

Students will zoom in on moments in poems in which speakers or characters do and say things that hold great importance to the meaning of the poem. Have students frame their findings with one or more poems as follows:

Poem	What the Character Says or Does	How the Character's Speech or Actions Are Important to the Poem
	.	

Wrap Up Check understanding as you guide students to briefly share what they have learned and produced today

Call students back together to discuss their work for the day. Ask students if they were successful in identifying moments when speakers or characters were doing and saying things that were important to the poem.

Then, solicit a few examples of moments students identified, reminding volunteers of the importance of text as evidence to justify their thinking.

Reading Lesson 7

▼ Teaching Objective

Readers interpret poems by considering the author's purpose.

Close Reading Opportunity

▼ Standards Alignment

RL.4.1, RL.4.10, SL.4.1a-d, L.4.1, L.4.6

▼ Materials

- "They Were My People" by Grace Nichols
- Copies of "In the Garden" by Emily Dickinson (see Appendix 4.7)

- Charting supplies or interactive whiteboard
- Poet's Purpose chart
- Student copies of Poet's Purpose chart
- Student poetry packets

▼ To the Teacher

"They Were My People" tells the story of slaves who worked in the sugar cane fields cutting, carrying, and crushing cane. The rhythm of the poem mirrors the rhythm of cutting the cane, at which slaves worked tirelessly "to the rhythm of the sunbeat." Emily Dickinson's poem "In the Garden" offers another purpose—to capture the wonder of nature in all of its simplicity and complexity through a bird, its beauty, and its hunger for a worm. Dickinson's poem offers us a commentary on society as Nichols's poem offers us a commentary on a slave's life. (For a really thorough example of how to do a close reading of Dickinson's poem, please see the close reading chapter in my first book in this series, *Be Core Ready*.)

▼ Procedure

Warm Up Gather the class to set the stage for today's learning

Ask students what they have observed about what compels poets to create a particular poem. What mood, intention or perspective seems to be motivating that poet? It is sometimes said that poems are a writer's way of making an argument, of making a case for something. It was Robert Frost who once said that he always wrote about what he was "for," not what he was "against." Connect to the work students have done writing and crafting their own poems. **ELL** Frontload the Lesson—Make Connections. ELLs benefit by seeing the ties between their work and referring back to their previous thinking. This is more of an opportunity to increase and practice their vocabulary.

> We've worked hard to think about what poems mean from our perspectives by looking carefully at the words the poet chose and the images they create for us. You've also been working on writing your own poems. Why have you chosen to write about particular topics? Why do you think specific poets write their poems?

Engage in a class discussion and see what your students are thinking as writers and readers of poetry. Emphasize with them that they have all made choices as poets—first by choosing poems to write from and pay tribute to, then by selecting a topic that matters to them, and finally by choosing the words, phrases, and structure that help them send their message out into the world.

This lesson is an opportunity to highlight several essential speaking and listening skills that are critical to holding a productive conversation. These skills include, but are certainly not limited to, asking questions to check for understanding, linking comments, and explaining ideas clearly. (SL.4.1c, SL.4.1d)

Teach Model what students need to learn and do

> Today I will introduce you to two poems that have different purposes. The first is "They Were My People." The title already poses many questions for me. The roots of this poem lie in telling an important story about a group of people. Let's read the poem and ask ourselves: What is the poet saying to the world? We call this the *poet's purpose*.

Read "They Were My People" to the students. Provide them with copies of the poem, or have a large copy available for discussion. If students do not draw their own conclusions about whom "my people" refers to, help them recognize that "my people" are slaves that worked the sugar cane fields. Connect that to the poet's purpose—to tell the story of slaves. She repeats phrases for emphasis and creates a rhythm in the poem that mirrors the rhythm of cutting the sugar cane over and over again.

Start a Poet's Purpose chart with students.

Poem	Poet's Purpose	How I Know (Evidence of Poet's Purpose from Poem and What I Know)
"They Were My People"	• To share the story of her people • To write about slavery • To convey the repetitive and grueling nature of working in the sugar cane fields	Title Repetition of words Role it played in American history

Try Guide students to quickly rehearse what they need to learn and do in preparation for practice

Guide students in reading another poem, focusing on the poet's purpose and how they uncover that purpose. For this lesson, we recommend Emily Dickinson's "In the Garden" because it offers a different purpose than "They Were My People." Dickinson's poem is complex but tied to lived experience for fourth graders. Read the poem to them and then direct them to work with a partner to discuss the poet's purpose and how they came to their conclusions. They should be prepared to share their thinking with the group. Poems on nature work particularly well for this portion of this lesson. In addition to Dickinson, we also recommend the work of Mary Oliver and short poems by Valerie Worth.

> Now it's your turn to try. Let's listen to our next poem, called "In the Garden." This poet has a very different purpose. Just like we did with "They Were My People" ask yourself, "Why do you think she wrote this poem? What message is she sending out into the world?" Remember to refer to specific words or phrases in the poem to support your thinking.

This poem has a more abstract message than "They Were My People." If the students need some coaching in getting their thinking going, you could give some examples. The poet sees a bird in a garden who eats a worm, drinks some dew, hops out of the way of a beetle, and darts his beady eyes around. All these are simple things the bird does. The observer then offers the bird a crumb and the bird flies away. The rest of the poem is hard to understand, but seems to compare the beauty of flight to moving through water. Some purposes of the poem could be how much there is to see in nature if we only stop to look; how sometimes our desire to participate in something instead of just observing it can make it stop; or how the act of a bird taking flight is one of the most miraculous things imaginable—nature is more beautiful and mysterious than we can ever know. After a few minutes, have partners share what they think the poet's purpose is. Add their thinking to your Poet's Purpose chart.

Clarify Briefly restate today's teaching objective and explain the practice tasks

> As you read from your poetry packets today, I want you to choose two poems and think about why each poet wrote the poem and what evidence you have for your thinking. Be ready to discuss your thinking with the class with evidence so back up your idea.

You may want to provide your students with individual copies of a Poet's Purpose chart or have them reproduce it in a notebook or computer document.

Practice Students work independently or in small groups to apply today's teaching objective

Students work independently. Each student chooses two poems to analyze to determine purpose. As students work and record their ideas, check in and provide support to students who need more guided practice.

Wrap Up Check understanding as you guide students to briefly share what they have learned and produced today

Have students share one poem they closely read and what they recorded on their Poet's Purpose chart. Challenge them to convince you that their interpretation holds water. Add their thinking to the class chart. Ask students who read the same poem whether they agree or disagree with their classmate's interpretation and to justify their own thinking. There are many ways to interpret a poem—the key is to support your thinking with reasoning and evidence.

 Collect your students Poet's Purpose charts and look for places where students accurately identified the poet's purpose with evidence from the text. ELL Assess for Content and Language Understanding—Formative Assessment

Milestone Performance Assessment

Determining Poet's Purpose

Use this checklist to assess student work in determining a poet's purpose.

Standards Alignment: RL.4.1, SL.4.1c, SL.4.1d

	Achieved	Notes
Identify a logical purpose for writing the poem.		
Provide relevant evidence to support thinking about the poet's purpose.		

> 66
> I was reading the dictionary. I thought it was a poem about everything.
>
> —Steven Wright
> 99

Reading Lesson 8 ···

▼ Teaching Objective

Readers will compare and contrast poems.

▼ Standards Alignment

RL.4.1, RL.4.2, RL.4.4, RL.4.5, RL.4.10, SL.4.1a-d, L.4.1, L.4.6

**Close Reading
Opportunity**

▼ Materials

- Robert Frost's "Stopping by Woods on a Snowy Evening"
- Ralph Fletcher's "Frost in the Woods"
- Charting supplies or interactive whiteboard
- Highlighting tools

▼ To the Teacher

Your students have been engaged in discussion that has led to comparisons between poems. This lesson will highlight the importance of looking within and across poems. Making connections between poems is something many of them are doing naturally at this point. This lesson draws attention to this important strategy and gives students an opportunity to read someone else's tribute poetry. (A tribute poem is one in which a poet mirrors elements of another poem in his or her work.) This lesson is a great opportunity to compare and contrast poems by the same poet or poems inspired by well-known works. Ralph Fletcher's poem "Frost in the Woods" is inspired by Frost's canonical "Stopping by Woods on a Snowy Evening."

▼ Procedure

Warm Up Gather the class to set the stage for today's learning

Gather your students and identify qualities of "poetry scholars." Note that you value close reading of text and that when scholars study poetry they

quote from the text itself. Remind students that rereading is a crucial factor to understanding poetry.

> Fourth graders, you have been working as poetry scholars, thinking critically about what poems mean and the purpose behind them. I want us to think about how we talk about lines and structures in poems that remind us of other poems. This is very important thinking, for it shows that you're making connections across these texts. We want to make those connections in different areas—structure, meaning, style, sound—to see how two poems compare in different ways.

Teach Model what students need to learn and do

Direct your students on their work for today—reading within and across two poems.

> Today we are going to read another poem by Robert Frost. When once asked what a poem of his meant, he famously said: "If I'd wanted you to know, I'd have told you in the poem." We are going to investigate the meaning and structure of this poem and become bold as poetry scholars. Then, we're going to read another's poet's twist on this poem and compare it to Frost's poem.

Read "Stopping by Woods on a Snowy Evening" to the students. Ask students to share their thinking. What do they think the poem is saying? What structural elements do they see Frost using? Refer students to their Clues We Use Bookmarks to help them with their interpretation. Record their thinking in an initial chart that can be used to help students with their Venn diagrams. **ELL** Provide Comprehensible Input—Graphic Organizers. This organizer will help your ELLs organize their thinking around the poetry work. Remember to add visuals where applicable to anchor nonlinguistic representations to the ideas.

There are many interesting points for discussion in this poem as the students analyze what the poem is saying. Why would the person care if the owner of the woods would not see him stopped in the night to look at the snow? Why do you think Frost spends so much of the poem focused on the horse and his discomfort at being stopped where they are? What was Frost's purpose in immediately switching from the uncomfortable questioning of the horse to more pleasant words such as easy, downy, and lovely? What do you think the promises might be that must be kept? Where do you think the rider and horse are going? Why would Frost repeat the last line?

After reading and discussing the poem, you can access a video of Frost discussing his work on the site Poetry Everywhere. http://www.pbs.org/wgbh/poetryeverywhere/

Next, share the poem "Frost in the Woods" by Ralph Fletcher with your students. Ask them: What do they think this poem is saying? How would they interpret this poem? What structural elements do they see Fletcher using? Refer students to their Clues We Use Bookmarks to help them with their interpretation. If students need some examples, you could point out that the poem starts right off the bat by saying that Uncle John lives in New Hampshire—identifying a human as the focus of the poem. How is that different from the setting of "Stopping by Woods"? The child and uncle engage in conversation, and the uncle recites part of a poem by Frost, which speaks to the child's heart. Even though they are out in nature, this poem seems to be more about human relationships. The uncle is teaching the child about not just nature, but about poetry, and life.

Use a highlighter online or offline to model for students how to mark things that are the same and things that are different. Highlight similarities, leave differences blank. Some things that might appear on the chart:

	"Stopping by Woods on a Snowy Evening"	"Frost in the Woods"
What the poem is saying	Person traveling through the woods with horse	Person is walking in the woods with his uncle
	Someone owns the woods	Renting the woods from God
	Stopping along the path, horse wonders why	Just the tromp tromp of their boots
	It's peaceful, dark, quiet, and snowy	Uncle recites from "Dust of Snow" as he reflects on their walk
	Still a long, long way to go, can't stop because he has promises to keep	Words echo inside child

	"Stopping by Woods on a Snowy Evening"	"Frost in the Woods"
Structural elements	Line breaks every four lines	Line breaks every two lines
	Lines are even, similar length	Lines are even, similar length
	Repetition in last stanza	Repetition of "I ask him____"
		He answers/says: "I'm/ I rent(ed)"

Try Guide students to quickly rehearse what they need to learn and do in preparation for practice

Invite students to come up and contribute to the highlighting process. Students should ask themselves what is the same and what is different.

Clarify Briefly restate today's teaching objective and explain the practice tasks

Clarify for your students that they will now be comparing and contrasting two poems on their own. They do not need to be original and tribute poems like the Frost and Fletcher poems. Students should start by choosing two poems that they think have something in common in terms of the message of the poems or in how they are structured.

Today in your poetry reading, I want you to compare and contrast two poems that you think have something in common either in what they are saying or in how they are structured. Start by analyzing one. What is the poem saying? How would you interpret it? What structural elements do you see? Try to identify some of the other elements that we have studied recently. Then, do the same for another poem. Highlight similarities, leave differences blank.

	Poem 1 Title	Poem 2 Title
What the poem is saying		
Structural elements		
Mood		
Strong images		
What characters do and say		
Poet's purpose		

Practice Students work independently or in small groups to apply today's teaching objective

Students will read and analyze two poems of their choosing with emphasis on what the poem is saying and the structural elements the poet uses. They will then compare and contrast the poems by highlighting things that are the same and things that are different.

Wrap Up Check understanding as you guide students to briefly share what they have learned and produced today

Gather students together and ask them to have their own charts handy. It's time to share with your students the significance of their work.

	Until I Saw the Sea by: Lillian Moore	Breakers by: Lillian Morrison
What is the poem saying?	Sea is beautiful and peaceful	Sea is beautiful yet very powerful and somewhat violent
Structural Elements	Repetition, short lines and white space for emphasis	Words compose a shape, looking like waves breaking on shore
Mood	Light and happy	nervous, unsettled by what nature might do
Strong Images	Wind folding the waves and the tide having the rhythm of a person breathing in and out	image of the tiger biting and clawing the shore
What characters do and say	shares all the amazing things she learned when she saw the sea	Sea is compared to a tiger who may eat away the shore with its big teeth
Poet's Purpose	To share the beauty of the sea	To have us think about the power of nature

 When you compare and contrast two poems, you are better able to see what makes poems distinct and different and where two poems overlap in their meaning and structure and where they are starkly different. Do your poems have more in common or more differences? Take a moment and explain at least one of your ideas to a partner. **ELL** Enabling Language Production—Increasing Interaction

This partner work represents a great opportunity to highlight several skills that are key to effective speaking and listening. Remind students

how to listen with care in respectful ways (SL.4.1b) and how to carefully explain their new understandings in light of your discussion on the importance of comparing and contrasting poems. (SL.4.1d)

 Collect student copies of charts for the structural and meaning comparisons they've made. **ELL** Assess for Content and Language Understanding—Formative Assessment

Milestone Performance Assessment

Comparing and Contrasting Poems

 Use this checklist to assess student work comparing and contrasting poems.

Standards Alignment: RL.4.1, RL.4.2, RL.4.4, RL.4.5, SL.4.1b, SL.4.1d

	Achieved	Notes
Describe what both poems are saying.		
Identify key elements of each poem: content, structure, mood, strong images, what characters say and do, and poet's purpose (may be uneven, but student should identify most of the elements).		
Highlight similarities between the poems.		

Reading Lesson 9 ·

▼ Teaching Objective

Readers will orally read poems with a strong voice to convey the author's message.

Close Reading Opportunity

▼ Standards Alignment

RL.4.1, RL.4.7, RL.4.10, SL.4.5, L.4.1, L.4.6

▼ Materials

- Charting supplies or interactive whiteboard
- How to Read Like a Poetry Performer chart
- Poetry Performer's Key
- "Poetry Recipe" by Ralph Fletcher

▼ To the Teacher

The goal of today's lesson is to help your students breathe life into the poems they've been reading in this lesson set and to see that these poems are meant to be read aloud and shared with the world. There are many wonderful examples of great poetry performances available online. We recommend searching for "poetry performances" or "poetry slams." Your students might also be interested in the history of the poetry slam movement and could do research on the Nuyorican Cafe in New York City or the influence of the Beat movement on the performance of poetry. You may find local poets in your area performing their poetry in cafes and bookstores. This would be a wonderful opportunity for a poetry field trip in which students can meet with poets in the field.

▼ Procedure

`Warm Up` Gather the class to set the stage for today's learning

You are using the clues poets create to help you better understand what the poet is saying and what messages they want to share in the world. Many poets wrote their pieces and didn't ever think many people would read them. Some of the poems we read together weren't famous until the poet had passed away and the work was found in his or her journals. Great art sometimes finds its way into the public eye that way. Some of these poems, though, were written so that they could be read and heard and shared over and over again.

`Teach` Model what students need to learn and do

 Begin a chart titled "How to Read Like a Poetry Performer." `ELL` Provide Comprehensible Input—Organizers.

Today I will read a poem aloud in a performance mode . . . `ELL` Provide Comprehensible Input—Models. Movement and acting out meaning offer a nonlinguistic way to share the meaning of the poem. I will use my body, hands, and voice to demonstrate the impact the poem has had on me.

Read the poem with emphasis on action words like *threw, kneading, picked up,* and *took a deep breath.* These are moments that can be exaggerated and performed for your student audience. (If you are not comfortable reading a poem aloud as a performance piece, use examples you find online.)

When you are finished, have students share what they noticed about your (or one they have viewed) performance and chart their thinking. They may note the following:

How to Read Like a Poetry Performer

- Use movement to express actions
- Voice emphasis of special words and phrases
- Adjust volume to match meaning of poem
- Pause for effect
- Read clearly so everyone can understand
- Use body language or hand gestures to express meaning

Have an enlarged copy available to model the planning you can do as a performer to prepare for reading a poem out loud. Have students help you identify and underline the action words. Put a star by words that you want to emphasize. Use a number sign for moments of pause. Create a performer's key for the class. Following are examples of some things you might want to include:

Poetry Performer's Key

Underline = Action words

* = Words that are important
# = Pause for effect
< = Make voice quieter
> = Make voice louder
Stick figure = Add body language or hand gestures

`Try` Guide students to quickly rehearse what they need to learn and do in preparation for practice

Now it's your turn to try. Choose a poem from your packet that you would like to perform. Once you're chosen your poem, use our performer's key to mark the poem with signals that will help you in your performance. When we're done you'll have a chance to practice performing these poems with a partner.

`Clarify` Briefly restate today's teaching objective and explain the practice tasks

When you are ready to perform your poem for a partner today, think about how you are going to act out the action words, which words you most want to emphasize, and where you want to pause for effect.

`Practice` Students work independently or in small groups to apply today's teaching objective

Students will share their poetry performance with a partner. This is a great lesson to extend into another day so that students have an opportunity to perform their poem choices for the class. Encourage partners to perform their poems a few times. Just as actors rehearse their performances many times before the big day, students can read and reread their selected poems several times to feel more comfortable and confident as poetry performers.

Wrap Up Check understanding as you guide students to briefly share what they have learned and produced today

Review with your students the fact that literacy is about reading, writing, speaking and listening. Emphasize that performing poems is a good example of the synergy of all four of these components.

Goal	Low-Tech	High-Tech
Students will learn about what it looks like and sounds like to perform poetry.	Students will watch their teacher perform a poem, noting what they see and hear.	Students will view poetry performers through digital videos such as those found on YouTube. There are many wonderful teen poetry slams available for viewing. One of our favorites is the Knicks Poetry Slam program. http://www.nba.com/knicks/community/poetryslam.html

Reading Lesson 10

▼ Teaching Objective

Readers reflect on core questions.

Close Reading Opportunity

▼ Standards Alignment

RL.4.1, RL.4.10, W.4.1a-d, W.4.4, W.4.10, SL.4.1a-d, L.4.1, L.4.6

▼ Materials

- Charting supplies or interactive whiteboard
- Core questions

▼ To the Teacher

This is the culmination of the lesson set. Providing time for your students to reflect on what they've learned is an important part of the learning process. It tells you what they have learned from your teaching and it can be used to inform your teaching of these lessons in the future. If you wish to have the students perform their poems for the entire class, be sure you provide time for that before this lesson.

▼ Procedure

Warm Up Gather the class to set the stage for today's learning

Congratulate your students on a job well done. Reading and interpreting poetry can be hard work, but our hope is that these lessons generate enthusiasm for this dynamic genre through complex and engaging texts. Your students should be proud of their close reading, analysis, partnerships, and independent poetry selections.

Engage your students in a discussion of their opinions on the experience of performing poetry. This is an important discussion to have to help students reflect on their own process before considering what they learned from viewing others.

Teach Model what students need to learn and do

Let us reflect on what we've learned about reading and interpreting poetry. One thing we worked on was crafting strong opinions and supporting our opinions with reasons or evidence from the text. We considered how to make our ideas clear and strong.

Engage the class in a discussion of the importance of careful and thoughtful interpretation of material, whether it be a poem or even viewing advertisements on television. Direct your students to the following core questions:

- What clues can we use to interpret poetry?
- What are the structures found in poetry?
- What techniques do poets use that I can use in my writing?
- What poetry mentors can I model my writing after?
- What language can I use to define and support my opinion?

Try Guide students to quickly rehearse what they need to learn and do in preparation for practice

 Choose one question from the previous list and lead the class in a discussion around this question. As the discussion unfolds, craft a shared response to the question. **ELL** Provide Comprehensible Input—Models. Modeling writing your ideas offers another language demonstration of sentence creation. It also offers possible sentence structures that your ELLs can us in their own work. Ideally, your class response should name other contexts to which students can transfer this learning.

Clarify Briefly restate today's teaching objective and explain the practice tasks

Today, you are going to write a response to another core question of your choosing. Remember to state your ideas using strong language and provide reasons and examples to support them!

Post the questions in a central location for students to refer back to as they work. Remind and guide students to structure their writing with:

- An introduction
- An answer to the question
- Examples from the reading and work in this lesson set
- Transitional phrases to connect their ideas
- A conclusion

Goal	Low-Tech	High-Tech
Students craft a written response to one core question.	Students answer the questions using pencil and paper, then share them orally. You could choose key snippets of their responses to include on a reflection bulletin board.	Students draft a response in a Word document, practicing their keyboarding skills. They can share this document with you by dragging it into a shared folder on Dropbox or sending it to you via email. In addition, students can post their reflections on a class blog. As homework, students could comment thoughtfully on the reflections of two (or more) of their classmates.

Practice Students work independently or in small groups to apply today's teaching objective

 Students individually craft responses to the question posed. **ELL** Enable Language Production—Reading and Writing. This is a good time to

check in with your ELLs who may need language support through scribing (writing their thoughts), sentence models, and verbal rehearsal of their thinking.

Wrap Up Check understanding as you guide students to briefly share what they have learned and produced today

 After students have had sufficient time to complete their responses, call the class together to share them. You should collect and save this assignment as evidence of student learning. **ELL** Assess for Content and Language Understanding—Summative Assessment

Milestone Performance Assessment

Reflection on Core Questions

Use this checklist to assess student work on written reflections on the core questions.

Standards Alignment: W.4.1a-d, W.4.4, W.4.10

	Achieved	Notes
Include an opening that introduces the topic of the reflection.		
Accurately answer selected core question.		
Provide examples and evidence for thinking from texts or experiences during lesson set to support ideas.		
Use transitional words and phrases to link ideas.		
Conclude with summarizing thought.		

Writing Lessons

The following table highlights the teaching objectives and standards alignment for all ten lessons across the four stages of the lesson set (introduce, define, extend, and assess). It also indicates which lessons contain special features to support ELLs, technology, speaking and listening, and formative ("milestone") assessments.

The Core Ready Writing Rubric that follows is designed to help you record each student's overall understanding across four levels of achievement as it relates to the lesson set goals. We recommend that you use this rubric at the end of the lesson set as a performance based assessment tool. Use the milestone performance assessments and checklists as tools to help you gauge student progress toward these goals, and reteach and differentiate as needed. See the foundational book, *Be Core Ready: Powerful, Effective Steps to Implementing and Achieving the Common Core State Standards,* for more information about the Core Ready Reading and Writing Rubrics.

The Core I.D.E.A. / Daily Writing Instruction at a Glance

Grade 4 Poetry Wars: Reading, Interpreting, and Debating Meaning in Poetry

Instructional Stages	Lesson #	Teaching Objective	Core Standards	Special Feature
Introduce: notice, explore, collect, note, immerse, surround, record, share	1	Writers consider their opinion of poetry through a poetry inventory.	RL.4.1 • RL.4.10 • W.4.4 • W.4.10 SL.4.1a–d • L.4.1 • L.4.6	Close Reading ELL
Define: name, identify, outline, clarify, select, plan	2	Writers look for poems that speak to them and that they can honor through tribute poetry writing.	RL.4.1 • RL.4.2 • RL.4.4 • RL.4.5 RL.4.10 • W.4.4 • W.4.10 • SL.4.1a–d L.4.1 •L.4.6	Close Reading ELL Tech
	3	Writers of poetry use line breaks and white space for impact.	W.4.4 • W.4.6 • W.4.10 • SL.4.1a SL.4.1b • L.4.1 • L.4.3b • L.4.6	Milestone Assessment
Extend: try, experiment, attempt, approximate, practice, explain, revise, refine	4	Writers of poetry use strong word choices to create strong images.	W.4.4 • W.4.6 • W.4.10 • SL.4.1a–d L.4.1 • L.4.6	Milestone Assessment
	5	Writers talk about what they notice in each other's poems.	SL.4.1 a–d • L.4.1 • L.4.6	ELL
	6	Writers create interpretations of poetry by crafting an opinion.	W.4.1a • W.4.10 • SL.4.1a–d • L.4.1 L.4.3 • L.4.6	Milestone Assessment
	7	Writers add on to their interpretations by providing reasons that are supported by evidence from the text.	W.4.1b–d • W.4.10 • SL.4.1a–d • L.4.1 L.4.3 • L.4.6	ELL Milestone Assessment
	8	Writers plan to defend their interpretations.	W.4.5 • SL.4.1a–d • SL.4.6 • L.4.1 • L.4.6	
	9	Debaters use the language of opinion and disagreement to defend their thinking.	SL.4.3 • SL.4.6 • L.4.1 • L.4.6	S&L
Assess: reflect, conclude, connect, share, recognize, respond	10	Writers reflect on their opinions of poetry by revisiting their poetry inventories.	RL.4.10 • W.4.4 • W.4.5 • W.4.10	Close Reading

Core Ready Writing Rubric

Grade 4 Poetry Wars: Reading, Interpreting, and Debating Meaning in Poetry

Lesson Set Goal	Emerging	Approaching	Achieving	Exceeding	Standards Alignment
Write poems in tribute to well-known works.	Student writes tribute poems with little evidence of success. Lacks connection to original poems.	Student writes tribute poems with some evidence of success. Connection to theme and structure of originals is weak.	Student successfully writes tribute poems. Connection to theme and structure of originals poems is clear.	Student writes exceptional tribute poems. Strong, insightful connection to theme and structure of original poems.	RL.4.1 RL.4.10 W.4.4 W.4.10
Use strong word choice to convey strong images.	Student shows little or no evidence of using strong word choice to convey strong images.	Student attempts to use strong words to convey images. But is infrequent, ineffective, or inaccurate at times.	Student frequently demonstrates ability to choose words that convey strong images.	Student always demonstrates several carefully chosen and/or sophisticated word choices that convey very clear, powerful images.	RL.4.4 W.4.4 W.4.6 W.4.10
Use line breaks and white space for impact.	Student shows little or no evidence of using line breaks and white space to impact meaning.	Student shows limited evidence of or ineffective use of line breaks and white space to impact meaning.	Student uses line breaks and white space in a way that clearly impacts meaning.	Student skillfully uses line breaks and white space to powerfully impact meaning of poem.	W.4.4 W.4.6 W.4.10
Write an interpretation of a poem supporting one's point of view with evidence from the poem.	Student makes a limited attempt or no attempt to write an interpretation of a poem supporting his/her point of view with evidence from the poem.	Student attempts with some evidence of success to write a plausible interpretation of a poem supporting his/her point of view with evidence from the poem.	Student writes a sound interpretation of a poem supporting his/her point of view with evidence from the poem.	Student writes an unusually insightful and well-developed interpretation of a poem supporting his/her point of view with evidence from the poem.	RL.4.1 RL.4.2 RL.4.4 RL.4.5 RL.4.10 W.4.1a W.4.4 W.4.10
Express and develop ideas in conversations with others.	Student makes little or no attempt to express and develop his/her ideas in conversations with others.	Student attempts with some success to express and develop his/her ideas in conversations with others. Gets off track at times.	Student generally expresses and develops his/her ideas in conversations with others. Generally focused and on task in conversation.	Student purposefully and effectively expresses and develops his/her ideas in conversations with others. Always focused and on task.	SL.4.1a–d SL.4.3 SL.4.6 L.4.1 L.4.6
With guidance and support from peers and adults, develop and strengthen writing as needed by planning, revising, and editing.	Student makes little or no attempt to develop and strengthen writing through planning, revising, and editing.	Student attempts with some success to develop and strengthen writing as needed by planning, revising, and editing.	Student develops and strengthens writing as needed by planning, revising, and editing. Some areas of the planning, revision, and editing may be more developed than others.	Student extensively develops and strengthens writing by planning, revising, and editing as needed.	W.4.5

Core Ready Writing Rubric, Grade 4, *continued*

Lesson Set Goal	Emerging	Approaching	Achieving	Exceeding	Standards Alignment
Refer to details and examples in a text when explaining what the text explicitly says and when drawing inferences from the text.	Student shows little or no evidence of active, purposeful reading or searching the text for specific information and evidence. Student makes little or no attempt to provide details and examples when explaining what the text says explicitly and is unable to draw inferences from the text.	Student shows some evidence of active purposeful reading and searching the text for specific information and evidence. Student may provide some details and examples, with marginal accuracy, when explaining what the text says explicitly and when drawing inferences from the text.	Student shows solid evidence of active, purposeful reading and searching the text for specific information and evidence. Student usually provides appropriate details and examples when explaining what the text says explicitly and when drawing inferences from the text.	Student demonstrates exceptional evidence of active, purposeful reading and searching the text for specific information and evidence. Student always provides accurate, explicit, and thoughtful details and examples when explaining what the text says explicitly and when drawing inferences from the text.	RL.4.1
Write an organized opinion piece that includes a clear introduction, point of view, supporting reasons, linking words and phrases, and a concluding statement.	Student writes an opinion piece with little or no evidence of an introduction or concluding statement. Does not articulate a clear point of view and supporting reasons are missing or insufficient. Omits linking words and phrases or uses them inconsistently.	Student writes an opinion piece and attempts to include an introductory and concluding statement. Attempts to identify a point of view but supporting reasons may be weak or irrelevant. Includes some linking words and phrases.	Student writes an opinion piece with a good introductory and concluding statement. Articulates a point of view and generally supports it with relevant supporting reasons. Generally uses linking words and phrases when appropriate.	Student writes an effective opinion piece with a strong introductory and concluding statement. Point of view is apparent and supported with clear and relevant reasons. Always uses linking words and phrases when appropriate.	W.4.1
By the end of the year, proficiently read and comprehend literature, including stories, dramas, and poetry in the grades 4–5 text complexity band, with scaffolding as needed at the high end of the range.	Student shows little or no evidence of reading and comprehending texts appropriate for the grade 4 text complexity band.	Student shows some evidence of reading and comprehending texts appropriate for the grade 4 text complexity band with independence and proficiency.	Student shows solid evidence of reading and comprehending texts appropriate for the grade 4 text complexity band independently and proficiently.	Student shows solid evidence of reading and comprehending texts above the grade 4 text complexity band independently and proficiently.	RL.4.10
Write routinely over extended time frames (time for research, reflection, and revision) and shorter time frames (a single sitting or a day or two) for a range of discipline-specific tasks, purposes, and audiences.	Student shows little or no evidence of writing routinely for short or long time frames for a range of discipline-specific tasks, purposes, and audiences.	Student shows some evidence of writing routinely for short and long time frames for a range of discipline-specific tasks, purposes, and audiences.	Student generally writes routinely for short and long time frames for a range of discipline-specific tasks, purposes, and audiences.	Student shows exceptional evidence of consistently and accurately writing for short and long time frames for a range of discipline-specific tasks, purposes, and audiences.	W.4.10
In collaborative discussions, demonstrate evidence of preparation for discussion and exhibit responsibility to the rules and roles of conversation.	In collaborative discussions, student comes unprepared and often disregards the rules and roles of conversation.	In collaborative discussions, student's preparation may be evident but ineffective or inconsistent. May occasionally disregard the rules and roles of conversation.	In collaborative discussions, student prepares adequately and draws on the preparation and other information about the topic to explore ideas under discussion. Usually observes the rules and roles of conversation.	In collaborative discussions, student arrives extremely well prepared for discussions and draws on the preparation and other information about the topic to explore ideas under discussion. Always observes the rules and roles of conversation.	SL.4.1a SL.4.1b

Core Ready Writing Rubric, Grade 4, *continued*

Lesson Set Goal	Emerging	Approaching	Achieving	Exceeding	Standards Alignment
In collaborative discussions, share and develop ideas in a manner that enhances understanding of topic. Contribute and respond to the content of the conversation in a productive and focused manner.	Student shows little or no evidence of engaging in collaborative discussions and makes little or no attempt to ask and answer questions, stay on topic, link his/her comments to the remarks of others, or to explain his/her own ideas and understanding in light of the discussion.	Student shows some evidence of engaging in collaborative discussions and with marginal success attempts to ask questions to check understanding of information presented, to stay on topic, link his/her comments to the remarks of others, and explain his/her own ideas and understanding in light of the discussion.	Student generally engages in a range of collaborative discussions and asks questions to check understanding of information presented, stays on topic most of the time, and frequently links his/her own ideas and understanding in light of the discussion.	Student effectively and consistently engages in a range of collaborative discussions and asks high level questions to check understanding of information presented, always stays on topic, and with great insight and attention to the comments of others links his/her own ideas and understanding in light of the discussion.	SL.4.1c SL.4.1d
Demonstrate knowledge of standard English and its conventions.	Student demonstrates little or no knowledge of standard English and its conventions.	Student demonstrates some evidence of knowledge of standard English and its conventions.	Student consistently demonstrates knowledge of standard English and its conventions.	Student demonstrates an exceptional understanding of standard English and its conventions.	L.4.1 L.4.2 L.4.3
Acquire and accurately use grade-appropriate conversational, general academic, and domain-specific vocabulary and phrases.	Student shows little or no evidence of the acquisition and use of grade-appropriate conversational and academic language.	Student shows some evidence of the acquisition and use of grade-appropriate conversational and academic language.	Student shows solid evidence of the acquisition and use of grade-appropriate conversational and academic language.	Student shows a high level of sophistication and precision when using grade-appropriate conversational and academic language.	L.4.6

Note: See the Core Ready Rubrics chart in the Welcome at the beginning of the book for descriptions of category headers.

Writing Lesson 1

▼ Teaching Objective

Writers consider their opinion of poetry through a poetry inventory.

Close Reading
Opportunity

▼ Standards Alignment

RL.4.1, RL.4.10, W.4.4, W.4.10, SL.4.1a-d, L.4.1, L.4.6

▼ Materials

- Poetry Inventory (see Appendix 4.8)
- *Love That Dog* by Sharon Creech

▼ To the Teacher

This lesson set is an opportunity to give your students space and support to share their opinions about poetry. Before this lesson set even begins, some of your students may have strong opinions about poetry. Today's lesson gives you the opportunity to tap into your students' beliefs and feelings about poetry. Do they see themselves as poets? Who are their favorite poets? What do they like and dislike about poetry? Once we come to know our students' initial opinions, we can understand how to better support them as readers and writers.

Love That Dog, by Sharon Creech, provides a wonderful read-aloud text for the duration of this writing lesson set. Today kicks off the reading of this book, which is told through Jack's poetic journal entries. At the beginning of this story, Jack does not see himself as a poet. Your students will be eager to hear how this fellow student comes to see himself differently. Consider viewing book trailers on *Love That Dog* created by students on YouTube to orient your students to the themes of the story—especially Jack's opinion in the beginning of the story that only girls write poetry. **ELL** Provide Comprehensible Input—Visuals. Video clips are a powerful way of conveying meaning through nonlinguistic media. These images can offer stronger ties to previous background knowledge and comprehension.

▼ Procedure

Warm Up Gather the class to set the stage for today's learning

Introduce your students to *Love That Dog*. Do a brief introduction of the book and then begin reading the book aloud. Pause to ask students what they notice about the format and style of this book. What do they think of the main character based on the first few pages?

> Fourth graders, today I want to introduce you to a new character, a boy named Jack, who, like you, is learning about poetry in school. I'm going to read the first few pages. Listen for how this story is different from other read-alouds you've heard. Listen for clues as to who Jack is and what his feelings about poetry are.

After reading a few pages, ask your students if some of them may feel like Jack—that poetry is for girls, that your brain might feel empty sometimes when you sit down to write a poem, and that poems can be hard to understand.

Teach Model what students need to learn and do

> Jack is showing us through his journal entries and poems that he has strong feelings about poetry but that he's also very capable as a poet. He has a story to tell and poetry seems to be giving him a way to tell it. I know I'm already wondering about the blue car and why it's important to him. So far this story seems to be a written exchange between Jack and his teacher, Miss Stretchberry, but we only hear about it through Jack's words. We know Miss Stretchberry is writing him back, though, based on the way he's telling his story.
>
> We all have opinions. Some of them are strong ones. And we all have opinions or beliefs about poetry. Some of you may see yourselves as poets. Some of you may not quite yet.
>
> Now that we've heard some of Jack's perspective, I want to hear yours. You may agree with Jack. You may disagree. Today you are going to complete a poetry inventory. An inventory is a survey that asks for your opinion and your background with poetry.

Try Guide students to quickly rehearse what they need to learn and do in preparation for practice

Before we take a look at today's inventory questions, put your thumb up if you like reading poetry. Put your thumb up if you like writing poetry. Now put your thumb up if you would like to learn more about poetry. Let's read through the inventory questions together.

Clarify Briefly restate today's teaching objective and explain the practice tasks

Read through the Poetry Inventory together as a class. Answer any questions your students may have. Use this as an opportunity for students to share their opinions and for you to gauge their understanding and background knowledge with poetry.

Practice Students work independently or in small groups to apply today's teaching objective

Students will complete the Poetry Inventory.

Wrap Up Check understanding as you guide students to briefly share what they have learned and produced today

Have students rate to what degree they consider themselves to be poets. Use a scale of 1 to 5 with 5 representing students who very strongly consider themselves poets and 1 representing students who would like to learn more about what it means to be a poet. Do this through a show of hands. It might be interesting to graph your students' responses and come back to this inventory at the end of the lesson set.

Continue reading from *Love That Dog*. This is a great ritual read-aloud to continue with for the duration of the lesson set. You may want to begin and end each lesson with some reading from this imaginative and engaging text.

> *A complete poem is one where an emotion finds the thought and the thought finds the words.*
>
> —Robert Frost

Writing Lesson 2

▼ Teaching Objective

Writers look for poems that speak to them and that they can honor through tribute poetry writing.

Close Reading Opportunity

▼ Standards Alignment

RL.4.1, L.4.2, RL.4.4, RL.4.5, RL.4.10, W.4.4, W.4.10, SL.4.1a-d, L.4.1, L.4.6

▼ Materials

- Student poetry packets
- *Stopping by Woods on a Snowy Evening* by Robert Frost
- Sample tribute poem (see Appendix 4.9, Tribute Poem Sample)

- Tools for writing
- *Love That Dog* by Sharon Creech

▼ To the Teacher

Students have read poems to find poems that speak to them. Today you're going to ask students to search for poetry mentors by collecting poems they are drawn to from the Internet, or you can direct students to their poetry packets and use these as the source of inspiration. If you have English language learners in your class, incorporate poems from students' native languages. **ELL** Enable Language Production—Reading and Writing. Native language is a valuable tool in connecting learning for your ELLs.

Warm Up — Gather the class to set the stage for today's learning

In our reading lesson, we searched for poems that spoke to us. You also received poetry packets full of poems. Put a thumb up if you have found several poems that you've enjoyed reading. Today you are going to hunt for poems again, but this time you are going to be reading with a new lens—that of a writer rather than a reader.

Teach — Model what students need to learn and do

Writers find inspiration from other writers. We're seeing that Jack in *Love That Dog* finds inspiration for his poems as he reads other poems in school. The structure and word choices that poets use have influenced the choices Jack is making as a writer. We see that when Jack repeats the phrase "So much depends on a _____," just like William Carlos Williams' poem The Red Wheelbarrow does. We also see that when Jack incorporates tiger sounds into his poem because he was inspired by William Blake's famous poem "The Tiger." Jack is going to continue to find inspiration for his poems by reading the great poems of others.

When you hear the word tribute what do you think of? Tribute means to honor. Jack honors the poems of William Carlos Williams and William Blake when he writes his poems in their spirit. Let's look at Jack's poems and the originals to see how Jack pays tribute to them as poets.

Create a list with your students of how Jack pays tribute to William Carlos Williams and William Blake. If you are further in your reading of *Love That Dog*, there may be other poets to include in your analysis.

Today you are going to read to see what poems you want to pay tribute to in the same way Jack pays tribute to William Carlos Williams and William Blake.

Try — Guide students to quickly rehearse what they need to learn and do

Direct students to the Tribute Poem Sample (see Appendix 4.9) and have students discuss with a partner specific ways this poet used the original poems (Frost's "Stopping by Woods on a Snowy Evening" and Fletcher's "Frost in the Woods") as an inspiration.

Next, have students read in their poetry packets and look for poems that they want to pay tribute to in their own writing. Direct students to put a star by any poems for which they are thinking of writing their own tribute poems.

Now that we've seen how Jack pays tribute to original poems and how other writers do it as well, it's time for you to read the poems in your poetry packet, looking out for those that you want to pay tribute to by mirroring your writing after theirs. Put a star next to the poems you're thinking of paying tribute to.

Clarify — Briefly restate today's teaching objective and explain the practice tasks

In your independent writing today, choose one of the poems you've starred and begin your own tribute version. Do you want to begin with the same first line or part of the first line? Do you want to repeat certain words or phrases just like the original does? Do you want to use the same number of stanzas? Do you want your lines to be about the same length as the original?

At the end of your poem write:

Inspired by _____ and fill in the blank with the name of the poet who inspired your work. This is another way we can honor this wonderful poetry.

Practice — Students work independently or in small groups to apply today's teaching objective

Students will choose one of the poems they starred in their packets and begin writing their own tribute version.

Wrap Up — Check understanding as you guide students to briefly share

Invite students to share their tribute poems. Share where you see them borrowing techniques and structures from the original poets and have them share how they have done so.

Goal	Low-Tech	High-Tech
Students will read in search of poems that speak to them for tribute poetry writing.	Students will read from books and copies of poems provided by the teacher.	Students will read from poetry websites such as Poetry Foundation, Poem Hunter, Poetry4Kids, and Giggle Poetry. www.poetryfoundation.org/ www.poemhunter.com/ www.poetry4kids.com/ www.gigglepoetry.com/ Create a class blog for student poets.

Writing Lesson 3 . . . .

▼ Teaching Objective

Writers of poetry use line breaks and white space for impact.

▼ Standards Alignment

W.4.4, W.4.6, W.4.10, SL.4.1a, SL.4.1b, L.4.1, L.4.3b, L.4.6

▼ Materials

- Poetry packets
- Tools for writing
- *Love That Dog* by Sharon Creech

▼ To the Teacher

This lesson is designed to mirror Reading Lesson 3 on poetic structures. In this lesson, students will be applying what they learned in reading to their writing by paying close attention to the use of line breaks and white space for poetic impact.

▼ Procedure

Warm Up Gather the class to set the stage for today's learning

Structure in writing refers to how the poet decides what words begin and end each line. It refers to whether there are patterns you can see in the poem, like words that rhyme at the end of each line. It refers to whether there is one stanza or many. In reading we've been learning about how poets use different structures to convey their messages. As writers these structures are very important.

Teach Model what students need to learn and do

Two structures that will be important to us as writers today are called line breaks and white space. Line breaks refer to how the poet begins and ends each line.

Does the poet end certain lines with rhyming words? Does the poet capitalize the start of each line? Does the poet use punctuation? All of these decisions are what poets must think about when they are determining line breaks.

Another structure poets use is called *white space*. That refers to the space between stanzas of poems. Stanza in Italian means "room." The stanzas in poems are like different rooms in the same house. When you're reading a new stanza it feels a little like walking into a new room in the poet's thinking. The white space signals to the readers that they are about to experience something new and different. Likewise, sometime poets use white space to make especially important words stand out. In some cases, white space has a close connection to the meaning of the poem, such as a poem about [demonstrate for students]:

going

down

the

stairs.

Both of these structures make a big impact on how we read the poem. In his February 7th entry, Jack reminds Miss Stretchberry of the importance of white space. Let's see what he says about this.

Read or reread this entry for students. Talk about why Jack wants his teacher to remember the white space between lines. Then, either refer to the poem you read during the reading lesson or choose a poem that shows the impact of white space. You can also choose a page from Jack's journal that uses white space and line breaks well. Use this as a model for students and the decisions they will make as writers when considering the importance of structure.

Try Guide students to quickly rehearse what they need to learn and do in preparation for practice

I want you to find a poem in your poetry packet that you think uses the structures of line breaks or white space well, and be ready to share what you found and why you think the structures make an impact on the meaning. Writers of poetry use structure as a way to convey big ideas, as a way to convince the reader of an idea that matters deeply to the poet.

Discuss with students which poems they chose and why. Focus the discussion on the structures of line breaks and white space.

Clarify Briefly restate today's teaching objective and explain the practice tasks

In your writing today, choose another poem from your packet to pay tribute to. This time I want you to focus on where you end a line and how you choose to begin a new one. Mirror what the original poet did with white space. Is there more than one stanza? Are the lines short or long? Your decisions will make an impact on the meaning of the poem.

Practice Students work independently or in small groups to apply today's teaching objective

Students will write tribute poems with emphasis on line breaks and white space. Some guiding questions for their work include:

- What parts of my poem should be grouped together or separated by line breaks?
- What parts of my poem should stand out and be surrounded by white space?
- How does the white space connect to the meaning of the poem?

Wrap Up Check understanding as you guide students to briefly share

Invite students to share their tribute poems with the group. Continue to comment on how you see your students paying tribute to the originals by focusing on line breaks and white space.

Writing Lesson 4 ·

▼ Teaching Objective

Writers of poetry use strong word choices to create strong images.

▼ Standards Alignment

W.4.4, W.4.6, W.4.10, SL.4.1a-d, L.4.1, L.4.6

▼ Materials

- Strong Images Plan chart
- Poetry packets
- Tools for writing
- "Fog" by Carl Sandburg (see Appendix 4.5)
- *Love That Dog* by Sharon Creech

▼ To the Teacher

In this lesson, students will be applying what they learned in reading to their writing by paying close attention to the use of strong word choices to create strong images in their readers' minds.

▼ Procedure

Warm Up Gather the class to set the stage for today's learning

In our reading lesson we read Carl Sandburg's poem "Fog" and observed how his word choices helped us really picture the fog as if it were alive and moving toward us. In just a few words he was able to create a vivid picture in our minds. We could see the fog sitting and then moving. By comparing the fog to a cat, Sandburg helped us imagine the fog as a living thing. Every word in this poem matters.

Teach Model what students need to learn and do

Share with students how they can plan their poetry writing with an emphasis on strong word choice for strong images.

> When I'm writing poems I pay attention to word choice to convey strong images, just like Carl Sandburg does. I plan in advance what I want to write about, what I'm going to compare it to, and what action words I'll use. Let's see how Sandburg may have planned this way:

Strong Images Plan

Thing I want to write about	The fog
What I'm going to compare it to	A cat
What action words I'll use	Sits, moves on

Try Guide students to quickly rehearse what they need to learn and do in preparation for practice

> Today you will read the poems you starred in your poetry packet and choose one that you can vividly picture in your mind. Notice how the writer used strong word choices to help you picture a scene. Did the poet use effective action words? Did the poet make comparisons the way Sandburg compared the fog to a cat? Complete a Strong Images Plan for your own poem:

Strong Images Plan

Thing I want to write about	
What I'm going to compare it to	
What action words I'll use	

Clarify Briefly restate today's teaching objective and explain the practice tasks

Today you are going to use your strong images plan to focus on the words you choose and the images you are creating in your readers' minds.

Practice Students work independently or in small groups to apply today's teaching objective

Students will write tribute poems, focusing on their word choices to convey strong images in their readers' minds.

Wrap Up Check understanding as you guide students to briefly share

Continue to invite students to share their tribute poems with the group. Remember to comment on how you see your students paying tribute to the originals by focusing on word choice to convey strong images.

Collect poetry and Strong Images Plans from students and look for places where students use strong word choices to convey strong images. **ELL** Assess for Content and Language Understanding—Formative Assessment.

Milestone Performance Assessment

Using Strong Imagery in Poetry

 Use this checklist to assess student tribute poems with strong images.

Standards Alignment: W.4.4, W.4.6, W.4.10

	Achieved	Notes
Compose a tribute poem based on an original poem.		
Attempt to create a strong image in the poem.		
Choose words that effectively convey the image.		

Writing Lesson 5 ·

▼ Teaching Objective

Writers talk about what they notice in each other's poems.

▼ Standards Alignment

SL.4.1a-d, L.4.1, L.4.6

▼ Materials

- Student tribute poems
- "Love That Boy" by Walter Dean Myers (in *Love That Dog*)
- Ways to Talk about Poetry chart
- Poetry sentence starters

▼ To the Teacher

This lesson builds on what Jack talks about when he reads Walter Dean Myers's poem "Love That Boy." Use his March 14th journal entry as a starting place for how your students can talk to each other about what they notice in each other's poems. Consider posting the following sentence starters for your students, which can help them discuss what they notice in each other's poems:

- This poem reminds me of when (personal connection). . . .
- This poem reminds me of (another poem, book, etc.). . . .
- I think the poet's message is _____.
- This poem makes me feel _____ because _____.
- _____ is a metaphor for _____.
- The big idea or theme of this poem is _____.
- This poem appeals to my senses (with examples). . . .
- This poem paints a picture of _____.
- I like how the poet _____.

- I noticed a technique this poet uses is _____.
- I have noticed that in many of this poet's poems _____.
- This poem is important to me because _____.
- The main idea of this poem is _____.
- My favorite part of the poem is _____ because _____.
- This poem reminds me of another poem we've read called _____ because _____.
- I think this because _____ (textual evidence to support your thinking).

▼ Procedure

Warm Up Gather the class to set the stage for today's learning

Now your students are ready to talk about what they notice about each other's poems.

> You've written several tribute poems and many of you have shared them with the class. Today you are going to choose your favorite to share with a partner and then you are going to talk about what you notice in each other's writing.

Teach Model what students need to learn and do

> I'm going to reread Jack's entry from March 14th. Let's listen for what Jack writes when he first reads Walter Dean Myers's poem titled "Love That Boy." Let's see why he likes it so much.

Read the entry to your students. Ask your students to reflect on Jack's response to "Love That Boy." What does Jack focus on in his response? Use Jack's response as a model for how students can form their own interpretations of poems. Among other remarks, they might say things like:

- He connects to the specific line about calling him in the morning because it reminds him of what his dad says.
- He connects to what he said to his dog, Skye, when he used to call the dog.

Start a Ways to Talk about Poetry chart. **ELL** Provide Compre-hensible Input—Graphic Organizer. Organizers offer support that ELLs can refer back to during their independent work. Consider adding visu-als and sketches where applicable as well as offering a small copy for their own folder.

Ways to Talk about Poetry

Make a connection to yourself.

Try Guide students to quickly rehearse what they need to learn and do in preparation for practice

> Now that we've seen Jack's response to "Love That Boy," what else do you think he could have commented on?

Have a discussion with your students about what they notice about the original Walter Dean Myers poem. Encourage them to talk about what words he repeats, his line breaks, his choices about capitalization, and his use of dialogue. Does the poem remind them of something from their own life? Does it remind them of another poem?

Continue with your Ways to Talk about Poetry chart.

Ways to Talk about Poetry

- Make a connection to yourself.

- Make a connection to another poem.

- Notice words that seem special.

- Talk about the actual words in the poem and what they say.

- Notice words that are repeated.

- Talk about the impact of line breaks.

- Talk about the impact of white space.

- Talk about the use of dialogue.

Clarify Briefly restate today's teaching objective and explain the practice tasks

> Today you are going to read your poem to a partner and then your partner will begin a conversation about the poem using our Ways to Talk about Poetry chart as a guide. Listen carefully to what your classmate has to say about your poem. At the end of class you are going to share what your partner noticed and commented on.

Practice Students work independently or in small groups to apply today's teaching objective

Students will share their poems with a partner and engage in an extended conversation initiated by the listener.

Wrap Up Check understanding as you guide students to briefly share

Have students share one thing their partner noticed about their poem. This is a great opportunity for students to report what their classmates said about their poem.

Writing Lesson 6 ·····························

▼ Teaching Objective

Writers create interpretations of poetry by crafting an opinion.

▼ Standards Alignment

W.4.1a, W.4.10, SL.4.1a-d, L.4.1, L.4.3, L.4.6

▼ Materials

- Opinion phrases list: I think . . . , In my opinion . . . , The way I see it . . . , As far as I'm concerned . . . , I suppose . . . , I suspect that . . . , I'm pretty sure that . . . , I'm convinced that . . . , I honestly feel that . . . , I strongly believe that . . . .

▼ Procedure

Warm Up Gather the class to set the stage for today's learning

Refer to yesterday's conversations about each other's poems. Remember that there are many possibly interpretations to poems, including the poems of your students. Continue to remind students of the importance of providing textual evidence when stating an opinion or giving an interpretation. Fourth graders, remember your work yesterday. You focused on reading your original poems with confidence and, equally as important, talking about each other's poems with care and respect. You noticed features you liked and shared them with one another. These kinds of focused conversations about poems help make poetry even more meaningful. They also help you set the stage for learning how to make the case for why one poem speaks to you or why you feel your interpretation of a poem is significant.

Teach Model what students need to learn and do

Today you are going to choose a poem and model how to write an opinion statement about this poem. Below we have included a sample opinion of William Carlos William's "The Red Wheelbarrow."

I'm going to share with you today the first poem that Jack read in school, "The Red Wheelbarrow." This is a poem that doesn't have many words but leaves a lot of things open for discussion. Listen as I share an opinion about the meaning of this poem. An opinion on the meaning of a poem is also called an interpretation of a poem. This poem has many interpretations despite (or maybe because of) its complete simplicity. Here is one possible interpretation. Notice how this piece of writing uses some of the phrases from our Opinion phrases list:

"In the poem, "The Red Wheelbarrow" I think that William Carlos Williams is writing about the potential of a simple object to have an important role in the world. This seems important because it made me stop and think about how many things are around me that I don't even notice a lot of the time. I strongly believe that if we paid more attention to our surroundings we would notice a lot more about what is happening in our lives."

When we write about our interpretations, we are often trying to convince someone that our opinion is valid or to excite someone about a new idea or new insight we have. We call this *persuasive writing*. When all of our writing is complete we are going to have poetry debates, defending and arguing that our interpretation is valid. We will support our interpretation with evidence from the poem.

To write your own opinion, you can use the following as a guide:

In the poem _____ I think that _____ is writing about _____.
This seems important because _____. I strongly believe that _____.

Opinion Phrases

- I think...
- In my opinion...
- The way I see it...
- I suspect that...
- I suppose...
- I believe that...
- I would argue...
- I honestly feel that...
- I'm convinced that...
- I found that...

Try Guide students to quickly rehearse what they need to learn and do in preparation for practice

Today you are going to write the beginning of your interpretation of a poem. Choose a poem from your packet. Ask yourself: what kind of case would I make for the way I would interpret this poem? Remember to use our opinion phrases list to help you with your thinking. You can also refer to your Clues We Use Bookmark to help you as you develop your interpretation.

Clarify Briefly restate today's teaching objective and explain the practice tasks

In your writing today, you are going to begin your poetry interpretation by stating your opinion about what the poem really means from your perspective. Remember to use our opinion phrases list to help you begin your piece.

Practice Students work independently or in small groups to apply today's teaching objective

Students will begin writing their poetry interpretations by stating their opinion about the meaning of the poem. Provide students with individual copies of the opinion phrases list to help them start their persuasive writing.

Wrap Up Check understanding as you guide students to briefly share

Have students share the poem they are writing about. Notice when students are writing about the same poem. Let them know it will be interesting to see who shares the same opinion about a particular poem and who disagrees.

Review the interpretations and take the opportunity to do one-to-one conferences with writers (either online via a system such as Google drive or face to face). **ELL** Assess for Content and Language Understanding—Formative Assessment.

Milestone Performance Assessment

Forming Opinions about Poetry Meaning

 Use this checklist to assess student work in developing opinions.

Standards Alignment: W.4.1a, SL.4.1a-d, L.4.3

	Achieved	Notes
Express an opinion about the meaning of the poem.		

	Achieved	Notes
Use appropriate academic language to express opinion (phrases).		
Demonstrate an understanding of how to form an interpretation using knowledge from previous lessons.		

Writing Lesson 7

▼ Teaching Objective

Writers add on to their interpretations by providing reasons that are supported by evidence from the text.

▼ Standards Alignment

W.4.1b-d, W.4.10, SL.4.1a-d, L.4.1, L.4.3, L.4.6

▼ Materials

- Poetry packets
- Student interpretations to date

▼ To the Teacher

Today you want students to add on to their opinions by citing specific words, lines, and structural evidence from the text. It will be important to model this with a poem your students have greatly enjoyed in either the reading or writing lessons.

▼ Procedure

Warm Up Gather the class to set the stage for today's learning

Remind students of the work they've done so far in establishing an opinion.

Teach Model what students need to learn and do

Today we're going to focus on the evidence that supports our opinions. Give reasons why we think the way we do to show that our opinions are well thought out and should be seriously considered.

Now turn to the review of a poem you've been crafting as a model for the class. Reread your opinion statement. Then, demonstrate finding specific evidence to support your opinion. Here's how your modeling could unfold:

Let me read my opinion statement again. "In the poem, "The Red Wheelbarrow" I think that William Carlos Williams is writing about the potential of a simple object to have an important role in the world. This seems important because it made me stop and think about how many things are around me that I don't even notice a lot of the time. I strongly believe that if we paid more attention about our surroundings we would notice a lot more about what is happening in our lives."

Now, let me list my reasoning across my fingers. One way to add on to this opinion is to provide the following reasons to support this opinion:

"First, I think the poem is about simplicity because the poem itself is so simple—just one sentence. Second, I think the objects (like the wheelbarrow and the rain and the chickens) are the focus because there is no action in the poem. Third, I think the poet really wants us to focus on the simplicity of the objects because he uses simple adjectives to describe them like "red" and "white." Finally, I think the poet thinks that these simple objects are so important because he starts his poem by telling us that so much depends on these things.

Demonstrate turning your thinking into sentences with examples. **ELL** Provide Comprehensible Input—Models. Sentence models offer a concrete example that helps students organize their speaking and writing in English. Consider practicing how this sounds several times so that they hear how these sentences sound when fluently spoken.

Did you notice how I started by rereading my opinion statement? Then I listed the reasons I have this opinion across my fingers. Next, I turned my reasons into sentences. My reasons are specific so the reader or listener can understand them. You can add on to your opinion by using the following sentence starters as a guide:

First, I think _____ because _____. Second, I think _____ because _____. Third, I think _____ because _____. Finally, I think _____ because _____.

Try Guide students to quickly rehearse what they need to learn and do in preparation for practice

Take a look at your opinion statement. Think for a moment. What are some reasons behind your opinion? Do you have examples from the text? Be sure that your reasons are specific enough to really support your opinion.

Give students a moment to think quietly. Then, ask them to share their thinking with a partner. Remind students to use the following sentence starters as a guide.

© Tatiana Belova / Fotolia

First, I think _____ because _____. Second, I think _____ because _____. Third, I think _____ because _____. Finally, I think _____ because _____.

Clarify Briefly restate today's teaching objective and explain the practice tasks

Today we are focusing on giving reasons to support our opinions. Let us be sure that they are closely related to our opinions.

Remind students to begin by stating their reasoning across their fingers.

Practice Students work independently or in small groups to apply today's teaching objective

Students independently review their opinions and provide reasons to support them.

Wrap Up Check understanding as you guide students to briefly share what they have learned and produced today

Choose one or two students to share their work with the class today. Collect the student interpretations done so far. Use this work to determine whether your students need additional guidance or practice with crafting strong opinions and supporting those opinions with relevant and specific reasons from the text. **ELL** Assess for Content and Language Understanding—Formative Assessment. This is the time to think about how ELLs are progressing with the language demands of the work that you have been doing. Use this as an opportunity to jot some notes on how to scaffold and support upcoming language demands.

Milestone Performance Assessment

Forming and Defending Opinions about Poetry Meaning

Use this checklist to assess student work on developing opinions.

Standards Alignment: W.4.1b-d, SL.4.1a-d, L.4.1, L.4.3

	Achieved	Notes
Express an opinion about the meaning of the poem.		
Use appropriate academic language to express opinion (phrases).		
Use evidence from the poem to support opinion.		

Writing Lesson 8 . . . .

▼ Teaching Objective

Writers plan to defend their interpretations.

▼ Standards Alignment

W.4.5, SL.4.1a-d, SL.4.6, L.4.1, L.4.6

▼ Materials

- Defense Notes page

▼ To the Teacher

Today is about helping your students prepare for their poetry defense. We want our students to care about the poems they've chosen and to defend their thinking using evidence from the text, but we don't want fourth graders rallying against each other. Rather, we suggest creative platforms for your poetry "debates." Try splitting your class into small groups for their poetry defenses rather than having the whole class agree or disagree with a writer's interpretation. This is also a fun opportunity to invite another class or grade level in to see whether they agree or disagree with how poems have been interpreted. You could create a poetry Hall of Fame in which students are arranged in poetry booths with the poem they've chosen to interpret on display and other students can come by their booth to hear what the interpreter thinks about the poem.

▼ Procedure

Warm Up Gather the class to set the stage for today's learning

Congratulate your class on their work writing powerful interpretations that ground their opinion of the poem's meaning with evidence from the poem. It is now time to plan for their poetry defense.

> Fourth graders, we have been working on creating writing powerful interpretations. You have concentrated on making sure your opinions are grounded in the words of the poems themselves. Now, it's time to plan for how you can defend your interpretation should someone else have a different opinion of the meaning of the poem.

Teach Model what students need to learn and do

> To help us defend our thinking, we are going to use a Defense Notes page to help us take notes on our opinions and prepare for what others might say.

My Defense	Disagreeing Opinions

> Let's look at my interpretation of _____. Watch as I turn my interpretation into bulleted notes. Now let's imagine what other interpretations of the poem might be.

Going back to our teacher who has been interpreting "The Red Wheelbarrow," the notes might be:

- simple sentence structure
- objects but no action
- simple adjectives
- opening line about so much depending on objects
- noticing simple objects makes us notice what is happening in our lives

Bullet points for disagreeing opinions might be:

- there is only one sentence, but it is complicated, with only one word on every other line

- there is no explicit action, but it is raining or has just rained and the chickens are probably active
- "red" and "white" are simple adjectives, but "glazed" has a more complex feel
- maybe the poet is almost joking or teasing about so much depending on these simple objects—they are not doing anything or causing anything at all to happen
- the point of the poem could be that simple objects have no impact at all on the world until people use them, so the thing the poet really believes everything depends on is people, not objects

Try Guide students to quickly rehearse what they need to learn and do in preparation for practice

Have students talk to a partner to generate what other interpretations of this poem might be. Then, come back together as a group and add everyone's thinking to the disagreeing opinions column in bulleted form.

Clarify Briefly restate today's teaching objective and explain the practice tasks

> In your independent practice today, you are going to first turn your interpretation into notes in the "my defense." Then, you are going to imagine what other interpretations of this poem might be.

Practice Students work independently or in small groups to apply today's teaching objective

Students will turn their interpretations into notes and further their plans for defense by taking notes on disagreeing opinions.

Wrap Up Check understanding as you guide students to briefly share

Have students share what was hard about preparing for disagreeing opinions.

> " The crown of literature is poetry.
> —Matthew Arnold "

Writing Lesson 9

▼ Teaching Objective

Debaters use the language of opinion and disagreement to defend their thinking.

▼ Standards Alignment

SL.4.3, SL.4.6, L.4.1, L.4.6

▼ Materials

- Opinion, agreement, and disagreement phrases lists

▼ To the Teacher

Today's lesson provides students with language that can help them express their opinions about the theme of a poem and learn to engage in respectful conversation with one another about their opinions. They may find they agree with a classmate or they may find they disagree. Giving them the language tools to respectfully discuss texts is an important part of becoming a speaker and a listener.

This is a great lesson for inviting a colleague in to help demonstrate how to share your interpretation and have someone else respectfully disagree.

▼ Procedure

Warm Up Gather the class to set the stage for today's learning

Let your students know that we all have opinions and that we want to have the language for expressing our opinions and disagreeing with someone else's opinions.

> Interpreting poetry often leads to differences of opinion. Being a poetry scholar not only means being able to engage with one another, but it also means using respectful language when you disagree. Let's take a look at some phrases we can use to express our opinions and to agree or disagree with someone else's opinions:

> Opinion phrases: I think . . . , In my opinion . . . , The way I see it . . . , As far as I'm concerned . . . , I suppose . . . , I suspect that . . . , I'm pretty sure that . . . , I'm convinced that . . . , I honestly feel that . . . , I strongly believe that . . . .

> Agreement phrases: I agree because . . . , I also feel that . . . .

> Disagreement phrases: I don't think that . . . , I don't agree . . . , Shouldn't we consider . . . , But what about . . . .

Teach Model what students need to learn and do

Model for students how to share an interpretation and how to agree and disagree.

> Today you are going to share your interpretations and hear the opinions of others in response to your interpretation. Listen as I share my interpretation of _____.

One teacher shared her interpretation of "The Red Whellbarrow" as follows:

> In my opinion, in "The Red Wheelbarrow" William Carlos Williams is writing about the potential of simple things to have important roles in the world. I strongly believe that if we paid more attention to our surroundings and the simple objects in them, we would notice and learn a lot more about what is happening in our lives.

> I'm convinced that the poet feels the same way because the poem is so simple. It is really just one sentence broken up in even parts. The way I see it, the poem really could not be more simple. The objects are very simple, only a wheelbarrow, rain, and chickens. The description of the objects also is simple—red and white are the main adjectives. I'm pretty sure that a poem can't get much simpler than that in its use of language. Plus, have you ever read anything where there is less action? As far as I am concerned, I like the poem, but absolutely nothing at all is actually happening in the poem. Finally, it is obvious to me that the poet shares my view, because he starts the poem by writing about how everything depends on these simple things.

But what about the opinion some people might have that the poet is actually just writing about how these objects just are what they are, simple things that have no effect on anything? I disagree because that would mean that the poet was joking or teasing when he wrote in the first line that everything depends on these simple objects. There is nothing in the simple language of the poem that gives any hint of any kind of teasing or joking feeling, so I am convinced that the poet was expressing his true feelings when he wrote about how important these simple objects are.

Try Guide students to quickly rehearse what they need to learn and do in preparation for practice

What language could you use to agree with my interpretation? What language could you use to disagree with my interpretation?

Clarify Briefly restate today's teaching objective and explain the practice tasks

Today you are going to share the interpretation of your poem and invite others to share their opinions.

Practice Students work independently or in small groups to apply today's teaching objective

Students will share their interpretations and invite others to share what they think the poem means and why. To make their opinions stronger, audience members should be encouraged to identify the reasons and evidence the speaker used and then explain whether they support or refute those ideas. (SL.4.3)

Wrap Up Check understanding as you guide students to briefly share

Have students share what they learned about voicing their opinions, especially when they disagree with someone else.

Writing Lesson 10 ·

▼ Teaching Objective

Writers reflect on their opinions of poetry by revisiting their poetry inventories.

▼ Standards Alignment

RL.4.10, W.4.5, W.4.4., W.4.10

▼ Materials

- Poetry inventories (completed in Writing Lesson 1)
- Colored pencils

▼ To the Teacher

This lesson brings the lesson set full circle. Your students have an opportunity today to revisit their original opinion of poetry from the start of the lesson set.

▼ Procedure

Warm Up Gather the class to set the stage for today's learning

Revisit the language of "interpretation" and "defense" and "argument." Explain that throughout life, knowing how to defend arguments about interpretation will serve your students well, whether they are arguing on behalf of a poem or something work related. Practicing interpretation and defense of it is good practice for life!

Students, you spent a lot of time reading poems with a critical eye and writing poems of your own. Remember when we first started this lesson set and first heard of Jack from *Love That Dog* and his opinion of poetry? How did his opinion of poetry change? How did his opinion of himself as a poet change?

Teach Model what students need to learn and do

Remember the Poetry Inventories we completed at the start of the lesson set? We all had opinions of poetry then. For some of us, our opinions may have changed just like Jack. Let's take a look at the Poetry Inventory from the start of the lesson set and how feelings or favorites have changed now.

Share with students your response to the Poetry Inventory and how some things may have changed for you, such as your favorite poet and whether you considered yourself a poet.

Try Guide students to quickly rehearse what they need to learn and do in preparation for practice

Distribute student's original Poetry Inventories. Have them read over their Poetry Inventories and then have them share with a partner the ways they've changed before responding in writing.

Clarify Briefly restate today's teaching objective and explain the practice tasks

Today in your independent practice, you are going to revise your Poetry Inventory to reflect your new growth. How has your opinion of poetry or of yourself as a poet changed?

Practice Students work independently or in small groups to apply today's teaching objective

Students will revise their original opinions.

Wrap Up Check understanding as you guide students to briefly share

Have students share with the class how their opinions have changed.

Language Companion Lesson: Poetry Punctuation · · · · · · ·

This lesson is best taught early in the lesson set (around the same time as Writing Lessons 4 and 5) so students can apply what they learn to their poetry writing.

▼ Teaching Objective

Poets choose punctuation carefully to enhance the meaning and mood of their poems.

▼ Standards Alignment

L.4.3b

▼ Materials

- Several poems that include ending punctuation for students to examine
- Whiteboard
- Charting materials

▼ To the Teacher

This lesson calls students' attention to the power of punctuation in poetry. Poets have lots of freedom when it comes to punctuation—more freedom than writers of prose. Poets make careful choices about which punctuation marks to include, where to include them, and where to leave them out altogether. They can even bend the rules and use punctuation in unusual and creative ways. All of these decisions can make a big difference in the meaning of the poem. In this lesson, we focus specifically on ending punctuation (periods, question marks, and exclamation points) as students explore and experiment with this fun aspect of poetry. The reading element of the lesson helps develop reading fluency as well.

▼ Procedure

Warm Up Gather the class to set the stage for today's learning

Provide students with sample poems in books or packets. Direct them to spend a few minutes exploring the poems with a partner. Ask them to focus on ending punctuation, especially periods, question marks, and exclamation points. Some guiding questions include the following:

- What do you notice?
- How often are these marks used?
- Does every poem include punctuation marks?
- Do all lines end with a punctuation mark?
- Where in the poem are they used most often?

Chart the students' findings.

Teach Model what students need to learn and do

Explain that today's lesson will focus on the choices poets make about punctuation marks.

> When it comes to punctuation, poetry has much looser rules than we normally have to follow when we write. When we write stories, reports, essays, and the like, we learn from kindergarten on that every sentence ends with a punctuation mark. Poets have a lot of freedom. Not every line needs a punctuation mark at the end. In fact, as we discovered in our exploration earlier, some poems have no punctuation at all. Poets understand, however, that punctuation marks can have a very powerful effect on the meaning of their poems.

Engage students in reading the following passage or a similar one.

ABCDEFG.

HIJK!

LMNOP?

QRSTU.

VWXYZ!

What did you do to your voice as you read these lines? Why?

Punctuation automatically sends the reader signals about the meaning of text. Let's pretend that this was a poem. Even though there are no real words, we already can use the punctuation as clues to the meaning of the passage. Let's look at another one:

ABCDEFG.

HIJK.

LMNOP.

QRSTU?

VWX?

YZ!

Where do you think the poet was most excited?

Where is the poet probably the calmest or most serious?

Where might the poet be full of wonder?

▼ Optional

Try Guide students to quickly rehearse what they need to learn and do in preparation for practice

You can see how punctuation alone can work to send the reader important information about the meaning of a poem. Now let's look at a section of a real poem to consider the effect of punctuation on the meaning.

Display the following (or a segment of another poem) on a whiteboard or other tool that allows easy erasure:

Cosmo

White ball of fluff
Round eyes like marbles
My best furry friend
Sits at the kitchen door
Looks out the window
Sends me off with a woof
When I go to school
I miss you all day long

Woof
    Woof
        Woof
Love my good buddy

See you later buddy

Read the poem.

What is the subject of the poem?

Who is talking?

What mood or emotions do you sense here?

Now experiment with adding ending punctuation in a variety of spots.

How does the punctuation affect the meaning of the poem?

How does the punctuation change the mood or emotions you sense in the poem?

How does the absence of punctuation affect parts of the poem?

Some possible variations:

Cosmo

White ball of fluff
Round eyes like marbles.
My best furry friend
Sits at the kitchen door.
Looks out the window.
Sends me off with a woof.
When I go to school
I miss you all day long.
Woof?
    Woof?
        Woof?
Love my good buddy.
See you later buddy?

Possible discussion points:

Periods seem to make the mood more serious.

The periods slow down the poem.

Feels sad, like the dog is disappointed. The question marks suggest that the dog wonders why the owner is leaving. The owner seems uncertain he will see the dog later at the end. Maybe the dog is sick?

Cosmo

White ball of fluff
Round eyes like marbles
My best furry friend
Sits at the kitchen door
Looks out the window
Sends me off with a woof!
When I go to school
I. miss. you. all. day. long!
Woof!
    Woof!
        Woof!
Love my good buddy!
See you later buddy!

Possible discussion points:

Feels happy. Flows quickly at the beginning.

Breaks rules by including periods after all of the words in a sentence (I miss you all day long.) This emphasizes how much the narrator misses the dog, suggests the day goes slowly for him.

At the end, exclamations make both narrator and dog seem excited. Dog and owner are calling to each other. Can picture them looking at each other as the narrator leaves.

▼ Optional

Clarify Briefly restate today's teaching objective and explain the practice tasks

We have seen what an impact punctuation can have on the meaning and mood of a poem! It is important for poets to make careful choices when adding punctuation.

▼ Optional

Practice Students work independently or in small groups to apply today's teaching objective

Direct students to experiment with various ending punctuation choices in the poems they are writing. Remind them to read the poem with the punctuation marks they want to try. They should ask themselves, which punctuation marks will help a reader understand the meaning of my poem?

Wrap Up Check understanding as you guide students to briefly share what they have learned and produced today

Have students share how they used ending punctuation in their poetry. Ask them to explain how the choices they made impact the meaning and mood of the poem.

GLOSSARY

alliteration: the repetition of the same sound at the beginning of words in a phrase or sentence.

assonance: similarity in sounds, especially vowel sounds in poetry; use of the same vowel sounds in the accented syllables but with different consonants, as in *deep* and *feet*.

author's purpose: the reason why an author writes something. For example, authors write to entertain, to inform, or to persuade.

hyperbole: in rhetoric, an obvious and deliberate exaggeration or overstatement, intended for effect and not to be taken literally. (Cf. litotes)

idiom: a phrase that cannot be understood through the meanings of each of its words.

imagery: images that are created in the mind while reading or looking at art.

metaphor: a phrase that describes something by comparing it to some other thing.

mood: the general emotion or feeling of a poem.

onomatopoeia: the formation or use of words whose sounds suggest the meanings of the words, such as *bang, moo,* or *jingle.*

personification: the act or technique of ascribing human attributes to nonhuman or inanimate things.

poem: a piece of writing different from ordinary writing in its special form, style, and language. Poems often express emotions and are considered to have beauty.

repetition: words or phrases that are repeated.

rhyme: a word that ends with the same sound as another word. *Hop* and *stop* are rhymes for *mop.*

simile: a figure of speech in which two different things are compared by using the word *like* or *as.*

theme: the main subject or topic.

white space: how a poem is arranged on the page, including line breaks, page layout and format, and spacing.

PD pd TOOLKIT™

Accompanying *Core Ready for Grades 3–5*, there is an online resource site with media tools that, together with the text, provides you with the tools you need to implement the lesson sets.

The PDToolkit for Pam Allyn's *Core Ready* Series is available free for 12 months after you use the password that comes with the box set for each grade band. After that, you can purchase access for an additional 12 months. If you did not purchase the box set, you can purchase a 12-month subscription at **http://pdtoolkit.pearson.com.** Be sure to explore and download the resources available at the website. Currently the following resources are available:

- Pearson Children's and Young Adult Literature Database
- Videos
- PowerPoint Presentations
- Student Artifacts

- Photos and Visual Media
- Handouts, Forms, and Posters to supplement your Core-aligned lesson plans
- Lessons and Homework Assignments
- Close Reading Guides and Samples
- Children's Core Literature Recommendations

In the future, we will continue to add additional resources. To learn more, please visit **http://pdtoolkit.pearson.com.**

Grade 5

Making the Case: Reading and Writing Editorials

- Introduction
- Standards Alignment
- Essential Skill Lenses (PARCC Framework)
- Core Questions
- Lesson Set Goals
- Choosing Core Texts
- Teacher's Notes
- Core Message to Students
- Building Academic Language
- Recognition
- Assessment
- Core Support for Diverse Learners
- Complementary Core Methods
- Core Connections at Home

Reading Lessons

Writing Lessons

Language Companion Lesson

Introduction

The Common Core State Standards call for students to be able to express their opinions clearly, present an organized and logical argument to support their claims, and write persuasively. As a result, we have the exciting opportunity to teach our students ways in which they can contribute their voices as concerned citizens of the world. This lesson set allows students to make direct connections between their work and learning at school and the issues and topics about which they are most interested and passionate. What a wonderful combination!

In support of the reading standards, this lesson pushes students to closely ana-

lyze a series of mentor editorials to gain a better command of the genre. In addition, students conduct a short research project, engaging with both print and digital sources, to gather information and evidence to support their point of view on a specific topic or issue.

Through writing their own editorials, students will gain a deeper understanding of the connection between audience and author's craft. Students will also practice stating a strong opinion and supporting that opinion by organizing their thoughts and research notes into logically ordered reasons.

Why This Lesson Set?

In this lesson set, students will:

- Read editorials closely to analyze the structure, features, content, and purpose of this genre

- Research self-chosen topics, take notes, and organize their ideas

- Compare and contrast multiple accounts of the same topic

- Examine and practice how to develop and present a strong argument to an audience

- Compose and publish organized editorials that express and support their opinions

Common Core State Standards Alignment

Reading Standards

RI.5.1 Quote accurately from a text when explaining what the text says explicitly and when drawing inferences from the text.

RI.5.2 Determine two or more main ideas of a text and explain how they are supported by key details; summarize the text.

RI.5.4 Determine the meaning of general academic and domain-specific words and phrases in a text relevant to a grade 5 topic or subject area.

RI.5.5 Compare and contrast the overall structure (e.g., chronology, comparison, cause/effect, problem/solution, description) of events, ideas, concepts, or information in two or more texts.

RI.5.6 Analyze multiple accounts of the same event or topic, noting important similarities and differences in the point of view they represent.

RI.5.7 Draw on information from multiple print or digital sources, demonstrating the ability to locate an answer to a question quickly or to solve a problem efficiently.

RI.5.8 Explain how an author uses reasons and evidence to support particular points in a text, identifying which reasons and evidence support which points.

RI.5.9 Integrate information from several texts on the same topic in order to write or speak about the subject knowledgeably.

RI.5.10 By the end of the year, independently and proficiently read and comprehend informational texts, including history/social studies, science, and technical texts at the high end of the grades 4–5 text complexity band.

Writing Standards

W.5.1 Write opinion pieces on topics or texts, supporting a point of view with reasons and information.

a. Introduce a topic or text clearly, state an opinion, and create an organizational structure in which ideas are logically grouped to support the writer's purpose.

b. Provide logically ordered reasons that are supported by facts and details.

c. Link opinion and reasons using words, phrases, and clauses (e.g., *consequently, specifically*).

d. Provide a concluding statement or section related to the opinion presented.

W.5.4 Produce clear and coherent writing in which the development and organization are appropriate to task, purpose, and audience. (Grade-specific expectations for writing types are defined previously in standards 1–3.)

W.5.5 With guidance and support from peers and adults, develop and strengthen writing as needed by planning, revising, editing, rewriting, or trying a new approach.

W.5.6 With some guidance and support from adults, use technology, including the Internet, to produce and publish writing as well as to interact and collaborate with others; demonstrate sufficient command of keyboarding skills to type a minimum of two pages in a single sitting.

W.5.7 Conduct a short research project that uses several sources to build knowledge through investigation of different aspects of a topic.

W.5.8 Recall relevant information from experiences or gather relevant information from print and digital sources; summarize or paraphrase information in notes and finished work and provide a list of sources.

W.5.9 Draw evidence from literary or informational texts to support analysis, reflection, and research. Apply grade 5 reading standards to literature (e.g., "Compare and contrast two or more characters, settings, or events in a story or a drama, drawing on specific details in the text [e.g., how characters interact]").

W.5.10 Write routinely over extended time frames (time for research, reflection, and revision) and shorter time frames (a single sitting or a day or two) for a range of discipline-specific tasks, purposes, and audiences.

Speaking and Listening Standards

SL.5.1 Engage effectively in a range of collaborative discussions (one-on-one, in groups, and teacher-led) with diverse partners on grade 5 topics and texts, building on others' ideas and expressing their own clearly.

a. Come to discussions prepared, having read or studied required material; explicitly draw on that preparation and other information known about the topic to explore ideas under discussion.

b. Follow agreed-on rules for discussions and carry out assigned roles.

c. Pose and respond to specific questions by making comments that contribute to the discussion and elaborate on the remarks of others.

d. Review the key ideas expressed and draw conclusions in light of information and knowledge gained from the discussions.

SL.5.2 Summarize a written text read aloud or information presented in diverse media and formats, including visually, quantitatively, and orally.

SL.5.4 Report on a topic or text or present an opinion, sequencing ideas logically and using appropriate facts and relevant, descriptive details to support main ideas or themes; speak clearly at an understandable pace.

SL.5.5 Include multimedia components (e.g., graphics, sound) and visual displays in presentations when appropriate to enhance the development of main ideas or themes.

SL.5.6 Adapt speech to a variety of contexts and tasks, using formal English when appropriate to task and situation.

Language Standards

L.5.1 Demonstrate command of the conventions of standard English grammar and usage when writing or speaking.

a. Explain the function of conjunctions, prepositions, and interjections

in general and their function in particular sentences.

b. Form and use the perfect (e.g., *I had walked; I have walked; I will have walked*) verb tenses.

c. Use verb tense to convey various times, sequences, states, and conditions.

d. Recognize and correct inappropriate shifts in verb tense.

e. Use correlative conjunctions (e.g., *either/or, neither/nor*).

L.5.2 Demonstrate command of the conventions of standard English capitalization, punctuation, and spelling when writing.

a. Use punctuation to separate items in a series.

b. Use a comma to separate an introductory element from the rest of the sentence.

c. Use a comma to set off the words *yes* and *no* (e.g., Yes, thank you), to set off a tag question from the rest of the sentence (e.g., It's true, isn't it?), and to indicate direct address (e.g., Is that you, Steve?).

d. Use underlining, quotation marks, or italics to indicate titles of works.

e. Spell grade-appropriate words correctly, consulting references as needed.

L.5.3 Use knowledge of language and its conventions when writing, speaking, reading, or listening.

a. Expand, combine, and reduce sentences for meaning, reader/listener interest, and style.

b. Compare and contrast the varieties of English (e.g., dialects, registers) used in stories, dramas, or poems.

L.5.6 Acquire and accurately use grade-appropriate general academic and domain-specific words and phrases, including those that signal contrast, addition, and other logical relationships (e.g., *however, although, nevertheless, similarly, moreover, in addition*).

Essential Skill Lenses (PARCC Framework)

As part of its proposal to the U.S. Department of Education, the multi-state Partnership for Assessment of Readiness for College and Careers (PARCC, 2011) developed model content frameworks for grades 3 to 11 in English Language Arts to serve as a bridge between the Common Core State Standards and the PARCC assessments in development at the time of this publication. In the grades 3 to 5 lesson sets, we expect students to engage in reading and writing through eight PARCC specified skill lenses that are rooted in the standards. The following table details how each skill lens is addressed across the lesson set.

	Reading	Writing
Cite Evidence	Students will be asked to cite the text as evidence throughout this lesson set. In particular, students analyze mentor editorials to find specific examples of how the author uses facts and details to support his or her point of view.	Students cite text as evidence to support their own opinions in their original editorials.
Analyze Content	There are many opportunities for students to analyze editorials to gain insight into the author's craft as well as how the author uses facts and details to support his or her opinion.	Students must analyze the print and digital resources they identify as relevant in order to collect evidence to use to support their statement of opinion. In addition, students frequently work in partnerships to analyze the writing of their classmates, and provide feedback.

	Reading	Writing
Study and Apply Grammar and Usage	Students must demonstrate the ability to convey their ideas clearly, using language that is appropriate to the situation and audience.	Students will analyze their own writing to improve its clarity, using an Editorials Checklist Appendix 5.9, as a guide.
Study and Apply Vocabulary	Students must become familiar with and use the vocabulary related to the genre of editorial. In addition, students must research key vocabulary related to their topic or issue.	Students must incorporate key vocabulary related to their topic or issue in an effort to gain credibility and strengthen their arguments.
Conduct Discussions	Students will engage in discussions of editorials daily. Rules and behaviors that foster productive conversation are a crucial element of this study.	There are many opportunities throughout this lesson set for students to share and discuss their work with partners as well as the entire class. Specifically, students draw conclusions from critical discussions of their work to make appropriate revisions that serve to strengthen their editorials.
Report Findings	Students are required to create an original editorial on a topic or issue of great concern and relevance to them.	Students are expected to publish and share their original editorials with their intended audience. In addition, students share and respond to the work of their classmates.
Phonics and Word Recognition	We recommend that teachers plan opportunities for students to build Reading Foundational Skills by exploring grade-level appropriate skills in the context of the core texts from each unit and applying this knowledge to their independent reading.	We recommend that teachers encourage students to apply Reading Foundational Skills in the context of their daily writing.
Fluency and Stamina	Through shared and partner readings of editorials, students will improve their fluency and stamina within a specific genre.	Throughout this lesson set, students will be asked to write across short and long time frames, crafting their own editorials section by section. This combination will support students as they develop their skills to write fluently and with purpose in a variety of situations.

Core Questions

The ability to write persuasively and to clearly communicate your opinions is an essential skill for fifth graders as they grow into becoming concerned, empowered citizens of the school, local, and global communities. These questions should remain at the core of your teaching. Refer back to them often, encouraging your class to share their thinking as it evolves.

- How can we use our writing to change the world?
- How can we use mentor texts to guide and inform our own work?
- How do you build a strong written argument?
- How and where can we look for reliable information to form and support our ideas?

Ready to Get Started?

Fifth graders are developing into opinionated, knowledgeable citizens of their school, local, and global communities. This lesson set is not only inspired by the call of the Common Core State Standards to highlight and hone students' abilities to write persuasively, but it is also inspired by our desire to help shape thoughtful, intelligent individuals who put their voices and ideas out into the world in responsible and effective ways.

Lesson Set Goals

Within this lesson set, there are many goals we want to help our students reach.

Reading Goals

- Identify the structures and features common to editorials and determine the purpose of an editorial considering multiple pieces of evidence from the text. (RI.5.1, RI.5.2, RI.5.5, RI.5.8, RI.5.10, W.5.1a, W.5.4, W.5.10, SL.5.1a–d, SL.5.2, L.5.1, L.5.6)

- Select a variety of print and digital resources about a topic of interest and take effective notes on reading. (RI.5.1, RI.5.7, RI.5.10, W.5.7, W.5.8, W.5.10, SL.5.2)

- Compare and contrast multiple editorials on the same topic. (RI.5.6, RI.5.7, RI.5.9, RI.5.10, W.5.7, W.5.8, W.5.10)

- Use mentor texts to analyze how writers craft introductions and conclusions and build up their arguments. (RI.5.1, RI.5.4, RI.5.8, RI.5.10, W.5.1a–d, W.5.10, SL.5.1a–d, L.5.1, L.5.6)

- Quote accurately from a text when explaining what the text explicitly says and when drawing inferences from the text. (RI.5.1)

- Write an organized opinion piece that includes a clear introduction, point of view, supporting reasons, linking words and phrases, and a concluding statement. (W.5.1)

- By the end of the year, independently and proficiently read and comprehend a variety of literature at the high end of the grades 4–5 text complexity band. (RI.5.10)

- Write routinely over extended time frames (time for research, reflection, and revision) and shorter time frames (a single sitting or a day or two) for a range of discipline-specific tasks, purposes, and audiences. (W.5.10)

- In collaborative discussions, demonstrate evidence of preparation for discussion and exhibit responsibility to the rules and roles of conversation. (SL.5.1a, SL.5.1b)

- In collaborative discussions, share and develop ideas in a manner that enhances understanding of topic. Contribute and respond to the content of the conversation in a productive and focused manner. (SL.5.1c, SL.5.1d)

- Demonstrate knowledge of standard English and its conventions. (L.5.1, L.5.2, L.5.3)

- Acquire and accurately use grade-appropriate conversational, general academic, and domain-specific vocabulary and phrases. (L.5.6)

Writing Goals

- Connect with an issue or topic that inspires the student to make his or her voice heard. (RI.5.8, RI.5.10, SL.5.1a–d)

- State individual opinions clearly. (W.5.1a, W.5.4, W.5.9, W.5.10)

- Seek out information from print and digital sources to use as evidence to support an opinion on a particular topic or issue. (RI.5.1, RI.5.7, RI.5.10, W.5.4, W.5.7, W.5.8, W.5.9, W.5.1.0)

- Reflect on the impact of audience on his or her writing. (W.5.4, W.5.10, SL.5.4, SL.5.6, L.5.1, L.5.6)

- Craft a logically organized argument composed of relevant facts and details in support of an opinion. (W.5.1a–d, W.5.4, W.5.9, W.5.10, SL.5.5)

- Determine how and where to publish his or her work to reach the intended audience. (W.5.6)

- With guidance and support from peers and adults, develop and strengthen writing as needed by planning, revising, editing, rewriting, or trying a new approach. (W.5.5)

- Quote accurately from a text when explaining what the text explicitly says and when drawing inferences from the text. (RI.5.1)

- Write an organized opinion piece that includes a clear introduction, point of view, supporting reasons, linking words and phrases, and a concluding statement. (W.5.1)

- By the end of the year, independently and proficiently read and comprehend a variety of literature at the high end of the grades 4–5 text complexity band. (RI.5.10)

- Write routinely over extended time frames (time for research, reflection, and revision) and shorter time frames (a single sitting or a day or two) for a range of discipline-specific tasks, purposes, and audiences. (W.5.10)

- In collaborative discussions, demonstrate evidence of preparation for discussion and exhibit responsibility to the rules and roles of conversation. (SL.5.1a, SL.5.1b)

- In collaborative discussions, share and develop ideas in a manner that enhances understanding of topic. Contribute and respond to the content of the conversation in a productive and focused manner. (SL.5.1c, SL.5.1d)

- Demonstrate knowledge of standard English and its conventions. (L.5.1, L.5.2, L.5.3)

- Acquire and accurately use grade-appropriate conversational, general academic, and domain-specific vocabulary and phrases. (L.5.6)

Choosing Core Texts

To prepare for this lesson set, you will need to gather a variety of editorials and opinion pieces that represent a range of reading levels and topics. One of the best sources for editorials is the newspaper. The reading level is usually perfectly appropriate for grade 5 readers, and typically there are several in most papers every day on topics that may be of local interest to your students. In addition, using editorials published in your local, regional, or city paper is a great way to foster cross-disciplinary discussions of current events.

Take this unit as an opportunity to get to know your students even better than you already do by asking specific questions about their interests, concerns, and thoughts about the world around them. What do they see as problems for people their age? What do they see as the critical problems of our world in this moment? Are there aspects of their school or neighborhood community that they would like to change? Enabling students to rely and facts and good argument skills to express their thoughts and concerns orally and in writing is powerful and, for that reason, we think you will find this to be an engaging and fulfilling lesson set.

Keeping in mind the broad range of interests held by students of differing genders, experiences, and cultures, we suggest the following resources for finding editorials to support the work in this lesson set:

- Your local, regional, or city newspaper
- *Science News for Kids* (an online resource at www.sciencenewsforkids.org), a companion publication to *Science News* aimed at a younger audience
- *Time for Kids* (both in print and online at www.timeforkids.com)
- *Scholastic News* (both in print and online)

A Note about Addressing Reading Standard 10: Range of Reading and Level of Text Complexity

This lesson set provides all students with opportunities to work with texts deemed appropriate for their grade levels, as well as texts at their specific reading levels. Through shared experiences and focused instruction, all students engage with and comprehend a wide range of texts within their grade-level complexity bands. We suggest a variety of high-quality, complex texts to use within the whole-class lessons, and we recommend a variety of additional titles in the section Choosing Core Texts to extend and enrich instruction. However, research strongly suggests that during independent practice and in small-group collaborations, all students need to work with texts they can read with a high level of accuracy and comprehension (i.e., at their developmentally appropriate reading levels) to significantly improve their reading (Allington, 2012; Ehri, Dreyer, Flugman, & Gross, 2007). Depending on individual needs and skills, a student's reading level may be above, within, or below in his or her grade-level band.

Teacher's Notes

An *editorial* is defined as a newspaper article that provides an opinion on a topical issue. At this point in the school year, we may know our students well, but can we articulate what is truly topical for our kids? Realistically, how often do we have the time or opportunity to speak at length with our students about the issues that concern them the most? This lesson set will be an eye-opening experience into the hearts, minds, and voices of your students.

Core Message to Students

It is your turn to speak out and make your voices heard, rationally, logically, and persuasively. How often have you heard or read a story on the news and thought to yourself, "I have something to say about that"? Or how many times have you listened to adults discuss an issue that concerns *you*, but they never ask your opinion? Well today is your day. Not only are we going to spend the next few weeks identifying the topics that concern you the most, we are also going to learn how you can effectively and powerfully put your opinions out into the world and be heard.

See Appendix 5.1 for an enlarged version to reproduce and share with students.

Questions for Close Reading

The Core Ready lessons include many rich opportunities to engage students in close reading of text that require them to ask and answer questions, draw conclusions, and use specific text evidence to support their thinking (Reading Anchor Standard 1). These opportunities are marked with a close reading icon. You may wish to extend these experiences using our recommended Core Texts or with texts of your choosing. Use the following questions as a resource to guide students through close reading experiences in any editorials.

- What is the author's argument?
- What reasons did the author supply to support the argument?
- What techniques/words did the author use to persuade you?
- Are there any other points or techniques that might have helped the author's case?

- What arguments would you pose to counter the author's opinion?
- Did the author successfully influence your opinion? Why or why not?
- Do you know anything about the author's background that influenced his or her point of view?
- Did the author include visual images? How did they impact the argument?
- How do you think the author prepared to write this?
- How does this argument relate to your life?

Building Academic Language

Following is a list of academic language to build your students' comprehension of the focus of this lesson set and facilitate their ability to talk and write about what they learn. There are words and phrases listed. Rather than introduce all the words at once, slowly add them to a learning wall as your teaching unfolds. See the glossary at the end of this chapter for definitions the words. Also listed are sentence frames that may be included on a sentence wall (Carrier & Tatum, 2006), a research-proven strategy for English language learners (Lewis, 1993; Nattinger, 1980), or as a handout to scaffold student use of the content words. Some students, especially English language learners, may need explicit practice in using the sentence frames. Encourage all students to regularly use these words and phrases in their conversations and writing.

Recognition

At the end of the lesson set, it is important to recognize the hard work your students have put into their learning and the way they've thought about themselves and others. At the end of this lesson set, students will have written editorials that put forth their reasoned and researched opinions on topics or

Core Words

acknowledge	opinion
argument	opposition
conclude	ordering
editor	periodical
editorial	position
evidence	stance

support

Core Phrases

Expressing Your Opinion

- In my opinion . . . based on the fact that. . . .

- I feel/think that . . . because. . . .

- Personally, I maintain that . . . due to. . . .

- It is my belief that . . . since. . . .

Adding More

- Also. . . .

- What's more. . . .

- In addition. . . .

- Furthermore. . . .

- In addition. . . .

- Most of all. . . .

- Not only will . . . , but . . . will also. . . .

Ordering

- First of all. . . .

- Second . . . , third . . . , etc.

- Then. . . .

- Next. . . .

- After that. . . .

- Finally. . . .

Acknowledging the Opposition

- Some say that . . . , yet. . . .

- It is true that . . . , but. . . .

- While it is true . . . , don't forget that. . . .

Showing

- For example. . . .

- For instance. . . .

- In this case. . . .

- It is obvious that. . . .

- Clearly. . . .

Concluding

- To sum up. . . .

- In conclusion. . . .

- In summary. . . .

- All things considered. . . .

- I have argued that. . . .

- It is clear that. . . .

issues that matter to them. Consider creating your own version of an open mic night for students to share their opinions by reading their work aloud to their classmates. Discuss with students how opinions often gain strength through the power of the spoken performance. Consider inviting families or another class in for a celebration of free speech to honor the hard work your students have done throughout the lesson set. Other engaging celebrations of learning include:

- Post your students' editorials in a prominent location in the school for others to stop and consider.
- Create an opinion-based newspaper with your students' editorials, inviting other students to respond thoughtfully.
- Create a current events corner in the classroom where students can read, reflect, and comment on issues addressed in local news publications.

Assessment

Assessment in this lesson set is both ongoing and culminating, meaning that we are constantly observing how students are making meaning and how they are interpreting new material. Throughout this lesson set, look for performance-based assessments, called Milestone Performance Assessments, each marked with an assessment icon. Milestone Performance Assessments are opportunities to notice and record data on Core standards-aligned indicators during the course of the lesson set. Use the results of these assessments to determine how well students are progressing toward the goals of the lesson set. Adjust the pace of your teaching and plan instructional support as needed.

We also encourage you to use the Reading and Writing Rubrics (also marked with assessment icons) with each lesson set to evaluate overall student performance on the Core standards-aligned lesson set goals. In this lesson set, the original editorials students write will be essential pieces of evidence when you assess student performance. The editorials can be analyzed and placed in a portfolio of student work.

In addition, we have provided a Speaking and Listening Checklist (Appendix 5.11) that provides observable Core Standards–aligned indicators to assess student performance as speakers and listeners. There are multiple opportunities in every Core Ready lesson set to make such observations. Use the checklist in its entirety to gather performance data over time or choose appropriate indicators to create a customized checklist to match a specific learning experience.

Core Support for Diverse Learners

This lesson set was created with the needs of a wide variety of learners in mind. Throughout the day to day lessons, you'll find examples of visual supports, graphic organizers, highlighted speaking and listening opportunities, and research-driven English language learner supports aimed at scaffolding instruction for all learners. However, we urge you to consider the following more specific challenges with which your students may need guided support. The next sections are written to spotlight important considerations as you move through the lesson sets.

Reading

Choosing texts that are at students' reading levels is essential for their reading success and reading identity. When finding texts make sure you have various levels represented in your classroom reading collection. Your students or some of your students may benefit from repeated exposure to a lesson's teaching objective over several days. This can be accomplished with the whole class or in small-group settings.

Closely monitor your students who are reading below grade level to determine if they are reading with accuracy and fluency to support comprehension. Encourage students to use context to confirm or self-correct word recognition and understanding and to reread when necessary. Refer to the Common Core Foundational Skills Standards both at the grade 5 level as well as the lower grade level standards for direct, explicit foundational skills support that your students reading below grade level may need.

Students conducting research for an editorial are likely to encounter a variety of multi-syllabic words that will require teacher support to decode and understand. In addition, your student researchers will often come across content-specific terms that may be unfamiliar. Refer to our Core Words guide for vocabulary that you may want to frontload with small groups of students. Be cognizant of unfamiliar language embedded within the topics you and your students choose for both whole-class teaching as well as independent reading and preview the texts you provide to students reading below grade level.

As you continue your work with students, use observational notes and reading assessment data to create two to three specific short-term goals for your students with diverse needs. For example, as stated above, these goals may be related to increasing word accuracy, building vocabulary, improving fluency, or enhancing comprehension. Throughout this lesson set, tailor your individualized and small-group instruction set so that it addresses and evaluates student progress toward these goals.

Writing

Inspired writers are motivated writers. Allowing students to choose the topic of their writing is critical for their ultimate success and their positive development of identity as a writer. When immersing your students in a new genre, form, or purpose for writing, be sure to emphasize the meaning and function this particular type of writing may have in their own lives. Many of your students will also benefit from exposure to strong mentor texts, examples of your own writing, and the experience of sharing their own work—both the final product and in process.

Many of your students, especially ELLs, may significantly benefit from the opportunity to sketch their opinion and supporting reasons before adding text. For example, some students will require extra support in writing to move from drawing to writing or to move from story mapping to sentences. This is especially helpful for visual learners and students who need to "sketch to stretch." Even your most proficient writers can benefit from this step, but many of your resistant writers will feel more comfortable with getting their ideas on paper through drawing first. Giving students some sentence starters can vastly help them focus on their ideas and have the stamina to get their thoughts on paper (refer to our Core Words and Core Phrases) such as:

In my opinion,

It is my belief that . . .

For example,

For instance,

To sum up,

In conclusion,

In summary,

All things considered,

I have argued that . . .

It is clear that . . .

As your students move from determining their ideas for their editorials and begin telling a sequential tale, provide your students with a variety of paper choices that are fifth grade appropriate. For students with fine motor control issues, providing students with a variety of paper choices that have handwriting lines with a dotted line in the middle can offer support as letter formation may require significant energy for some writers. Also consider having some students type and electronically publish their editorials rather than handwrite them if that is a medium more conducive to their writing success.

We want our fifth graders to share their editorials with an audience and supporting them as developing writers is essential. In addition to providing students with topic choice and the opportunity to draw prior to writing, we can provide further scaffolding by having students orally rehearse their editorials with us or with a peer. For some students, the oral rehearsal will provide a springboard to writing. For others, they will have greater success dictating their editorial to you.

As with the reading lessons, your students may benefit from several days on a single lesson's teaching objective. This can be done with the whole class or in small-group settings.

English Language Learners

While it is always our goal as teachers to get to know all of our students deeply both in and out of the classroom setting, this work is perhaps more critical when considering our English language learners. Honoring families' cultural traditions and experiences is important to getting to know, understand and work with your students in meaningful ways.

English language learners are learning about editorials alongside native English speakers in your classroom, but they are also simultaneously learning English. For our English language learners, it is essential to simultaneously develop their ability to easily hold conversations about their reading and writing and build their academic language base. Goldenberg (2008) defines "academic English" as the more abstract, complex, and challenging language that permits us to participate successfully in mainstream classroom instruction. English language learners will over time be responsible for understanding and producing academic English both orally and in writing. However, language acquisition is a process and our English language learners range in their development of English language acquisition. We urge you to consider your students along a spectrum of language acquisition from students new to this country to those who are proficient conversationally to those who have native-like proficiency.

Refer to the English language learner icons throughout this lesson set for ways to shelter instruction for English language learners. These elements will help English language learners participate successfully in the whole-group lesson and support the development of their language skills. While these moments during instruction are designed to support English language learners, recent research has shown that a separate ELD (English language development) block targeted at oral English language development will further support your students in their language acquisition.

Students with growing English proficiency will benefit from a Editorial Word Wall to build vocabulary (refer to our Core Words and Phrases). A sentence word wall to give them sentence starters to help with conversation will also offer students another layer of support. Some students may benefit from having their own personalized copies of these words to keep in their reading or writing notebooks for quick reference. Visual aids will further support students and give them a reference to what words are important to this study and what they mean.

Some students will benefit from several days on the same teaching objective. You may consider gathering small groups of readers or writers for repeated instruction or using one-on-one conferences as an opportunity to revisit teaching objectives.

Complementary Core Methods

Read-Aloud

Take this opportunity to share a wide variety of editorials from various sources during read-aloud. Make sure to include editorials that vary in length and topic. Use your knowledge of students' interests to select editorials that will inspire and excite your class. When appropriate, use your read-aloud as another chance for students to practice one or two of the following skills:

- Asking and answering questions about a text, using portions of the text as evidence in their responses
- Identifying and exploring the meanings of new vocabulary words

- Identifying editorial structures
- Discussing a respectful and thoughtful response to the editorial

Shared Reading

Shared reading provides a wonderful opportunity to implement repeated reading of strong editorials and other forms of persuasive writing aloud together. Focus on choosing a variety of types of persuasive writing for this experience. Consider sharing informational articles, reports, persuasive letters, and brochures with your class. Following are some prompts you may want to use in your conversations about these texts:

- What do we notice about this piece of persuasive writing?
- What reasons and evidence does the author give to support his or her opinion?
- Summarize the author's argument.

Shared Writing

Shared writing provides an opportunity to write editorials and other forms of persuasive writing together. Use this time to:

- Determine topics or issues that inspire or are of great concern to the class.
- Try various types of introductions and conclusions.
- Craft an argument to support a shared opinion.
- Draft a shared editorial or persuasive letter.
- Address an issue or topic of concern within the school community.

Core Connections at Home

Invite families to read the newspaper or watch the news as a family, asking students to report back on their findings. What issues or topics are of great concern to their families? Ask families to draft a shared editorial, relying on their student to guide the structure of their writing. Display these editorials along with the work students complete in class.

Reading Lessons

The following table highlights the teaching objectives and standards alignment for all 10 lessons across the four stages of the lesson set (Introduce, Define, Extend, and Assess). It also indicates which lessons contain special features to support ELLs, technology, speaking and listening, and formative ("Milestone") assessments.

The Core Ready Reading Rubric is designed to help you record each student's overall understanding across four levels of achievement as it relates to the lesson set goals. We recommend that you use this rubric at the end of the lesson set as a performance-based assessment tool. Use the Milestone Performance Assessments as tools to help you gauge student progress toward these goals, and reteach and differentiate as needed. See the foundational book, *Be Core Ready: Powerful, Effective Steps to Implementing and Achieving the Common Core State Standards,* for more information about the Core Ready Reading and Writing Rubrics.

The Core I.D.E.A. / Daily Reading Instruction At-a-Glance

Instructional State	Lesson	Teaching Objective	Core Standards	Special Features
Introduce: notice, explore, collect, note, immerse, surround, record, share	1	Readers notice the structure and features of editorials.	RI.5.1 • RI.5.5 • RI.5.8 • RI.5.10 SL.5.1a–d • L.5.1 • L.5.6	Close Reading ELL S&L
	2	Readers can identify the purpose of an editorial, as well as any supporting evidence.	RI.5.1 • RI.5.2 • RI.5.8 • RI.5.10 SL.5.1a–d • L.5.1 • L.5.6	Close Reading ELL
Define: name, identify, outline, clarify, select, plan	3	Readers choose a topic which they are interested in and gather related research materials.	RI.5.7 • W.5.7 • SL.5.1a SL.5.1b • L.5.6	ELL
	4	Readers research and take notes on a topic about which they are interested.	RI.5.1 • RI.5.7 • RI.5.10 • W.5.4 W.5.7 • W.5.8 • W.5.10 • SL.5.1a SL.5.1b • L.5.6	Close Reading ELL Milestone Assessment
Extend: try, experiment, attempt, approximate, practice, explain, revise, refine	5	Readers round out their research by turning to and effectively navigating online resources.	RI.5.7 • RI.5.10 • W.5.7 • W.5.8 W.5.10 • SL.5.1a • SL.5.1b SL.5.2 • L.5.6	ELL
	6	Readers compare and contrast multiple accounts of the same topic or event.	RI.5.6 • RI.5.7 • RI.5.9 • RI.5.10 W.5.7 • W.5.8 • W.5.10 • SL.5.1a SL.5.1b • L.5.1 • L.5.6	ELL
	7	Readers revisit mentor texts to analyze the craft of introducing an issue.	RI.5.1 • RI.5.8 • RI.5.10 • W.5.1a W.5.4 • W.5.10 • SL.5.1a • SL.5.1b L.5.1 • L.5.6	Close Reading ELL
	8	Readers revisit mentor texts to analyze how writers build an argument.	RI.5.1 • RI.5.8 • RI.5.10 • W.5.1a–c W.5.4 • W.5.10 • SL.5.1a–d L.5.1 • L.5.6	Close Reading ELL
	9	Readers revisit mentor texts to analyze how writers craft strong conclusions.	RI.5.1 • RI.5.4 • RI.5.10 • W.5.1d SL.5.1a–d • L.5.1 • L.5.6	Close Reading ELL
Assess: reflect, conclude, connect, share, recognize, respond	10	Readers reflect on the core questions.	RI.5.10 • W.5.4 • W.5.10 • SL.5.1a–d L.5.1 • L.5.6	ELL Milestone Assessment Tech

Grade 5 Making the Case: Reading and Writing Editorials

Lesson Set Goal	Emerging	Approaching	Achieving	Exceeding	Standards Alignment
Identify the structures and features common to editorials and determine the purpose of an editorial considering multiple pieces of evidence from the text.	Student does not identify the structures and features common to editorials and/or does not determine the purpose of an editorial. Student makes little or no attempt to use any textual evidence.	Student identifies some of the structures and features common to editorials and determines the purpose of an editorial with some success. Student attempts to consider some pieces of evidence from the text.	Student generally identifies the structures and features common to editorials and determines the purpose of an editorial. Student considers multiple pieces of evidence from the text.	Student consistently identifies all of the structures and features common to editorials and determines the purpose of an editorial. Student flawlessly considers multiple pieces of evidence from the text.	RI.5.1 RI.5.2 RI.5.5 RI.5.8 RI.5.10 W.5.1a W.5.4 W.5.10 SL.5.1a–d SL.5.2 L.5.1 L.5.6
Select a variety of print and digital resources about a topic of interest and take effective notes on the reading.	Student selects few resources. Neglects a balance between print and digital. Student's resources are not relevant. Student may attempt to take notes, but they are ineffective.	Student attempts to select a variety of print and digital resources. Resources are not all relevant. Student takes some notes, but they are unclear or disorganized at times.	Student generally is able to successfully select a variety of relevant print and digital resources about a topic of interest. Takes effective notes.	Student consistently selects a wide variety of relevant digital and print resources about a topic of interest. Student takes exemplary notes on the topic.	RI.5.1 RI.5.7 RI.5.10 W.5.7 W.5.8 W.5.10 SL.5.2
Compare and contrast multiple editorials on the same topic.	Student shows little or no evidence of success comparing and contrasting any editorials.	Student attempts to compare and contrast editorials on the same topic. Findings are inaccurate, unclear, or incomplete at times.	Student generally is able to successfully compare and contrast editorials on the same topic. Findings are generally accurate, clear, and complete.	Student successfully compares and contrasts editorials on the same topic. Findings are consistently accurate, clear, and complete. Shows great insight or infer subtle ideas in the text.	RI.5.6 RI.5.7 RI.5.9 RI.5.10 W.5.7 W.5.8 W.5.10
Use mentor texts to analyze how writers craft introductions and conclusions and build up their arguments.	Student demonstrates little or no success using a mentor text to support his or her writing. No clear connections between mentor and own writing.	Student attempts to use mentor texts to support some aspects of writing including introductions, conclusions, and/or the buildup of arguments. Connections present, but may be underdeveloped.	Student accurately uses mentor texts to analyze how writers craft introductions and conclusions and build up their arguments. Clear connection between mentor and own writing.	Student skillfully uses mentor texts to analyze how writers craft introductions and conclusions and build up their arguments in a way that powerfully influences own writing.	RI.5.1 RI.5.4 RI.5.8 RI.5.10 W.5.1a–d W.5.10 SL.5.1a–d L.5.1 L.5.6

Lesson Set Goal	Emerging	Approaching	Achieving	Exceeding	Standards Alignment
Accurately quote from a text when explaining what the text explicitly says and when drawing inferences from the text.	Student shows little or no evidence of active, purposeful reading or searching the text for specific quotes, information, and evidence. Student makes little or no attempt to provide accurate details and examples when explaining what the text says explicitly and is unable to draw inferences from the text.	Student shows some evidence of active, purposeful reading and searching the text for specific quotes, information, and evidence. Student provides some details and examples, with limited accuracy, when explaining what the text says explicitly and when drawing inferences from the text.	Student shows evidence of active, purposeful reading and searching the text for specific quotes, information, and evidence. Student usually provides appropriate and accurate details and examples when explaining what the text says explicitly and when drawing inferences from the text.	Student consistently demonstrates exceptional evidence of active, purposeful reading and searching the text for specific information and evidence. Student always provides accurate and thoughtful details and examples when explaining what the text says explicitly and when drawing inferences from the text.	RL.5.1
Write an organized opinion piece that includes a clear introduction, point of view, supporting reasons, linking words and phrases, and a concluding statement.	Student writes an opinion piece with little or no evidence of introduction and concluding statements. Does not articulate a clear point of view and supporting reasons are missing or insufficient. Omits linking words and phrases or uses them inconsistently.	Student writes an opinion piece and attempts to include introductory and concluding statements. Attempts to identify a point of view but supporting reasons may be weak or irrelevant. Includes some linking words and phrases.	Student writes an opinion piece with solid introductory and concluding statements. Articulates a point of view and supports it with relevant supporting reasons. Uses linking words and phrases when appropriate.	Student writes a highly effective opinion piece with a powerful and engaging introduction and concluding statement. Point of view is articulated and supported with several clear and relevant reasons. Consistently uses linking words and phrases when appropriate.	W.5.1
By the end of the year, independently and proficiently read and comprehend a variety of informational texts at the high end of the grades 4–5 text complexity band.	Student shows little or no evidence of reading and comprehending texts appropriate for the grade 5 text complexity band.	Student shows inconsistent evidence of independently and proficiently reading and comprehending texts appropriate for the grade 5 text complexity band.	Student shows solid evidence of independently and proficiently reading and comprehending texts appropriate for the grade 5 text complexity band.	Student shows solid evidence of independently and proficiently reading and comprehending texts above the grade 5 text complexity band.	RI.5.10
Writes routinely over extended time frames (time for research, reflection, and revision) and shorter time frames (a single sitting or a day or two) for a range of discipline-specific tasks, purposes, and audiences.	Student shows little or no evidence of writing routinely for short or long time frames for a range of discipline-specific tasks, purposes, and audiences.	Student shows some evidence of writing routinely for short and long time frames for a range of discipline-specific tasks, purposes, and audiences.	Student shows solid evidence of writing routinely for short and long time frames for a range of discipline-specific tasks, purposes, and audiences.	Student shows exceptional evidence of consistently and accurately writing for short and long time frames for a range of discipline-specific tasks, purposes, and audiences.	W.5.10
In collaborative discussions, demonstrate evidence of preparation for discussion and exhibit responsibility to the rules and roles of conversation.	In collaborative discussions, student comes unprepared and often disregards the rules and roles of conversation.	In collaborative discussions, student's preparation is evident but ineffective or inconsistent. Occasionally disregards the rules and roles of conversation.	In collaborative discussions, student prepares adequately and draws on the preparation and other information about the topic to explore ideas under discussion. Usually observes the rules and roles of conversation.	In collaborative discussions, student arrives extremely well prepared for discussions and draws on the preparation and other information about the topic to explore ideas under discussion. Always observes the rules and roles of conversation.	SL.5.1a SL.5.1b

Lesson Set Goal	Emerging	Approaching	Achieving	Exceeding	Standards Alignment
In collaborative discussions, share and develop ideas in a manner that enhances understanding of topic. Contribute and respond to the content of the conversation in a productive and focused manner.	Student shows little or no evidence of engaging in collaborative discussions and makes little or no attempt to ask and answer questions, stay on topic, link his or her comments to the remarks of others, or to explain his or her own ideas and understanding in light of the discussion.	Student shows some evidence of engaging in collaborative discussions and with marginal success attempts to ask questions to check understanding of information presented, to stay on topic, link his or her comments to the remarks of others, and explain his or her own ideas and understanding in light of the discussion.	Student engages in a range of collaborative discussions and asks questions to check understanding of information presented, stays on topic most of the time, and frequently links his or her own ideas and understanding in light of the discussion.	Student effectively and consistently engages in a range of collaborative discussions and asks high level questions to check understanding of information presented, always stays on topic, and with great insight and attention to the comments of others links his or her own ideas and understanding in light of the discussion.	SL.5.1c SL.5.1d
Demonstrate knowledge of standard English and its conventions.	Student demonstrates little or no knowledge of standard English and its conventions.	Student demonstrates some evidence of knowledge of standard English and its conventions.	Student consistently demonstrates knowledge of standard English and its conventions.	Student demonstrates an exceptional understanding of standard English and its conventions.	L.5.1 L.5.2 L.5.3
Acquire and accurately use grade-appropriate conversational, general academic, and domain-specific vocabulary and phrases.	Student shows little or no evidence of the acquisition and use of grade-appropriate conversational and academic language.	Student shows some evidence of the acquisition and use of grade-appropriate conversational and academic language.	Student shows solid evidence of the acquisition and use of grade-appropriate conversational and academic language.	Student shows a high level of sophistication and precision with the acquisition and use of grade-appropriate conversational and academic language.	L.5.6

Note: See the Core Ready Rubrics chart in the Welcome at the beginning of the book for descriptions of category headers.

Reading Lesson 1

▼ Teaching Objective

Readers notice the structure and features of editorials.

Close Reading Opportunity

▼ Standards Alignment

RI.5.1, RI.5.5, RI.5.8, RI.5.10, SL.5.1a–d, L.5.1, L.5.6

▼ Materials

- Various examples of editorials representing a range of topics
- Chart paper or interactive whiteboard
- Several copies of your local newspaper
- An editorial on offshore drilling written by a fifth grade student and attached here in the appendix

▼ To the Teacher

This lesson focuses on identifying the text structures and features most commonly used in editorials and then using this knowledge to research and write an original editorial. In this lesson set, students will not only engage with informational text in order to research a topic about which they are interested, they will also conduct close readings of key mentor texts. In the lower grades, students hopefully have been introduced to the idea of writing persuasively by crafting strong opinions and supported their opinions with textual evidence. You can build on and extend this prior knowledge in this lesson. (Do not worry, though, if this is the first introduction to persuasive reading and writing for your students—no particular prior student learning is required to make this lesson set successful.)

To give students an adequate amount of time to immerse themselves in the genre of editorials, this lesson is best implemented across more than one day of instruction.

Prior to teaching this lesson, create a simple T-chart. **ELL** Provide Comprehensible Input—Organizers. This organizer will help your ELLs understand the features of an editorial; you should include examples or copies of these features for a visual reference. Title the chart "What We Noticed about Editorials." You will use this chart throughout this lesson to record the structures and features of an editorial, as well as examples of these different elements.

▼ Procedure

Warm Up | Gather the class to set the stage for today's learning

Writers use words to persuade an audience of an idea, a feeling, a perspective. Writers create arguments fortified by solid evidence to convince an audience their idea, feeling, or perspective has merit. When have you ever felt confident enough to try to persuade someone of something and why?

ELL Frontload the Lesson—Activate Prior Knowledge. Reminding of previous works offers a connection and foundation for the upcoming work. This is also a time that they can clarify any questions that they may have before they continue with the work.

Allow students a moment to think about and respond to this question. Use their responses to help you gauge the class's current understanding of the power of persuasion.

Teach | Model what students need to learn and do

For the next few weeks, we are going to be reading, writing, and studying editorials. An editorial is an article that presents your opinion on an issue that matters to you. It is a writer's way of presenting a strong and forceful argument. Usually this issue is a hot topic, meaning it is an issue that many other people care about as well. Let's look in today's paper to find the editorial section and get a quick idea of the topics that people are writing about right now. **ELL** Identify and Communicate Content and Language Objectives—Key Content Vocabulary. Take this time to help your ELLs understand the issues that are current, which may be based more in this country than hot topics that they are hearing about at home around their home country. If possible, ask them to bring in native language blogs and news resources and share some topics that are relevant in their home countries.

Using current news, turn to the editorial or opinion section and read a few of the titles aloud. Think aloud about topics that seem to be "of the moment."

Writing a solid editorial is an art. There are certain components, structures, and features of this kind of writing that are going to be important for us to notice and use in our own work. Today, we are going to immerse ourselves in this genre by reading a variety of editorials with a partner. Before we do that, however, I'd like to read an example of an editorial together first.

Read an example of an editorial aloud to the class. **ELL** Provide Comprehensible Input—Models. When preparing for the model, think of ideas or vocabulary that you may need to define or provide contextual clues around in order for your ELLs comprehension. You can certainly choose to use a well-written editorial of your selection. For the purposes of this lesson set, we have chosen to use an editorial about offshore drilling written by a fifth grader, attached here in the appendix.

As you read the editorial aloud to the class, pause and notice various structures used by the author. Add your observations to the What We Noticed about Editorials chart you created. **ELL** Provide Comprehensible Input—Graphic Organizers. Here is one way your modeling could unfold.

Read the first full paragraph aloud.

"Imagine that Florida, instead of having white, beautiful beaches, had black and desolate shorelines from an oil spill! Florida must ban nearshore oildrilling permanently!"

Right away, I notice that this author begins with a sentence that catches my attention. She creates a strong image of Florida beaches being black and desolate. The author has definitely captured my interest from the beginning and made me want to read more.

On your T-chart, add "interesting lead or hook" to the left side. On the right side, jot the first sentence of this editorial as an example.

What We Noticed About Editorials
First Place: Elementary School

Interesting lead or hook	- Grabs the reader by clearly stating what the law about nearshore drilling should be for Florida. - Makes it clear that nearshore drilling is an enemy
Logically ordered paragraphs/reasons	- Flows well, including a grabbing opening, clear reasons as to why nearshore drilling hurts Florida and ends with a thought-provoking question to engage reader to take a stance against near shore drilling
Research-based support for the opinion (facts)	- supports the idea that Florida needs tourism because it brings in so much money to the economy - shares how much damage the offshore drilling brought to the Florida economy

Try Guide students to quickly rehearse what they need to learn and do in preparation for practice

Now it's your turn to do some careful listening. As I read the last two paragraphs of this editorial, listen carefully to see if you can identify some of the structures or features this author used to prove her point. What tools, tricks, or strategies is she using to clearly state and back up her opinion?

Read the remainder of the editorial.

"According to www.stateofflorida.com, Florida has 2,276 miles of shoreline, of which 663 miles are famous beaches. Nearshore oil drilling would harm the beauty and the environment along Florida shorelines. Besides, an oil spill would destroy the wildlife, and would devastate the tourism, fishing and water-sport industries. These industries are sources of major income to Florida. According to Visit Florida, tourism alone brought about 1 million jobs and $65.5 billion revenue to Florida on 2007. It generated $3.9 billion sales tax to Florida government that year. Florida cannot risk losing these vital industries and its most beautiful resource, its shorelines and beaches.

For the above reasons, Florida must prohibit nearshore oil drilling." Kim-Anh Vo, fifth grader

Now, ask students to share what they noticed about the author's craft. What tricks or strategies did the author use to clearly state and back up her opinion in this final portion of the editorial? Add your observations to the class T-chart as you go. Some things you may want to guide your students to notice include:

- A strong and clearly stated opinion
- Logically ordered paragraphs and reasons
- Research-based support for the opinion (facts)

Clarify Briefly restate today's teaching objective and explain the practice tasks

Today we are going to immerse ourselves in editorials by reading a variety of editorials written about a range of topics and issues. We've already spent some time closely reading one example of an editorial and jotting down the various tools and strategies the author used to clearly state and back up her opinion. As you read through several editorials with a partner today, I want you to pay attention to these structures and features of editorials. How do the authors craft their opinions and put together persuasive editorials? When we gather together again at the end of our reading time, each partnership will share at least one thing they noticed about how an editorial is constructed, as well as an example of that observation.

Practice Students work independently or in small groups to apply today's teaching objective

With partners, students read editorials on a range of topics and issues. **ELL** Enable Language Production—Increasing Interaction. You can partner ELLs with partners who speak their native language to increase transfer between languages. You could also partner ELLs in triads, where one partner speaks only English, one speaks English and the native language, and then your ELL, as this offers many models of language. Students focus on the craft of writing editorials by noticing the structures and features included in their reading, rather than focusing exclusively on the topics and issues being discussed.

The Practice and Wrap Up sections of this lesson highlight the importance of coming to class discussions prepared and explicitly drawing on that preparation to explore the ideas under discussion. (SL.5.1a)

Wrap Up Check understanding as you guide students to briefly share what they have learned and produced today

Gather the class and ask partners to share their observations.

How did the author craft his or her opinion and put together a persuasive editorial?

As students share what they noticed, they should also provide an example from their reading for the class.

Reading Lesson 2

▼ **Teaching Objective**

Readers can identify the purpose and audience of an editorial.

Close Reading Opportunity

▼ **Standards Alignment**

RI.5.1, RI.5.2, RI.5.8, RI.5.10, SL.5.1a–d, L.5.1, L.5.6

▼ Materials

- "Big Food, Big Soda: Ban Supersized Drinks" (See Appendix 5.3)
- "Texting Instead of Talking: Are Text Messages Destroying Communication?" (See Appendix 5.4)
- "Zoos: Good for Animals and People" (See Appendix 5.5)
- Charting supplies or interactive whiteboard

▼ To the Teacher

This lesson continues your students' immersion in the genre of editorials. Today's focus, however, is on identifying the *purposes* of editorial writing. Editorials are written for a variety of purposes. For example, some editorials are published to influence public opinion, others intend to promote critical thinking, and sometimes editorials encourage people to take action on an issue. Authors of editorials must think carefully about their purpose and consider their audience while crafting their writing, a skill we want to instill in our fifth grade writers as well.

▼ Procedure

Warm Up Gather the class to set the stage for today's learning

Indicate your What We Noticed about Editorials chart.

> So far we have explored the different structures and features editorial writers rely on to grab people's attention, state their opinions, and back up their ideas. Let's take a moment to review some of what we have observed about this genre so far.

Briefly review your chart with students.

Teach Model what students need to learn and do

> Today we're going to think more deeply about the purpose of editorials as well as their intended audience. Whom is the author writing for? We know that the authors of editorials care deeply about their topics. The purpose of an editorial is to persuade not just private opinion but public opinion. This

means the author wants us to do something collectively as a result of reading this piece. What action does the author want the intended audience to take?

Explain to the class that authors of editorials have a specific purpose in mind as they craft their writing. They also have a clear idea of who their audience is and what they would like them to do after reading the editorial. In general, there are three purposes to editorials. As you introduce and discuss each of these purposes, record them for students to refer back to on a chart titled "Purposes of Editorials." **ELL** Provide Comprehensible Input— Organizers. Remember to include visuals from the articles to demonstrate text features.

- To influence public opinion
- To encourage people to think critically about themselves or their actions
- To motivate people to take action

Model reading an editorial and identifying the author's desired audience and purpose. For the purposes of this lesson, we have chosen to use "Texting Instead of Talking" (available in Appendix 5.4) as a shared text. Distribute copies of this text to students so they can follow along as you read selected portions.

Begin by reading the editorial out loud for the class as students follow along. Then, think aloud with your students about the intended audience (students) for this particular editorial. **ELL** Provide Comprehensible Input— Models. This modeling will offer support for your ELLs when they are looking through text on their own.

> I think the audience for this editorial is students. I noticed several times throughout the editorial the author refers to parents, adults, or grownups and even mentions that one of the benefits of sending a text message is to "let our mom know we made it across the street safely." This is not something you would say if you were writing for adults, because they have been crossing the street safely, and by themselves, for many, many years. Also, the research study the author used as an example includes facts about the number of text messages young people write each month, and the overall topic was very relevant to young people, who obviously write a lot of text messages.

Try Guide students to quickly rehearse what they need to learn and do in preparation for practice

Now that I've thought aloud about the intended audience of this editorial, I want you to turn and talk with a partner about the author's purpose behind writing this editorial about the impact of texting versus talking on our relationships with our friends. What do you think the author wants us to *do* after reading his or her work?

Give students an opportunity to discuss this question in pairs. **ELL** Enable Language Production—Increasing Interaction. You can aid partnerships in talk and language structures by listening into partnerships with ELLs. You can support if needed by offering support to extend language during their share. Circulate and listen in on student conversations. Then, gather the class once again and ask a few partners to share their thinking. Guide the class to see that one justifiable purpose of this editorial is to encourage people to think critically about themselves, specifically the impact of texting on their lives by asking whether the common assumption that texting is a negative thing is actually true. It argues texting can have a positive influence on people's communication skills and experiences, if not done too often. Refer specifically to the last section of the editorial as textual evidence of this purpose. Highlight the use of direct quotations as textual evidence.

Clarify Briefly restate today's teaching objective and explain the practice tasks

Authors of editorials have an audience and a purpose in mind when they craft their opinions. Today, we discussed three different purposes an author may have when writing an editorial: to influence public opinion, to encourage people to think critically about themselves or their actions, or to motivate people to take action. I want you to read through these two new editorials and then work with your partner to determine who is the audience, discuss the author's purpose, and then find evidence from the text in the form of direct quotations to support your thinking. Be sure to refer back to the chart we created as you read today.

Practice Students work independently or in small groups to apply today's teaching objective

Distribute copies of "Zoos: Good for Animals and People" (Appendix 5.5) and "Big Food, Big Soda: Ban Supersized Drinks" (Appendix 5.3) to students. Students read these editorials in pairs, focusing on determin-

ing the *purpose* of each editorial. **ELL** Enable Language Production—Increasing Interaction. Students identify specific evidence from the text to support their thinking about the author's purpose. If students can justify more than one purpose citing evidence, encourage these interpretations also.

Wrap Up Check understanding as you guide students to briefly share what they have learned and produced today

Gather the class to discuss each of the editorials. Have partners share their thinking regarding the author's purpose for writing that particular editorial. Use the following questions to guide your discussion:

- Who is the intended audience for this editorial?
- What is the author's purpose? What do you believe he or she wants the audience to *do* after reading this piece?
- How do you know? Do you have direct evidence from the text to support your thinking about purpose?

For instance, the audience in "Big Food, Big Soda: Ban Supersized Drinks" would be the local authorities in charge of determining whether to pass a restriction on the size of sugary drinks that stores and restaurants are allowed to sell. But it is also the citizens of the town, for if the writer of the editorial can convince the citizens to support the ban on supersized drinks, they will make their views known to the authorities. The purpose is to encourage the leaders of the town to give ban supersized sugary drinks. The direct evidence from the text is the statement encouraging people to call the leaders of the town to support the ban, and the medical evidence proving that the health risks of too much sugar are real and dangerous. Another thing to notice is how the author attempts to anticipate the counterarguments by including a section about how an unhealthy society costs all of us more money, and even with the restriction, people will still be able to get as much sugar by simply drinking smaller portions of soda.

> *I have found you an argument; but I am not obliged to find you an understanding.*
>
> —Samuel Johnson

Reading Lesson 3 ....

▼ Teaching Objective

Readers choose a topic they are interested in and gather related research materials.

Close Reading Opportunity

▼ Standards Alignment

RI.5.7, W.5.7, SL.5.1a, SL.5.1b, L.5.6

▼ Materials

- "The Importance of Owning a Dog" (see Appendix 5.2, Sample Editorial)
- Students should have easy access to their free writing (created during Writing Lesson 1—the reading and writing lesson sets work best when taught in tandem)
- What Matters to Us chart (created during Writing Lesson 1—which was taught in tandem with Reading Lesson 1)

▼ To the Teacher

Navigating, selecting, and integrating resources both in print and on the Internet are a hallmark of the Common Core State Standards, particularly for fifth graders. These lesson sets will emphasize both modes.

▼ Procedure

Warm Up — Gather the class to set the stage for today's learning

> During our writing work yesterday, we spent time thinking and writing about the issues that concern us the most and might inspire us to write an editorial. You did some free writing on a variety of topics.

Take a moment and review the list of topics and issues you created with your class during Writing Lesson 1.

Teach — Model what students need to learn and do

> Today you will each select an issue to pursue, choosing a topic about which you are passionate and interested.

Take a moment to reflect on your own passions and concerns, using the list you created with students to help you select an issue about which you are passionate and would like to write an editorial. For the purposes of this lesson set, we have created an editorial about the importance of owning a dog (see Appendix 5.2, Sample Editorial); however, you are also free to choose a topic close to your heart and to compose your own editorial as a model for the class.

> Everybody's interests and passions are different. Some of you will choose to write about an issue that impacts this classroom, others will have opinions about issues that affect our community, and some of you might use this editorial as a chance to share your concerns about more global problems. In this sample editorial, the author is passionate about owning a dog, and also wants to sway public opinion so that many follow his lead. **ELL** Frontload the Lesson—Make Connections. Creating connections for your ELLs helps them to ground their thinking and vocabulary in something tangible. Consider connecting ideas into their native language to increase and extend their thinking.

It is time to model for students how to select and gather print resources from the library.

Demonstrate using your topic to generate a list of key words to use in a library search. Here is one way your modeling could unfold using the topic of dog ownership.

> I know that a strong editorial includes supporting evidence from experts or other reliable sources. I need to do some research to find evidence to support my opinion that owning a dog is a great thing for a family. We're going to begin our search for resources in the library, so I'm going to start by creating a list of key terms related to my topic that I can use to search the library for print resources. (Internet searches will be addressed later in this lesson set, but most certainly can also be introduced now if that is your school's primary source for research.)

Jot your ideas down in a list as you think aloud. Following are some ideas for search terms to include in your list. **ELL** Provide Comprehensible Input—Models. This model will help ELLs see how to brainstorm search terms, as well as have the time to clarify possible search terms.

- Pet ownership
- Dog ownership
- Families and pets

Try Guide students to quickly rehearse what they need to learn and do in preparation for practice

Now it's your turn. I'd like each of you to take a moment and reflect on the issues and concerns that inspire us as a class. Look at the chart we created together and read through your writing. Choose an issue about which you have a strong opinion.

Give students a moment to come up with a topic or issue about which they have a strong opinion. **ELL** Enable Language Production—Listening and Speaking. This is a time for your ELLs to clarify and extend their thinking and English vocabulary around their ideas. Ask students to briefly share their ideas for topics.

Clarify Briefly restate today's teaching objective and explain the practice tasks

We are preparing to write editorials in order to convince others and make our voices heard on an issue or topic that matters to us. Part of our preparation involves gathering resources and finding evidence to support our opinion. Today we are conducting a search for print materials by creating a list of key words.

Practice Students work independently or in small groups to apply today's teaching objective

Students work independently to generate a list of key words to guide their search. Students work independently to use their key words to uncover material for their editorials.

© pressmaster / Fotolia

Wrap Up Check understanding as you guide students to briefly share what they have learned and produced today

Gather the class to reflect on today's work. Lead the class in a discussion focused on the process of finding print resources as well as determining the *usefulness* of the resources they uncovered. Below is a list of questions to help guide your conversation.

- Were you able to find resources in the library?
- Are your resources useful?
- Do they provide you with information that will help support your point of view on your chosen topic?
- How did you determine which resources were useful and which were not?

Reading Lesson 4

▼ Teaching Objective

Readers research and take notes on a topic about which they are interested.

Close Reading Opportunity

▼ Standards Alignment

RI.5.1, RI.5.7, RI.5.10, W.5.4, W.5.7, W.5.8, W.5.10, SL.5.1a, SL.5.1b, L.5.6

▼ Materials

- Sample excerpt of informational text from a book (can be on any topic)
- Charting supplies or interactive whiteboard

▼ To the Teacher

Knowing when to paraphrase and when to use a direct quotation in note taking is a sophisticated skill for fifth graders. The research students are doing for this lesson set is fairly narrow; they are simply reading to find evidence that supports their opinion, rather than looking for a large amount of information to answer a broad question. Therefore, this lesson provides the perfect opportunity to reinforce the difference between paraphrasing and using direct quotation and provides students with the chance to practice the process of deciding which tool would be the most effective.

▼ Procedure

Warm Up Gather the class to set the stage for today's learning

Fifth graders, the idea of taking notes as you read informational text is not new to you, but this year we are really going to focus on this vital aspect of research and improve our note-taking skills. Note taking is designed to help in two ways: to remember what you read and to organize and build evidence for an argument. **ELL** Frontload the Lesson—Activate Prior Knowledge.

Allow several students to share their thoughts on both positive and negative experiences they've had with note taking. Students may comment that note taking allows us to record the important pieces of information so we can remember and use them later. Inaccurate notes, or notes that don't take down the important points, don't help us later on since we forget the main ideas or things jumble together in our memory and we can't use them in our writing. Affirm the idea that note taking is most impactful when it feels purposeful.

What are some strategies for note taking that have worked for you in the past?

Again, allow students the chance to share their ideas with the class. Hopefully, students have had a great deal of practice in note taking in previous years and, as a result, they should have a general idea of what notes look like and how to organize them. If your sense is that many of the students are weak in the area of note taking, take some extra time here to review the fundamental purposes of taking notes before delving into the specifics of this lesson.

Teach Model what students need to learn and do

Today we are going to focus on two important skills in note taking: paraphrasing and using direct quotations. Paraphrasing means you record what you have learned in your own words. You do not copy word for word. Changing a few words here and there is also not paraphrasing. Paraphrasing is a skill and it takes practice. When you successfully paraphrase another person's idea, you read what the author wrote, take it in, and then record the idea in your own words. When you practice, try to do this without looking at all at the original text. Paraphrasing is most useful when you want to take a note about the author's main or big ideas. Sometimes an author says something exactly right, so that it is worth it to actually quote the words. This is also best used when you are trying to capture main ideas. When you use a direct quotation, you copy the sentence or idea exactly as it appears in the original text, using quotation marks and giving credit to the original author. There is also a time when you are not paraphrasing or quoting, but simply recording important facts. For instance, if you were researching the sun and came across these sentences, quick recording of facts would be the way to take notes: "The sun is 93 million miles from the earth. It takes light about eight and a half minutes to travel all the way from the sun to the earth. Think of what can happen in that time—a fast runner can go more than two miles, the Nathan's Coney Island hot dog eating champ can eat 57 hot dogs, and 4,167 bottles of Tabasco sauce come rolling off the assembly line, all while the beams of light are making their way from the sun to us. The sun seems so close, so warm, and nearby. But it is farther than we can almost imagine. If you somehow were able to get in your car and drive at a highway speed of 60 miles an hour through space, without ever stopping for gas, you would arrive in 177 years."

Model for students the difference between paraphrasing and writing direct quotations in their notes. Choose a piece of informational text on any topic (for the purposes of this lesson, it does not have to relate back to the topic of your editorial). Ideally, choose a print resource like the books your students will be using to take notes during the Practice portion of this lesson.

Select a paragraph from the book. The purpose of this exercise is to model for students the difference between paraphrasing and using a direct quotation, so the subject matter of the excerpt is less important. Read the paragraph aloud to the class. Highlight an important piece of information from the paragraph. Then, model how to paraphrase the same idea in your own words using the following strategy: look, say, cover, write, check. **ELL Provide Comprehensible Input—Models. This vocabulary strategy will support your ELLs as they encounter new words and ideas. You may need to offer models at different levels to account for the different levels of English proficiency in the class.** First, *look* at (or read) the portion of text you would like to paraphrase. Then, *say* the information in your own words as an oral rehearsal of what you intend to write. Next, *cover* the text and *write* your notes. Finally, *check* (or reread) what you wrote to make sure it is accurate.

Now, model for your class how to write down a direct quotation from the same paragraph. **ELL Provide Comprehensible Input—Models.** Think aloud about your use of quotation marks, the need to copy the text exactly, and writing down the source. Keeping track of related sources is essential as students are working to integrate and take notes from a variety of sources. Following is an example how to set up a direct quotation: (author's name) in (name of book) at (page number) writes, "(direct quote)."

Lead the class in a brief discussion about the similarities and differences of these two tools. During this discussion, highlight some rules of thumb for students to use when deciding whether paraphrasing or direct quotation is the best choice for their notes. Add these to a chart titled,

"Paraphrase or Direct Quote?" **ELL Provide Comprehensible Input—Organizers. This is a helpful organizer for your ELLs to demonstrate "examples and non-examples" of what they can try in their work. Consider using various levels of vocabulary to meet the needs of the different language proficiencies.** Some rules of thumb to incorporate into your conversation and your charting are:

- Paraphrase when you think that the words of the other writer are too difficult for your readers.
- Paraphrase when *what* the author says is more important than *how* the author says it.
- Quote directly when using a fact that is presented in an unusual or interesting way.
- Quote directly when you want to use another writer's exact words so you do not plagiarize.

Try Guide students to quickly rehearse what they need to learn and do in preparation for practice

Give students an opportunity to try paraphrasing and using direct quotations. Select another paragraph from the text you used during the Teach portion of this lesson. Read it aloud to your class. Then, guide your students through the processes of paraphrasing the information (relying on the strategy of look, say, cover, write, check) and using a direct quote correctly.

Clarify Briefly restate today's teaching objective and explain the practice tasks

Today you are going to dig into your resources and take notes when you identify information that supports your opinion. As you are taking notes to use as evidence in your final editorial, think about when it is best to paraphrase information and when it is best to use a direct quotation. Use the chart we created together as a guide to help you make these decisions.

Practice Students work independently or in small groups to apply today's teaching objective

Students independently read the resources they have gathered during Reading Lesson 3. Students take notes on information that supports their opinion, relying on the strategies of paraphrasing and direct quotation.

© Jacek Chabraszewski / Fotolia

Wrap Up Check understanding as you guide students to briefly share what they have learned and produced today

Gather the class to discuss the process of note taking. Use the following questions to guide your reflection:

- How did you organize your notes?

- How did you decide when to paraphrase? When to use a direct quote? Can you give an example?

- In rereading your notes, do you feel that they will be helpful to you?

Milestone Performance Assessment

Note-Taking Strategies

 Use this checklist to assess student notes at this point.

Standards Alignment: RI.5.1, RI.5.7, RI.5.10, W.5.4, W.5.7, W.5.8, W.5.10, SL.5.1a, SL.5.1b, L.5.6

	Achieved	Notes
Develop a system to organize notes.		
Paraphrase information from sources.		
Record direct quotes from sources; use quotes and credit sources.		
Keep a list of sources used.		

Reading Lesson 5 ·

▼ Teaching Objective

Readers round out their research by turning to and navigating online resources effectively.

▼ Standards Alignment

RI.5.7, RI.5.10, W.5.7, W.5.8, W.5.10, SL.5.1a, SL.5.1b, SL.5.2, L.5.6

▼ Materials

- Internet access for each student
- Notes on your editorial topic

▼ To the Teacher

Today's lesson continues our expanded focus on gathering multiple relevant print and digital resources by asking students to find and gather information from Internet sites. Be aware that although our students may seem expert in using technology, conducting a digital search can still be a daunting task for many fifth graders to actually navigate fluidly and independently. They need to select key words, enter them into a search engine, navigate through the wealth of resources that are generated in order to determine which are relevant as well as which are most reliable, and then read through useful sites in order to find information that supports their opinions. All of this requires skillful decision making and strong reading skills. The work in this lesson concentrates on determining the reliability of an online resource, a skill that is crucial to effective research.

▼ Procedure

Warm Up Gather the class to set the stage for today's learning

Hold a brief discussion with your class.

> Consider information you have searched for recently online. We often search for information when we have a specific question in mind, and the more specific we are in our search, the more effective it will be. Think about a topic you searched and the steps you took. You used logical thinking skills to craft a question for the search bar, to select words that would give you the most success, and then you sifted through lots of results to get to where you wanted to be.

Allow several students to share their experiences with searching the Internet for specific information.

Teach Model what students need to learn and do

Students are well on their way to collecting a substantial amount of evidence to support their opinions for their editorials.

> In the last lessons we looked for information in print resources. Today we are going to conduct an Internet search to locate additional resources for you to rely on when constructing your final editorial.

Explain that searching for information on the Internet requires creating key words to type into a search engine. Take a moment to ensure that students are familiar with the term *search engine*. A search engine is a website that easily allows the user to comb the Internet for information related to the key terms entered in the search bar. Popular search engines to hold up as examples are Google, Bing, Yahoo!, and Ask.

Make the clear connection between using key words to search for information in a library catalog and for information on the Internet.

> Earlier in this lesson set, you created a list of key words to help you locate information in the library catalog. Here are the words I used to search for information about dog ownership.

Display the search terms you used when looking for information in the library catalog.

- Pet ownership
- Dog ownership
- Families and pets

Point out that the biggest difference between these two types of searching is the level of specificity required of the key word search terms.

> The Internet has more information than any one library could possibly hold, so I need to be more specific in my search terms.

> For example, if I typed "families and pets" into a search engine, I would get too much information to look through in return, and much of it might not be helpful to me personally. I need to be more specific when thinking about search terms to use in an Internet search.

Generate a list of more specific search terms to enter into a search engine like Google, thinking aloud about what exactly makes these terms more specific. Here are a few examples of more specific search terms:

- How dog ownership benefits families
- Positive benefits of dog ownership
- Raising a dog
- Good dogs around children
- Responsibilities of dog ownership

> When I was searching the library catalog, I used the search term "dog ownership" to help me find information. Now that I am taking my search to the Internet, I need to make my key words more specific. Let me think about the exact

kind of information I need to support my opinion. I am looking for information about how dog ownership benefits familes. So, I'm going to use those exact words in the search bar—"how dog ownership benefits families."

Choose a search engine for students to use. Model entering your key words into the search bar.

Try Guide students to quickly rehearse what they need to learn and do in preparation for practice

Demonstrate how to read through the link titles, the address of the link, as well as the first two lines of text below the link (the thumbnail description). Select a link that looks promising based on the thumbnail description. **ELL** Provide Comprehensible Input—Models. Think aloud about your decision for the class to hear your thought process.

Now, take a moment to scan the website you have selected along with your students. Model studying the homepage and skimming it for facts and information that may be useful as evidence to support your opinion. Decide whether or not the website provides useful information. Then, ask your students to help identify specific pieces of information you might use in your editorial to further support your opinion.

Take a moment and read the information on the homepage on your own. Look for specific information that supports the opinion that dog ownership is a good idea for families.

Add any relevant information to your notes, using paraphrasing or direct quotes as appropriate.

As you model Internet searches, consider the translation feature that online translation sites offer, where a whole website can be translated into several languages. This can be a helpful support for your ELLs proficient in their native language.

Clarify Briefly restate today's teaching objective and explain the practice tasks

To prepare for writing our own editorials, let us be sure that we've collected enough information to use as evidence to support our opinions. You will now create a highly specific list of search terms to help you conduct an online search about your topic.

Practice Students work independently or in small groups to apply today's teaching objective

Students create a list of specific search terms to use in an Internet search. Each student conducts an online search for information, considering relevancy as they scan the resulting webpage for useful information and additional links to follow.

Wrap Up Check understanding as you guide students to briefly share what they have learned and produced today

Gather the class to reflect on today's work. Ask students to keep their list of search terms nearby for easy reference.

Search terms need to be specific, and specially created just for you, by you. The search engine question bar is waiting for you to create sharp and focused words that will lead the way. Let's share examples from today that worked well for you.

Here are some other question to use to guide your class' reflection:

- What search terms did you try?
- Did you find your search results to be useful? How did you modify your search to get to more useful results?
- How did you decide which resources you would use and which resources would not be as useful?

Reading Lesson 6 ·

▼ Teaching Objective

Readers compare and contrast multiple accounts of the same topic or event.

▼ Standards Alignment

RI.5.6, RI.5.7, RI.5.9, RI.5.10, W.5.7, W.5.8, W.5.10, SL.5.1a, SL.5.1b, L.5.1, L.5.6

▼ Materials

- Charting supplies or interactive whiteboard
- Internet access for students
- "Big Food, Big Soda: Ban Supersized Drinks" (See Appendix 5.3)

▼ To the Teacher

Strong editorials effectively refute the stance of the opposition. We want to encourage our fifth graders to do more than simply state that the opposition is wrong. We want them to dip their toes into researching opposing viewpoints in an effort to understand and more persuasively disarm them.

Dog Ownership

Point of View	Opposing Opinion
-loyal friend	-may scare friends or neighbors
-promotes responsibility	-takes too much time to take care of a dog
-promotes exercise	- limits types of exercise to walking or running
-offers unconditional love	- wants to be with you all the time

▼ Procedure

Warm Up Gather the class to set the stage for today's learning

Conduct a quick opinion poll of your students on a topic of interest such as "Should schools allow candy to be sold in the cafeteria?" or "Should schools allow students to carry cell phones in class?" Ask students on both sides of the argument explain the reason for their opinion. Ask:

> If you were writing an editorial on your view, do you think it would be important to research what those on the opposing side think? Why?

Allow students to freely share their thinking on this question.

Teach Model what students need to learn and do

Discuss the importance of researching opposing points of view.

> Sophisticated authors of editorials are smart. They know that there are people out there who will disagree with their opinions. Instead of ignoring those people, authors of strong editorials are bold enough to acknowledge the opposite point of view in their editorials. They research the opposite point of view, learning enough about it to pick it apart and further strengthen their own argument.

Turn to your own work to model determining opposing points of view. Begin a simple T-chart, labeling one side "point of view" and the other side "opposing opinion." **ELL** Provide Comprehensible Input—Graphic Organizers. Add your own opinion to the left side of the chart. Then think aloud about the opposing opinion, adding that to the chart as well.

> My opinion is that owning a dog is good for families because dogs push people to get more exercise, make great friends, and help kids learn to be more responsible. So the opposite point of view would be that owning a dog is NOT good for families. But why? I need to say more than just "owning a dog is not a good idea." Let me try to think more concretely about why someone would think owning a dog is NOT a good idea for a family.

Think aloud, placing yourself in the shoes of the opposition. Add an opposing opinion to your chart. You might write something like "Owning a dog is not a good idea for families because of the expense and amount of time caring for a dog requires." Fully understanding the opposing point of view may be difficult for some students. What if they can't conceive of any reasons behind the opposite point of view? The Internet is a great tool for quickly resolving this issue. Guide students to use the opposite point of view as a search term. Then, reinforcing the teaching you did during Reading Lesson 5, remind students how to navigate search results to quickly find the answer to their question while relying on reliable sources. Emphasize to students that they do not need to do as in depth research about the opposite point of view as their own position; the Internet is one resource they can turn to if they have difficulty coming up with more detail about opposing opinions.

Try Guide students to quickly rehearse what they need to learn and do in preparation for practice

> In the editorial "Big Food, Big Soda: Ban Supersized Drinks," (Appendix 5.3) the author's opinion is that giant-sized sodas should be banned because they pose significant health risks.

Add this point of view to the left side of your T-chart.

> What would the opposite opinion sound like?

Ask students to take a moment to think about this question. **ELL** Enable Language Production—Listening and Speaking. During this time, it is important to model the language and sentence structures that you want your ELLs to be able to use and master. These structures can offer support as they are working to convey their thinking. Then have students share some possibilities. Guide the class in a discussion of this question, helping them arrive at a relevant opposing opinion such as "People should be free to decide what kind of food they eat and how much is enough."

Now work with your class to think about what they need to find out about the alternative point of view to be able to successfully refute it. Remind students that it is not necessary to conduct a huge research study; emphasize that it is an important skill to be able quickly find the answer to their question.

Clarify Briefly restate today's teaching objective and explain the practice tasks

> Strong editorials acknowledge the opposing point of view as a way to gain credibility and make their arguments even more convincing. Today, I want you to identify the opinion that opposes your point of view. Then, I want you to do some quick research to get a better understanding of this opinion in order to help you adequately address it in your own editorial. We are powerful writers and researchers and we enjoy a little debate.

Practice Students work independently and/or in small groups to apply today's teaching objective

Students work independently to identify and articulate the opinion that opposes their own point of view. Then, students focus on using their Internet search skills to skim text to find out more about the opposing point of view.

Wrap Up Check understanding as you guide students to briefly share what they have learned and produced today

Gather students together. Ask several volunteers to share the topic of their editorial, their opinion, and the opposing opinion. Add these ideas to the T-chart you began during the Teach portion of this lesson.

Reading Lesson 7

▼ **Teaching Objective**

Readers revisit mentor texts to analyze the craft of introducing an issue.

Close Reading Opportunity

▼ **Standards Alignment**

RI.5.1, RI.5.8, RI.5.10, W.5.1a, W.5.4, W.5.10, SL.5.1a, SL.5.1b, L.5.1, L.5.6

▼ Materials

- Student copies of "Big Food, Big Soda: Ban Supersized Drinks" (Appendix 5.3)
- Student copies of "Texting Instead of Talking: How One Type of Communicating Destroys Communication" (Appendix 5.4)

▼ To the Teacher

For the next several lessons, your students will revisit mentor editorials, conducting a close reading of these texts to help them better understand the particulars of this new genre. Prior to the start of this lesson, create a chart titled "Elements of a Strong Editorial." You will use this chart in the next three reading lessons and refer to it in several of your writing lessons. Here is an example of a simple format for this chart:

Elements of a Strong Editorial

Element	Examples and ideas
Introduction	
Strong opinion statement	
Logically ordered reasons	
Concluding statement	

▼ Procedure

Warm Up Gather the class to set the stage for today's learning

Ask students to vote on which editorial from the lesson set so far they think is the most convincing. Have volunteers explain why. Explain that today's lesson will focus on examining strong editorials to determine what makes them so effective. This will prepare students to write their own convincing editorials.

Teach Model what students need to learn and do

Whenever I am getting ready to write in a new genre or style, I spend time studying the writing of mentor authors to get a feel for how my writing should be structured or sound. For the next few days, we're going to reread of some select mentor texts in order to prepare ourselves to write our own editorials.

Show the class the Elements of a Strong Editorial chart you have created in advance. **ELL Provide Comprehensible Input—Graphic Organizers.** Tell the class that today you are going to focus on examining the beginnings of editorials. What strategies or tools do authors use to capture the reader's attention?

Ask students to take out their copies of "Big Food, Big Soda: Ban Supersized Drinks." Read the first full paragraph aloud as students follow along. Think aloud about how the author captures your attention by posing a thought-provoking question in this introduction. Add "ask thought-provoking question" to the Introduction section of your chart. **ELL Provide Comprehensible Input—Models. This model will be a reference or your ELLs when they are working independently. Think of ways you can incorporate visuals to offer a nonlinguistic tie to the work.**

Try Guide students to quickly rehearse what they need to learn and do in preparation for practice

Now ask students to take out their copies of "Texting Instead of Talking: How One Type of Communicating Destroys Communication." Tell students to read the introduction, or first paragraph, of this editorial with a partner. Once they have finished reading, partners should discuss how the author of this editorial grabbed their attention and introduced her topic.

Allow students enough time to read and discuss the beginning of this editorial. Circulate, listen in on, and support conversations between partners. Then, gather the class and have partners share their thinking. Guide the class toward recognizing that this editorial begins with a general description of a familiar experience—texting. Add "share an example" to the Introduction section of your chart.

Clarify Briefly restate today's teaching objective and explain the practice tasks

I'd like to add a few more options and examples of engaging beginnings for our editorial work. Today, read and study several mentor editorials with a partner, focusing on the introductions or first few paragraphs. How did the authors grab your attention? What tool or strategy can we add to our chart? Each partnership should be prepared to share one new idea and a specific example from a mentor text when we gather together again at the end of our reading time. (SL.5.1a)

Practice Students work independently or in small groups to apply today's teaching objective

 Students study the introductions of mentor editorials with a partner, focusing on naming the strategy or tool the author used to engage their audience. **ELL** Enable Language Production—Increasing Interaction. This interaction offers another model for ELLs to practice this activity with a partner. If the ELL is a newer English speaker, consider the triad model to help model editorial introductions in English. Students should focus on naming the strategy or tool the author used to engage his or her audience.

Wrap Up Check understanding as you guide students to briefly share what they have learned and produced today

Gather the class. Have partners share the strategy or tool they identified in the introduction of a mentor editorial. Add student ideas to the Examples and Ideas sections of your chart. Allow your students to name the strategies and tools used by authors; this type of ownership builds confidence and often makes a complex idea, such as author's craft, more accessible for all students. **ELL** Identify and Communicate Content and Language Objectives—Simplify Language. This is an opportunity to think of the various stages of language acquisition that you have in the class. Think of how you can model and incorporate a variety of sentence structures to support those levels when sharing strategies and tools. Be sure to have students also share an explicit example from their text. Ask "What was it about this type of introduction that grabbed your attention?"

>
> *I pass with relief from the tossing sea of Cause and Theory to the firm ground of Result and Fact.*
>
> —Winston Churchill

Reading Lesson 8

▼ Teaching Objective

Readers revisit mentor texts to analyze how writers build their arguments.

Close Reading Opportunity

▼ Standards Alignment

RI.5.1, RI.5.8, RI.5.10, W.5.1a–c, W.5.4, W.5.10, SL.5.1a–d, L.5.1, L.5.6

▼ Materials

- Student notes
- Analysis of an Editorial graphic organizer (see Appendix 5.6)
- Student copies of "Zoos: Good for Animals and People," (Appendix 5.5)

▼ To the Teacher

You'll notice that Reading Lesson 8 is very similar to Reading Lesson 7. As we mentioned in Reading Lesson 7, this cluster of lessons (7–9) asks students to engage deeply with mentor editorials as a way to familiarize themselves with the structures and craft of this genre. Not only will this type of analysis help students as they begin to write their own editorials as part of our writing lesson set, it will also promote increased fluency as students encounter these types of texts in the future.

▼ Procedure

Warm Up Gather the class to set the stage for today's learning

Recap Reading Lesson 7's work with examining mentor texts. Explain that today, the lens will be on how our mentor texts present an argument.

Teach   Model what students need to learn and do

An editorial begins with an engaging introduction and strong statement of opinion, then moves on to reveal an argument that supports that opinion. That's where our research comes in to play. Today we're going to return to our mentor texts to study how authors of editorials build strong arguments by using precise language and research.

Introduce students to the Analysis of an Editorial graphic organizer. **ELL** Provide Comprehensible Input—Graphic Organizers. Now, ask students to take out their copies of "Zoos: Good for Animals and People." Take a moment to remember and reread the author's opinion. (Zoos are beneficial spaces for both animals and people.) Jot this opinion down on the Analysis of an Editorial graphic organizer.

Highlight the author's use of headings to organize the argument into logical and easy-to-follow categories.

> Right away, as I glance through this editorial, I notice the headings the author uses. These headings help to organize the author's argument into logical categories that are easy for the reader to follow.

Read the first section of the editorial (Keeping Animals Happy and Healthy) aloud to the class as they follow along. Think aloud about how the author begins to build an argument that supports her opinion. **ELL** Provide Comprehensible Input—Models.

> This main idea of this first section is that zoos keep animals happy and healthy by building authentic habitats and making sure they stay disease free. The author uses examples of how zoos accomplish this to support her opinion that zoos are beneficial for animals and people. So really, this section begins to build the author's argument by supporting the first part of her opinion—zoos are good for *animals*. That was a logical place to begin. Let me look for some really specific examples from the text that show how the author used these studies to support the first part of her opinion.

Go back into the text and indicate for students specific sentences and paragraphs within this first section that support the author's opinion. Jot these examples from the text in the first bubble on your graphic organizer. Then, in the box below, write a sentence or two that explains *how* this piece of evidence supports the opinion given by the author. Some specific textual evidence from the editorial includes:

- Zoos use plants, trees, and food familiar to the animals to create authentic habitats for them.
- Zoos are able to help sick animals so that they do not become vulnerable to natural prey, as they would in the wild.

> Did you notice how I analyzed the text to learn about the ways an author builds an argument in an editorial? First, I reread a section of the editorial. Then, I thought about the section's main idea and how it worked to support the author's opinion. Last, I went back into the text another time to find specific examples or evidence the author used to support the particular point she was making in her writing.

Try   Guide students to quickly rehearse what they need to learn and do in preparation for practice

Now ask students to read the next section of "Zoos: Good for Animals and People" (Protecting the Species). Once they have finished reading, students should discuss with a partner how the author of this editorial used this next section to further her argument. Support partner conversations by providing them with three questions to guide their conversations:

1. What is the main idea of this section?
2. How does this section work to support the author's opinion?
3. What specific examples can we pull from the text?

Allow students enough time to read and discuss this section of the editorial. Circulate, listen in on, and support conversations between partners. Then, gather the class and have partners share their thinking. Record relevant answers on the Analysis of an Editorial graphic organizer.

Clarify   Briefly restate today's teaching objective and explain the practice tasks

> Authors of editorials build convincing arguments by logically ordering their evidence and presenting it in dynamic ways. Today, I'd like you to read and study several mentor editorials with a partner, focusing on how the author built his or her argument. Use the Analysis of an Editorial graphic organizer to support your work and record your thinking.

Practice Students work independently or in small groups to apply today's teaching objective

Students study the body or argument of mentor editorials with a partner, focusing on identifying specific pieces of text as evidence that support particular points or aspects of the author's opinion. **ELL** Enable Language Production—Increasing Interaction. This is a good opportunity to listen in on and see how to best scaffold and support language structures in partnerships. It is also an opportunity to understand the amount of language your ELLs bring to their work. They should focus on identifying specific pieces of text as evidence that support particular points or aspects of the author's opinion.

Wrap Up Check understanding as you guide students to briefly share what they have learned and produced today

Gather the class. Have one or two partnerships share their analysis with the class. Now turn to your Elements of a Strong Editorial chart. **ELL** Provide Comprehensible Input—Graphic Organizers.

I'd like to record some of our mentor authors' techniques for building strong arguments on our chart, so we can refer back to these ideas as we are writing our own editorials. What have we learned about the argument in an editorial?

Reading Lesson 9

▼ Teaching Objective

Readers revisit mentor texts to analyze how writers craft strong conclusions.

Close Reading Opportunity

▼ Standards Alignment

RI.5.1, RI.5.4, RI.5.10, W.5.1d, SL.5.1a–d, L.5.1, L.5.6

▼ Materials

- Student copies of "Zoos: Good for Animals and People" (Appendix 5.5)
- Charting supplies or interactive whiteboard

▼ Procedure

Warm Up Gather the class to set the stage for today's learning

Ask students to take out their copies of "Zoos: Good for Animals and People." Take a moment to reread the editorial as students follow along. Then hold a brief discussion guided by the following questions:

- What is this author's opinion?
- What reasons does the author give to support her opinion?
- Can you find a specific piece of text as evidence?

Teach Model what students need to learn and do

Today we're going to return to our mentor texts one last time to study how authors of editorials conclude their writing with power and leave the reader thinking.

Reread the concluding paragraph of "Zoos: Good for Animals and People." Think aloud about the tools or strategies the author uses to craft a strong conclusion.

In this final paragraph, or the conclusion of this editorial, the author restates her opinion and the main reasons in support of that opinion. Then the author ends with the strong statement that leaves me thinking about the power and possibility of zoos. Let's turn back to the text and see exactly is written.

Return to the final sentence of the editorial, modeling how to highlight a specific example from the text as evidence of the author's craft. **ELL** Provide Comprehensible Input—Models.

Did you notice how I analyzed the text to learn about how the author crafted a strong conclusion? First, I first reread the entire editorial to remind myself of the author's opinion and argument. Then, I zeroed in on the conclusion, reading it again. Last, I thought about what the author did—what tricks and strategies she used in her writing—to craft such a strong conclusion, and then I identified a specific line or two as an example of that strategy.

Try Guide students to quickly rehearse what they need to learn and do in preparation for practice

We have spent the last several lessons analyzing mentor texts to help us better understand the genre of editorials, as well as to familiarize ourselves with various strategies authors use when crafting strong editorials. Each time we've returned to a mentor text to do this type of analysis, we've relied on a similar process. The approach of closely analyzing a specific text is an important one—we get to be better readers and writers by studying the work of those authors who already have their voices out in the world. So let's take a moment and chart that technique for ourselves, remembering that we can add on to and revise this process as we become even stronger readers.

Ask students to discuss the steps they have taken over the last few days to analyze a text for a specific purpose. **ELL** Identify and Communicate Content and Language Objectives—Repeat. Repetition offers your ELLs more time to practice their steps that they are working on to be able to analyze text. This will sound different depending on language proficiency level. What did they do first? What did they do next? Circulate around the room, listening in on students' conversations and supporting their ideas. In particular, listen for key strategies or ideas that you would like to highlight on the resulting process chart.

Title the chart "The Process of Analyzing a Text." **ELL** Provide Comprehensible Input—Organizers. Then share some of the thinking you overheard and ask students to add more. Guide your class toward creating a chart that emphasizes the following steps in their own words:

- Reread the entire short text (or portion of the longer text) being studied to orient yourself.
- Think about the purpose of your analysis. What are you looking for?

- Return to the text to find specific examples of your thinking.
- Share your ideas and findings in your own words, using the text as evidence (paraphrasing or using direct quotations) to support your thinking.

Clarify Briefly restate today's teaching objective and explain the practice tasks

Authors of editorials conclude their work with powerful summaries of their opinions and arguments. That isn't always an easy thing to do. Today, I'd like you to read and study several mentor editorials with a partner, focusing on the author's conclusion. Each partnership should be ready to share at least one strong example when we gather together again at the end of our reading time. (SL.5.1a)

Practice Students work independently or in small groups to apply today's teaching objective

Students study the conclusions of mentor editorials with a partner. **ELL** Enable Language Production—Increasing Interaction, focusing on choosing a strong sample to share with the class.

Wrap Up Check understanding as you guide students to briefly share what they have learned and produced today

Gather the class. Have several partnerships share their analysis with the class. Then ask students, "What made this conclusion feel more powerful than other conclusions you read today? How can this example help you in your own writing?" Add students' thinking to your Elements of a Strong Editorial chart. **ELL** Provide Comprehensible Input—Organizers.

Reading Lesson 10 . . . .

▼ Teaching Objective

Readers reflect on the core questions.

▼ Standards Alignment

RI.5.10, W.5.4, W.5.10, SL.5.1a–d, L.5.1, L.5.6

▼ Materials

- Chart that lists the core questions for this lesson set

▼ To the Teacher

Reflection is an essential part of this work. It provides students with the necessary time to think about and articulate their own learning, as well as develop and express their identities as readers and writers. Helping students pause and think about what they've learned and what they've enjoyed will have long-lasting effects. This is something you may also want to discuss with families when they visit your classroom or through newsletters or other communications you send home. Emphasize with students that identifying an author's opinions and related reasoning will be a skill that will serve them throughout their lives, no matter what path they choose to take.

▼ Procedure

Warm Up Gather the class to set the stage for today's learning

You have learned so much as readers over these last few weeks. I've watched you confidently conduct your own research, read the work of others to determine their opinions, and analyze their related arguments.

Teach Model what students need to learn and do

Today I want us to take some time to reflect on everything we've learned by studying and creating our own editorials. One thing we learned was that crafting a strong persuasive argument to support your opinion is an art. Now that we've finished going through this process ourselves, I want us to reflect on this question: "How do you build a strong written argument?"

Try Guide students to quickly rehearse what they need to learn and do in preparation for practice

Lead the class in a discussion around this question. As the discussion unfolds, begin to craft a shared response to the question. **ELL** Provide Comprehensible Input—Models. Shared responses will help your ELLs have an example of how they can craft their thinking.

Clarify Briefly restate today's teaching objective and explain the practice tasks

It's important to take some time to reflect on your learning after completing a project. This helps make what you learn stay in your brain so you can use it later. I want to know what you have learned about yourself as a reader

through this process. Today, you are going to write a response to one of our core questions.

Post the questions in a central location for students to refer back as they work.

- How can we use our writing to change the world?
- How can we use mentor texts to guide and inform our own work?
- How and where can we look for information?

Remind and guide students to structure their writing with:

- An introduction
- An answer to the question
- Examples from the reading and work in this lesson set
- Transitional phrases to connect their ideas
- A conclusion

Practice Students work independently or in small groups to apply today's teaching objective

Students individually craft responses to the core questions posed. **ELL** Enable Language Production—Reading and Writing. This is an informal time for you to support ELLs language acquisition in "real time." You may find it helpful to carry sticky notes for quick support and modeling. This is also an opportunity for ELLs to ask for support or clarification in a smaller scale setting.

Goal	Low-Tech	High-Tech
Students craft a written response to one or two reflection questions.	Students answer the questions using pencil and paper. Students share their responses orally. You could choose key snippets of their responses to write up and create a reflection bulletin board.	Students draft a response in a Word document, practicing their keyboarding skills. They can share this document with you by dragging it into a shared folder on Dropbox or via email. In addition, students can post their reflections to a class blog to share with their peers. As homework, students could comment thoughtfully on the reflections of two (or more) of their classmates. Create a VoiceThread to post and preserve audio and visual representations of class reflections on the core questions.

Wrap Up Check understanding as you guide students to briefly share what they have learned and produced today

 After students have had sufficient time to complete their responses, call the class together to share their ideas. Collect student work to assess their understanding of reading and conducting research using multiple informational resources. Let this information help you determine where students need additional guidance or support. **ELL** Assess for Content and Language Understanding—Summative Assessment.

Milestone Performance Assessment

Reflection on Core Questions

 Use this checklist to assess student work on their written reflections on the core questions.

Standards Alignment: RI.5.10, W.5.4, W.5.10, SL.5.1a–d, L.5.1, L.5.6

	Achieved	Notes
Include an opening that introduces the topic of the reflection.		
Accurately answer selected core questions.		
Provide examples and evidence for thinking from texts and/or experiences during the lesson set to support ideas.		
Use transitional words and phrases to link ideas.		
Conclude with summarizing thought.		

Grade 5

Writing Lessons

The following table highlights the teaching objectives and standards alignment for all 10 lessons across the four stages of the lesson set (Introduce, Define, Extend, and Assess). It also indicates which lessons contain special features to support ELLs, technology, speaking and listening, and formative ("Milestone") assessments.

The Core Ready Writing Rubric that follows is designed to help you record each student's overall understanding across four levels of achievement as it relates to the lesson set goals. We recommend that you use this rubric at the end of the lesson set as a performance based assessment tool. Use the Milestone Performance Assessments as tools to help you gauge student progress toward these goals, and reteach and differentiate as needed. See the foundational book, *Be Core Ready: Powerful, Effective Steps to Implementing and Achieving the Common Core State Standards,* for more information about the Core Ready Reading and Writing Rubrics.

Grade 5   Making the Case: Reading and Writing Editorials

Instructional State	Lesson	Teaching Objective	Core Standards	Special Features
Introduce: notice, explore, collect, note, immerse, surround, record, share	1	Writers think about the issues that inspire them to make their voices heard.	W.5.4 • W.5.6 • W.5.10 • SL.5.1a–d L.5.1 • L.5.6	ELL S&L Tech
	2	Writers analyze mentor texts and respond in writing.	RI.5.8 • RI.5.10 • W.5.1 • W.5.4 W.5.6 • W.5.9a • W.5.10 • SL.5.1a–d L.5.1 • L.5.6	ELL Milestone Assessment S&L
Define: name, identify, outline, clarify, select, plan	3	Writers consider their audience.	W.5.4 • W.5.10 • SL.5.1a–d L.5.1 • L.5.6	ELL S&L
	4	Writers craft strong opinion statements about an issue.	W.5.1a • W.5.4 • W.5.7 SL.5.1a–d • L.5.1 • L.5.6	ELL Milestone Assessment S&L
Extend: try, experiment, attempt, approximate, practice, explain, revise, refine	5	Writers plan how their argument will unfold.	W.5.1b • W.5.4 • W.5.5 • W.5.7 W.5.8 • SL.5.1a–d • L.5.1 • L.5.6	ELL Tech
	6	Writers choose visual images to integrate into and strengthen their writing.	W.5.5 • W.5.7 • W.5.8 • SL.5.1a SL.5.1b • SL.5.5 • L.5.1 • L.5.6	ELL Tech
	7	Writers craft powerful, engaging, and clear introductions.	W.5.1a • W.5.4 • W.5.5 • W.5.7 W.5.8 • SL.5.1a–d • L.5.1 • L.5.6	ELL S&L
	8	Writers draft organized and logical arguments to support their opinion.	W.5.1a–c • W.5.4 • W.5.5 • W.5.7 SL.5.1a–d • L.5.1 • L.5.6	ELL Milestone Assessment S&L
	9	Writers craft strong, relevant conclusions.	W.5.1d • W.5.4 • W.5.5 • W.5.7 W.5.8 • SL.5.1a–d • L.5.1 • L.5.6	ELL S&L
Assess: reflect, conclude, connect, share, recognize, respond	10	Writers publish and respond to editorials.	W.5.6 • W.5.7 • W.5.8 • SL.5.1a–d SL.5.4 • SL.5.6 • L.5.1 • L.5.2 L.5.3 • L.5.6	ELL Milestone Assessment Tech

Core Ready Writing Rubric

Grade 5   Making the Case: Reading and Writing Editorials

Lesson Set Goal	Emerging	Approaching	Achieving	Exceeding	Standards Alignment
Connect with an issue or topic that inspires the student to make his or her voice heard.	Makes little or no successful attempt to connect with an issue or topic that inspires him or her to make his or her voice heard.	Attempts to connect with an issue or topic that inspires him or her to make his or her voice heard. May have difficulty choosing topic or articulating why it is inspiring.	Connects with an issue or topic that inspires him or her to make his or her voice heard. Can articulate why it is inspiring.	Connects with an issue or topic that inspires him or her to make his or her voice heard. Articulates a particularly insightful connection or reason for inspiration.	RI.5.8 RI.5.10 SL.5.1a–d
State individual opinions clearly.	Makes little or no successful attempt to state his or her opinion clearly.	Attempts, with some success, to state his or her opinion. May lack focus or clarity.	States his or her opinion with appropriate focus and clarity.	States his or her opinion with exceptional focus and clarity.	W.5.1a W.5.4 W.5.9 W.5.10
Seek out information from print and digital sources to use as evidence to support the opinion on a particular topic or issue.	Makes little or no successful attempt to seek out information from print and digital sources to use as evidence to support his or her opinion on a particular topic or issue.	Attempts, with some evidence of success, to seek out information from print and digital sources to use as evidence to support his or her opinion on a particular topic or issue. Some information may be more relevant and appropriate than others.	Seeks out information that is mostly relevant and appropriate from print and digital sources to use as evidence to support his or her opinion on a particular topic or issue.	Seeks out information that is extremely relevant and appropriate from digital sources to use as evidence to support his or her opinion on a particular topic or issue.	RI.5.1 RI.5.7 RI.5.10 W.5.4 W.5.7 W.5.8 W.5.9 W.1.0
Reflect on the impact of the audience on his or her writing.	Shows little or no evidence or reflecting on the impact of audience on his or her writing. No relationship between writing and audience evident.	Attempts with some success to reflect on the impact of audience on his or her writing. Relationship between writing and audience is somewhat unclear.	Reflects on the impact of audience on his or her writing. Clear relationship between writing and audience.	Shows an exceptional ability to reflect on the impact of audience on his or her writing. Very strong relationship between writing and audience.	W.5.4 W.5.10 SL.5.4 SL.5.6 L.5.1 L.5.6
Craft a logically organized argument composed of relevant facts and details in support of an opinion.	Shows little or no evidence of success crafting an argument composed of facts and details in support of his or her opinion. Lacks focus, organization, and support.	Attempts, with some success, to craft a logically organized argument composed of relevant facts and details in support of his or her opinion. Argument may lack sufficient focus, organization, and support.	Crafts a logically organized argument composed of relevant facts and details in support of his or her opinion. Argument is basically focused, organized, and supported.	Crafts an exceptionally logical and well-organized argument that is clearly focused and comprised of multiple relevant facts and details in support of his or her opinion.	W.5.1a–d W.5.4 W.5.9 W.5.10 SL.5.5
Determine how and where to publish his or her work to reach the intended audience.	Makes little or no successful attempt to determine how and where to publish his or her work to reach the intended audience. No logical rationale for choice.	Attempts to determine how and where to publish his or her work to reach the intended audience. Rationale for choices may be somewhat off track or unclear.	Determines how and where to publish his or her work to reach the intended audience. Rationale for choices is logical and clear.	Determines with extraordinary insight how and where to publish his or her work to reach the intended audience. Presents a very thoughtful rationale for choices.	W.5.6

Lesson Set Goal	Emerging	Approaching	Achieving	Exceeding	Standards Alignment
With guidance and support from peers and adults, develop and strengthen writing as needed by planning, revising, editing, rewriting, or trying a new approach.	Student makes little or no attempt to develop and strengthen writing through planning, revising, and editing.	Student attempts to develop and strengthen writing as needed by planning, revising, and editing.	Student develops and strengthens writing as needed by planning, revising, and editing. Some areas of the planning, revision, and editing may be more developed than others.	Student extensively develops and strengthens writing by planning, revising, and editing as needed.	W.5.5
Quote accurately from a text when explaining what the text explicitly says and when drawing inferences from the text.	Student shows little or no evidence of active, purposeful reading or searching the text for specific quotes, information, and evidence. Student makes little or no attempt to provide accurate details and examples when explaining what the text says explicitly and is unable to draw inferences from the text.	Student shows some evidence of active, purposeful reading and searching the text for specific quotes, information, and evidence. Student may provide some details and examples, with limited accuracy, when explaining what the text says explicitly and when drawing inferences from the text.	Student shows solid evidence of active, purposeful reading and searching the text for specific quotes, information, and evidence. Student usually provides appropriate and accurate details and examples when explaining what the text says explicitly and when drawing inferences from the text.	Student demonstrates exceptional evidence of active, purposeful reading and searching the text for specific information and evidence. Student provides accurate, explicit, and thoughtful details and examples when explaining what the text says explicitly and when drawing inferences from the text.	RI.5.1
Write an organized opinion piece that includes a clear introduction, point of view, supporting reasons, linking words and phrases, and a concluding statement.	Student writes an opinion piece with little or no evidence of introductory or concluding statements. Does not articulate a clear point of view and supporting reasons are missing or insufficient. Omits linking words and phrases or uses them inconsistently.	Student writes an opinion piece and attempts to include introductory and concluding statements. Attempts to identify a point of view but supporting reasons are weak or irrelevant. Includes some linking words and phrases.	Student writes an opinion piece with solid introductory and concluding statements. Articulates a point of view and supports it with relevant evidence and reasons. Uses linking words and phrases when appropriate.	Student writes an effective opinion piece with strong introductory and concluding statements. Point of view is apparent and supported with clear and relevant reasons. Consistently uses linking words and phrases when appropriate.	W.5.1
By the end of the year, independently and proficiently read and comprehend a variety of informational texts at the high end of the grades 4–5 text complexity band.	Student shows little or no evidence of reading and comprehending texts appropriate for the grade 5 text complexity band.	Student shows inconsistent evidence of independently and proficiently reading and comprehending texts appropriate for the grade 5 text complexity band.	Student shows solid evidence of independently and proficiently reading and comprehending texts appropriate for the grade 5 text complexity band.	Student shows solid evidence of independently and proficiently reading and comprehending texts above the grade 5 text complexity band.	RI.5.10
Write routinely over extended time frames (time for research, reflection, and revision) and shorter time frames (a single sitting or a day or two) for a range of discipline-specific tasks, purposes, and audiences.	Student shows little or no evidence of writing routinely for short or long time frames for a range of discipline-specific tasks, purposes, and audiences.	Student shows some evidence of writing routinely for short and long time frames for a range of discipline-specific tasks, purposes, and audiences.	Student shows solid evidence of writing routinely for short and long time frames for a range of discipline-specific tasks, purposes, and audiences.	Student shows exceptional evidence of consistently and accurately writing for short and long time frames for a range of discipline-specific tasks, purposes, and audiences.	W.5.10

Core Ready Writing Rubric, Grade 5, *continued*

Lesson Set Goal	Emerging	Approaching	Achieving	Exceeding	Standards Alignment
In collaborative discussions, demonstrate evidence of preparation for discussion and exhibit responsibility to the rules and roles of conversation.	In collaborative discussions, student comes unprepared and often disregards the rules and roles of conversation.	In collaborative discussions, student's preparation may be evident but ineffective or inconsistent. May occasionally disregard the rules and roles of conversation.	In collaborative discussions, student prepares adequately and draws on the preparation and other information about the topic to explore the ideas under discussion. Usually observes the rules and roles of conversation.	In collaborative discussions, student arrives extremely well prepared for discussions and draws on the preparation and other information about the topic to explore ideas under discussion. Always observes the rules and roles of conversation.	SL.5.1a SL.5.1b
In collaborative discussions, share and develop ideas in a manner that enhances understanding of topic. Contribute and respond to the content of the conversation in a productive and focused manner.	Student shows little or no evidence of engaging in collaborative discussions and makes little or no attempt to ask and answer questions, stay on topic, link his or her comments to the remarks of others, or to explain his or her own ideas and understanding in light of the discussion.	Student shows some evidence of engaging in collaborative discussions and with marginal success attempts to ask questions to check understanding of information presented, to stay on topic, link his or her comments to the remarks of others, and explain his or her own ideas and understanding in light of the discussion.	Student engages in a range of collaborative discussions and asks questions to check understanding of information presented, stays on topic most of the time, and frequently links his or her own ideas and understanding in light of the discussion.	Student effectively and consistently engages in a range of collaborative discussions and asks high level questions to check understanding of information presented, always stays on topic, and with great insight and attention to the comments of others links his or her own ideas and understanding in light of the discussion.	SL.5.1c SL.5.1d
Demonstrate knowledge of standard English and its conventions.	Student demonstrates little or no knowledge of standard English and its conventions.	Student demonstrates some evidence of knowledge of standard English and its conventions.	Student consistently demonstrates knowledge of standard English and its conventions.	Student demonstrates an exceptional understanding of standard English and its conventions.	L.5.1 L.5.2 L.5.3
Acquire and accurately use grade-appropriate conversational, general academic, and domain-specific vocabulary and phrases.	Student shows little or no evidence of the acquisition and use of grade-appropriate conversational and academic language.	Student shows some evidence of the acquisition and use of grade-appropriate conversational and academic language.	Student shows solid evidence of the acquisition and use of grade-appropriate conversational and academic language.	Student shows a high level of sophistication and precision with the acquisition and use of grade-appropriate conversational and academic language.	L.5.6

Note: See the Core Ready Rubrics chart in the Welcome at the beginning of the book for descriptions of category headers.

Writing Lesson 1 ●

▼ Teaching Objective

Writers think about the issues that inspire them to make their voices heard.

▼ Standards Alignment

W.5.4, W.5.6, W.5.10, SL.5.1a–d, L.5.1, L.5.6

▼ Materials

- Charting supplies or interactive whiteboard

▼ To the Teacher

The following lesson allows students the opportunity to explore issues that matter to them. Allowing students to write about topics that feel important to them will inspire higher-quality writing.

▼ Procedure

Warm Up Gather the class to set the stage for today's learning

Gather your students. Announce that for the next few weeks you will be focusing on the issues and opinions they care about most.

> Fifth graders, we are all engaged members of this classroom, our school, our neighborhood communities, and the world. We see things happening around us and have our own concerns about issues that affect us every day. What are some of the concerns you have about our classroom, our school, our neighborhood, or the world? What issues feel the most important to you right now?

Allow students to share and discuss the issues and concerns that are important to them. **ELL** Frontload the Lesson—Activate Prior Knowledge. During this time, you can consider ELLs brainstorming important issues in their native language if they are newer arrivals. A bilingual student can help them translate and share their concerns that are important to them. Jot down a few of these ideas on a chart titled "What Matters to Us" to refer back to later in your teaching.

Teach Model what students need to learn and do

For the next few weeks, we are going to study and author our own editorials. An editorial is an article that presents an opinion on a topic or issue and then proceeds to give reasons to support that opinion. **ELL** Identify and Communicate Content and Language Objectives—Key Content Vocabulary. ELLs benefit from explicit vocabulary instruction when encountering new ideas and novel content. Consider the native language connection where possible as well as visualizing or providing examples of any relevant definitions. The first step, however, is thinking about an issue or topic that you feel strongly about. This is your opportunity to make your voice heard in a real way, so what do you want to say? What opinions do you want to put out in the world?

Think aloud about a topic that is important to you. You can select an issue that feels close to your heart or, for the purposes of this lesson set, we have chosen the issue of animal adoption. As you think aloud about your topic, take this opportunity to demonstrate to students that there is a wide variety of topics that can be relevant, from issues of global health to more local concerns in your neighborhood, school, or family. The point is for students to choose a topic they feel inspired to write about, rather than guiding students to choose a topic of general concern for all individuals. **ELL** Frontload the Lesson—Make Connections. ELLs bring a lot of background knowledge and interests from their native language and concerns from their home country. Think of ways you can honor and incorporate these things into their topic choice. Here is how your modeling could unfold if animal adoption were important to you:

> The news is filled with topics for our editorials—from stories about hungry children in countries far away to information about the struggles of our planet. I think about all of these things, as well as issues that are more local such as the lack of a coffeemaker in the teachers' room. But, as many of you know, animal adoption is a cause that is near and dear to my heart. I believe that all families should consider rescuing a pet of some sort—dogs, cats, fish, turtles, whatever! There are a lot of animals that need good homes.

Explain to the class that you are going to begin this journey with a free write. The purpose of a free write is for students to get their ideas down on paper in a way that makes the most sense to them. It is an opportunity for them to explore a topic or issue without the constraints of a particular genre or format. See the following table for both low- and high-tech options for this writing.

Goal	Low-Tech	High-Tech
Students compose at least two pages of freewriting that explores a topic or issue about which the student feels passionate.	Students write freely in a notebook or on loose-leaf paper.	Students write freely using a word processing program such as Word or Pages, demonstrating the keyboarding skills necessary to compose two pages in a single sitting.

Although it is not necessary to take the time to model composing an entire free write in front of students, you do want to provide students with some guidance as to aspects of their topic or issue to consider, such as:

- What is your opinion about this topic or issue?
- Why do you feel inspired to write about this topic or issue?
- What is your personal experience with this topic or issue?
- How do you want to change people's actions or thinking about this topic or issue?

Chart each of these questions for students to refer to as needed while they write. **ELL** Provide Comprehensible Input—Organizers. Be sure to take a moment to ensure that students understand each of these questions before moving on, using your own topic as a model for answering these questions orally.

Try Guide students to quickly rehearse what they need to learn and do in preparation for practice

So what are you thinking about? What issues or topics concern you the most and inspire you to make your voice heard? Turn and share your ideas with a partner.

As students share with one another, take this opportunity to reinforce the importance of several essential speaking and listening skills, such as following agreed-on rules for being a respectful listener (even when you don't agree with what your partner is saying). (SL.5.1b)

Animal Adoption

People who want pets for their families should adopt from animal shelters. Sadly, there are countless animals sitting in shelters with no families to love. When my family wanted to get a dog, we visited the local animal shelter. In visiting, we found the animals in to be healthy, fully vaccinated, and friendly.

Luckily, during our visit to the shelter, we found an adorable dog. After playing with him, we decided that this dog was a perfect match for us! So, we brought him home.

> Everyone has been happy since we brought Jake home. Finding Jake was good for all of us. We did not have to spend a lot of money, he came to us healthy, and he loves us as much as we love him! Jake seems has been loyal and loving since the day we brought him home. Who would not want a healthy, friendly pet who has so much love to offer?

Gather the class after they have had sufficient time to discuss their initial ideas with a partner. Ask students, "Are there any issues or topics you feel like we need to add to the chart we started earlier in this lesson?" Allow students time to share their ideas and add them to your What Matters To Us chart as appropriate.

Clarify Briefly restate today's teaching objective and explain the practice tasks

Send the group off to write freely about their chosen topic or issue.

Today I want you to just get your ideas about this topic or issue down on the paper. You can let your writing take you where ever you feel like you need to go. I'd like each of you to write at least two pages today. If you feel stuck, don't forget to check in with the list of questions I posted for you to consider. They will really help to get your thinking going again!

Practice Students work independently or in small groups to apply today's teaching objective

Students work independently to write at least two pages about the topic or issue that inspires them to make their voices heard. As students work, check in with various individuals and briefly discuss the topic or issue they have chosen to focus on. Guide students who may need additional support selecting an issue (large or small) that lends itself to editorial writing.

Wrap Up Check understanding as you guide students to briefly share what they have learned and produced today

Ask students to have their writing available to discuss with a partner. Instruct partners to share several ideas that surfaced for them during their freewriting. **ELL** Enable Language Production—Increasing Interaction. During partner time, consider making partnerships where all the partners speak the Native Language so that partners have a forum of clarification in either language.

This Wrap Up presents a wonderful opportunity to highlight and reinforce essential speaking and listening skills, such as listening with respect and care as your partner speaks, as well as posing questions that specifically relate to the topic or issue being addressed. (SL.5.1b, SL.5.1c)

Writing Lesson 2

▼ Teaching Objective

Writers analyze mentor texts and respond in writing.

▼ Standards Alignment

RI.5.8, RI.5.10, W.5.1, W.5.4, W.5.6, W.5.9a, W.5.10, SL.5.1a–d, L.5.1, L.5.6

▼ Materials

- Student copies of "Big Food, Big Soda: Ban Supersized Drinks" (Appendix 5.3)
- Method for highlighting text
- Take a Closer Look Question Sheet (see Appendix 5.7)

▼ To the Teacher

The purpose of today's lesson is to introduce students to the structure of an editorial. This lesson serves as a first pass of this essential material and is meant to provide students with a broad overview of the genre. Subsequent lessons in both the reading and writing lesson sets will address each aspect of an editorial in greater detail.

▼ Procedure

Warm Up Gather the class to set the stage for today's learning

Fifth graders, now that you have chosen the issues you want to write about we need to get writing and make your voices heard. Now that we have your initial ideas captured on paper, it's time to think about the structure of an editorial. Understanding the structure of an editorial will help us give shape to our argument and allow us to speak our minds in a way that is powerful.

Teach Model what students need to learn and do

Explain to the class that editorials have several distinct parts: an introduction, a statement of opinion, an argument, and a conclusion. Take the time to introduce and define each of these parts, charting notes about each as you go. **ELL** Identify and Communicate Content and Language Objectives—Key Content Vocabulary. **ELL** Provide Comprehensible Input—Organizers. This organizer will offer the structure that your ELLs need to understand about editorials. Make sure it is easy for them to access visually, either displayed or through their own personal copy. Here are some brief definitions of each section:

- Introduction: The introduction needs to grab the attention of your reader. It should also briefly explain the issue or topic to be discussed.

- Statement of opinion: Use strong language to clearly state your opinion. This is your chance to get the audience's mind ready for the argument you are about to present.

- Argument: The argument in an editorial is made up of a series of logically organized reasons. These reasons are usually based on research.

- Conclusion: The conclusion provides a solution to the issue and/or challenges the reader to think differently. Your goal is to end with a punch that summarizes your opinion and argument.

Now, share with your class an example of an editorial. You can choose any well-written editorial from a recent local or national newspaper; however, for the purposes of this lesson set, we are using an example of an editorial written about the health dangers associated with supersized soda.

Distribute student copies of "Big Food, Big Soda: Ban Supersized Drinks." Read the editorial aloud as students follow along. Then, turn back to the text and model for students how to code the editorial to highlight each of the parts you discussed earlier. **ELL** Provide Comprehensible Input—Models. Be sure to refer back to the chart you created about the various parts of an editorial in order to encourage students to do the same in their own work.

Highlight the introduction section with yellow. Then, label that section "introduction." **ELL** Provide Comprehensible Input—Visuals.

Look at this—the introduction for this editorial is an entire section.

Next, highlight the opinion statement with green. Label that section "opinion statement."

Did you notice where in the introduction the author placed her opinion? It's in the last two full sentences in the introduction. That makes sense—she introduced us to the issue of self-esteem and then stated her opinion. Now, we're ready for her argument.

Try Guide students to quickly rehearse what they need to learn and do in preparation for practice

Work with students to code the argument. Choose a different color to highlight each of the reasons presented to support the opinion given in this editorial. Through class discussion, guide students to identify each of the reasons given by the author. As you code your editorial, students should be coding their copy of the editorial as well. Then, ask students to pair up to identify, highlight, and label the conclusion.

Clarify Briefly restate today's teaching objective and explain the practice tasks

As we prepare to write our own editorials about issues we are passionate about, it's important to become familiar with the structure of this genre. We've highlighted this mentor editorial to show the introduction, statement of opinion, argument, and conclusion. Now I want you to take a closer look at this editorial and think more deeply about some of these questions in writing.

Introduce the class to the Take a Closer Look Question sheet. Take a moment to read through it and be sure that students understand what is being asked.

Practice Students work independently or in small groups to apply today's teaching objective

Students work independently to more deeply analyze this editorial in writing using the Take a Closer Look Question sheet. Students focus on the opinion and argument presented in the editorial, identifying the reasons and evidence used to support the point of view of the author.

Wrap Up Check understanding as you guide students to briefly share what they have learned and produced today

Gather the class, asking each of them to have their work handy (SL.5.1a). Then, discuss the questions asked on the Take a Closer Look Question sheet. Lead the class in a discussion.

What were the author's main points? How did the author use reasons and evidence to support particular points within this editorial?

Collect and analyze student work. Can students successfully articulate the reasons given by an author to support a particular point? Use your analysis to guide future teaching. Do you need to spend additional time practicing this skill with the entire class or perhaps a small group? **ELL** Assess for Content and Language Understandings—Formative Assessment. Take this time to think about language that might have been confusing or need further clarification when looking at the formative assessment, this can help drive further scaffolds in future lessons.

Milestone Performance Assessment

Analyzing Editorial Components

Use this checklist to assess the Taking a Closer Look Question sheets.

Standards Alignment: RI.5.8, RI.5.10, W.5.1, W.5.4, W.5.6, W.5.9a, W.5.10, SL.5.1a–d, L.5.1, L.5.6

	Achieved	Notes
Identify the opinion(s) expressed in the editorial.		
Identify evidence and reasons that support the opinion(s).		
Explain how reasons or pieces of evidence support the opinion(s).		

There is occasions and causes why and wherefore in all things.

—William Shakespeare

Writing Lesson 3

▼ Teaching Objective
Writers consider their audience.

▼ Standards Alignment
W.5.4, W.5.10, SL.5.1a–d, L.5.1, L.5.6

▼ Materials

- Students should have their free writes from Writing Lesson 1

▼ Procedure

Warm Up Gather the class to set the stage for today's learning

Let's review what you've accomplished so far. You've chosen a topic or issue to express your opinion about, you have your thinking captured in writing, and you have an idea of the basic structure of a strong editorial. We're almost ready to get started writing, but first we need to consider our audience. Who do you want to read your work? How are you going to reach them?

Teach Model what students need to learn and do

Explain to the class that editorials are written with a desired audience in mind. The intended audience influences all aspects of the editorial—how the author constructs his or her argument, the tone of the editorial, even the author's word choice. **ELL** Identify and Communicate Content and Language Objectives—Key Content Vocabulary. This may be a time that you try to connect vocabulary to native language through bilingual students in the class translating or through online translation sites. You can also restate the information in different ways, scaffolding the content until it becomes comprehensible through various examples. Sometimes authors target a group of people they would like to move to action; these are people who usually are inclined to agree with the author's point of view and just need a push to get motivated to create change. Other times, authors target a group of people whose thoughts they want to influence or challenge; these are usually people who disagree with the author's point of view.

Model thinking about the audience for your editorial. **ELL** Provide Comprehensible Input—Models.

When I think about the audience of my editorial, two different groups of people come to mind. I could write for an audience of readers who don't particularly care about or understand animals who need to be adopted and try to change their thinking. Although, if there are people who don't like animals, I'm not sure how I'm going to change their minds. Or, I could write for an audience of readers who already love animals and perhaps just need a convincing push to visit their local adoption shelter. That seems like a good fit for me.

Demonstrate writing a few sentences to describe your intended audience. **ELL** Provide Comprehensible Input—Models.

Try Guide students to quickly rehearse what they need to learn and do in preparation for practice

Now that I've identified my intended audience, I have to think about how I'm going to reach them. Where can I publish or display my work? I need to think about how I'm going to get my message to these kinds of families.

Ask students to turn and talk, sharing with one another ideas for how to bring your message to the intended audience. **ELL** Enable Language Production—Increasing Interaction. You can aid partnerships in talk and language structures by listening in on partnerships with ELLs. You can support if needed by offering input to extend language during their brainstorm. Listen in and encourage students to push their thinking beyond the newspaper. Consider the following questions to guide their thinking:

- Are there online sites or locations you can consider?
- Are there physical locations your audience tends to visit?

Once students have had a few moments to share their ideas, work with the class to compose several shared sentences to finish identifying your intended audience and how you plan to reach them.

Clarify Briefly restate today's teaching objective and explain the practice tasks

It's important to consider your audience when writing an editorial. Your intended audience will impact the tone of your editorial, the language you choose, and the reasons you use to support your point of view. Today I want each of you to think about the audience you'd like to reach. Then, write a brief paragraph describing your audience, as well as some ideas about where you might publish your work to ensure that it reaches that audience.

Practice Students work independently or in small groups to apply today's teaching objective

Students work independently to identify and describe the intended audience for their editorial as well as how they plan to reach that audience. Students should be prepared to share and discuss their work at the end of the writing period. (SL.5.1a)

Students can use the following guiding questions:

- What is the purpose of your piece?
- Who might your audience be?
- Do they agree with you and need inspiration to act?
- Do they disagree with you and need convincing reasons to change?
- How can you connect with or relate to this audience through the tone of your writing? Be more casual? More formal?
- How can you make it likely that they will read your message?
  - Consider how you will publish your message.
  - Consider locations and resources to distribute it.

Wrap Up Check understanding as you guide students to briefly share what they have learned and produced today

Divide your class into small groups of three or four students each. Then, ask students to share their ideas about audience with one another. **ELL Enable Language Production—Increasing Interaction.** Emphasize speaking and listening skills such as listening respectfully, posing questions, and making comments that contribute to the speaker's ideas about audience. (SL.5.1b, SL.5.1c)

Writing Lesson 4 ···

▼ Teaching Objective

Writers craft strong opinion statements about an issue.

▼ Standards Alignment

W.5.1a, W.5.4, W.5.7, SL.5.1a–d, L.5.1, L.5.6

▼ Materials

- "Big Food, Big Soda: Ban Supersized Drinks" (Appendix 5.3)
- "The Importance of Owning a Dog" (see Appendix 5.2)
- Charting supplies or interactive whiteboard

▼ Procedure

Warm Up Gather the class to set the stage for today's learning

Now that you've identified your audience, it's time to begin writing by crafting a strong opinion statement to drive your editorial. It sounds like an easy thing to do—after all, you're just writing a sentence or two expressing how you really feel. But today we're going to think deeply about how to craft this statement to be as powerful as possible by asking:

- How can I express my opinion clearly and succinctly?
- What strong language choices can I use to state my opinion more powerfully?

Teach Model what students need to learn and do

Turn back to "Big Food, Big Soda: Ban Supersized Drinks" the editorial you coded during Writing Lesson 2. Return to the opinion statement you highlighted with students (the last two sentences in the first section of the editorial). Briefly discuss this opinion statement with your students.

Is this opinion statement clear? What do you notice?

Explain to the class that their opinion statement will be embedded within their introduction. Therefore, it is important to use words and phrases that signal to the reader that an opinion is coming. Introduce several phrases or sentence starters for students to rely on in their own writing. (See the Core Phrases in the introduction to the lesson set for more possibilities.) Chart these phrases for students to refer back to during their own work. **ELL Provide Comprehensible Input—Organizers.** These structures and sentence ideas are a helpful tool for ELLs to use when formulating their thinking. If needed, practice how they sound in context through examples at their language proficiency level. Here are a few to consider:

- In my opinion. . . .
- I feel/think that. . . .
- Personally. . . .
- It is my belief that. . . .

Now it's time to model using a combination of these phrases and strong language choices to clearly and succinctly state your opinion. **ELL** Provide Comprehensible Input—Models. Do this by crafting an opinion statement for your own editorial in front of the class. (If you wish, you can use the sample editorial supplied for you in Appendix 5.2. Simply pull out the opinion statement to use during this lesson.)

Write "In my opinion, adopting a dog seems like a no brainer because there are too many dogs currently living in shelters that need a good home and too many reasons why having a dog can make your life better."

> Did you notice how I began my opinion statement with one of the phrases we discussed earlier? The words "in my opinion" signal to the reader that my opinion is coming and that they need to pay attention. I also used the words "no brainer" to make the action I want my readers to take sound obvious. This is also a very casual phrase, which helps to establish the friendly tone I'd like to achieve in my editorial. Finally, I summarize and highlight some of the reasons I plan to use in my argument at the end of this sentence.

Try Guide students to quickly rehearse what they need to learn and do in preparation for practice

> Let's take another look at the opinion the author expressed in "Big Food, Big Soda: Ban Supersized Drinks." I think we can make it even stronger by using some of the phrases that signal an opinion. I also think we can choose stronger language that packs a more powerful punch.

Work with students to rewrite the opinion from "Big Food, Big Soda: Ban Supersized Drinks." Begin this revised opinion statement with one of the signal words or phrases and discuss stronger language choices with your class. Attempt to express this opinion in one clear and succinct sentence.

Clarify Briefly restate today's teaching objective and explain the practice tasks

The opinion statement might be the most important part of your editorial. It is essential that you signal to your reader that your opinion is coming by using some of the key phrases we discussed today. As you work to craft your opinion statement today, be sure to ask yourself:

- How can I express my opinion clearly and succinctly?
- What strong language choices can I use to state my opinion more powerfully?

Practice Students work independently or in small groups to apply today's teaching objective

Students work independently to craft strong opinion statements to use in their editorials. Students should be prepared to share and discuss their opinions with a partner at the end of the writing time. (SL.5.1a)

© iofoto / Fotolia

Gather the class and ask students to share their opinion statements with a partner. **ELL** Enable Language Production—Increasing Interaction. This is an important time for partners to support each other in their work. You can listen in to partnerships with newer ELLs to support their thinking and extend their vocabulary. Partners should demonstrate careful listening, as well as an ability to ask questions or make comments that aid the speaker in improving his or her work. In response, students review the comments made and decide on revisions that should be made to strengthen their opinion statement. (SL.5.1b–d)

Writing Lesson 5

▼ Teaching Objective

Writers plan how their argument will unfold.

▼ Standards Alignment

W.5.1b, W.5.4, W.5.5, W.5.7, W.5.8, SL.5.1a–d, L.5.1, L.5.6

▼ Materials

- Speaking My Mind graphic organizer (see Appendix 5.8)
- Parts of an Editorial chart (created with the class during Writing Lesson 2)
- Student free writing (composed during Writing Lesson 1)
- Student writing about audience (composed during Writing Lesson 3)
- Student research (compiled during Reading Lessons 3–5) should be handy for student reference during the Try portion of this lesson

▼ Procedure

Warm Up Gather the class to set the stage for today's learning

We have been working hard to develop strong and clear opinions that we can share with the world. Today is an important day—we are going to begin to plan out our arguments using a graphic organizer. Before we begin, who can remind me, what are the components of a strong edito-

rial? **ELL** Frontload the Lesson—Activate Prior Knowledge. Activating prior knowledge can help ELLs brainstorm the words that they may need in English to explain what they already understand about the topic.

As students share the various parts of an editorial, be sure to have them define each part.

Teach Model what students need to learn and do

Introduce students to the Speaking My Mind graphic organizer. **ELL** Provide Comprehensible Input—Organizers. Remember to include small examples or visuals in your organizer to offer a visual tie to editorial parts. Draw students' attention back to the Parts of an Editorial chart you created during Writing Lesson 2. Reiterate the key parts of an editorial as you explain the graphic organizer, focusing your attention on any aspects that students may have forgotten.

Students, so far you have studied the structure of editorials, chosen a topic you're passionate about, drafted a strong opinion statement, and compiled research to support your opinion. Now it's time to use the Speaking My Mind graphic organizer to pull all of these pieces together and help you organize your writing in a logical way so that the reader can easily follow your train of thought and reasoning.

Demonstrate filling out the beginning of the Speaking My Mind graphic organizer for the class. **ELL** Provide Comprehensible Input—Models. Think aloud about how you already have many of the pieces figured out and simply need to transfer them to the graphic organizer to help you plan the flow of your writing. For example, students should be able to easily move their statement of opinion over to the graphic organizer.

Now turn to your research notes. Model skimming through your notes to organize them into broad categories. Think aloud about how can you easily combine the evidence you've gathered into three or four strong reasons to support your point of view. For example, you might notice several statements about how dogs push people to be more active. Circle these statements in red. Then, scan the remainder of your notes for any similar statements and circle those in red as well. You've now coded your notes, highlighting one reason (dogs push people to be more active) that you can add to your graphic organizer.

Try Guide students to quickly rehearse what they need to learn and do in preparation for practice

Instruct students to take out the notes they've gathered on their issue or topic. Tell them to begin to read through their notes and identify one reason to support their point of view and circle it in red. Students should read through the remainder of their notes to circle similar evidence in red as well.

 Once students have had a moment to complete this task, ask them to turn and share their point of view and this first bit of reasoning with a partner. **ELL** Enable Language Production—Increasing Interaction. Partner time offers a chance for ELLs to ask for clarification in English and practice their thinking in English. As you circulate, aid ELLs if you hear them struggle by modeling sentence structures if needed.

Clarify Briefly restate today's teaching objective and explain the practice tasks

Authors of editorials do a lot of preparation before they begin to write. Today, our focus has been on creating a logical plan for our argument using the Speaking My Mind graphic organizer. Each of you will use this graphic organizer to plan your arguments, which is the final step before we start writing. Be prepared to share your graphic organizer with a partner.

Practice Students work independently or in small groups to apply today's teaching objective

Students synthesize information from their freewriting and research, as well as knowledge of their intended audience, as they create a plan for logically structuring their editorial. Students record this plan on the Speaking My Mind graphic organizer.

Wrap Up Check understanding as you guide students to briefly share what they have learned and produced today

Ask students to share and explain their graphic organizers with a partner. Partners should pay close attention and respond directly to the organization of their partner's argument. Partners can use the following questions as a guide:

- Is the argument organized?
- Are the reasons given to support the opinion relevant?
- Is there anything missing or confusing about your partner's plan?

 Collect and analyze student work at the end of this lesson. Use this analysis to determine whether students (either the whole class or a small group) need additional support creating clear and relevant reasons substantiated by research to support their opinions. **ELL** Assess for Content and Language Understandings—Formative Assessment. You can take this time to analyze the language needs of your ELLs and plan how to support them as you progress through the lessons.

Milestone Performance Assessment
Planning for Effective Editorials

Use this checklist to assess student Speaking My Mind graphic organizers.

Standards Alignment: W.5.1b, W.5.4, W.5.5, W.5.7, W.5.8, SL.5.1a–d, L.5.1, L.5.6

	Achieved	Notes
Express a strong opinion statement.		
Provide at least three logical reasons to support opinion.		
Develop reasons with evidence and research.		

Writing Lesson 6

▼ Teaching Objective

Writers choose visual images to integrate into and strengthen their writing.

▼ Standards Alignment

W.5.5, W.5.7, W.5.8, SL.5.1a, SL.5.1b, SL.5.5, L.5.1, L.5.6

▼ Materials

- Recent copy of your local newspaper
- "Big Food, Big Soda: Ban Supersized Drinks" (Appendix 5.3)
- "Texting Instead of Talking: Are Text Messages Destroying Communication?" (Appendix 5.4)
- "Zoos: Good for Animals and People" (Appendix 5.5)
- Speaking My Mind graphic organizers (completed during Writing Lesson 5)
- Computers with Internet access (for high-tech option)
- Drawing supplies (for low-tech option)

▼ To the Teacher

A picture of worth a thousand words. This lesson encourages students to consider the potential power of visual images on an editorial.

▼ Procedure

Warm Up Gather the class to set the stage for today's learning

Share with students a current copy of your local or other newspaper. Choose several articles with strong accompanying visuals to discuss. Focusing on one article at a time, read the title and summarize the content. Then give students a moment to take a longer look at the image that accompanies the article. Ask, "How does this image help you to better understand this story? In what ways does it make this news story more powerful?"

Teach Model what students need to learn and do

Images certainly are powerful tools that can help strengthen and clarity to your point of view. Let's take a look at some of the mentor texts we've returned to again and again throughout this lesson set.

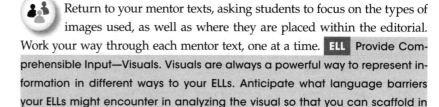 Return to your mentor texts, asking students to focus on the types of images used, as well as where they are placed within the editorial. Work your way through each mentor text, one at a time. **ELL Provide Comprehensible Input—Visuals. Visuals are always a powerful way to represent information in different ways to your ELLs. Anticipate what language barriers your ELLs might encounter in analyzing the visual so that you can scaffold in the moment.** For each article, ask:

- What images do you see?
- Where are these images located within the editorial?
- Why do you think the author chose to put the image in that particular location?
- How does the image included serve to enhance the point of view of the article?

Guide students toward understanding that strong visuals can work to make an author's point of view even more powerful by reinforcing certain images in the minds of the reader.

I'd like all of us to consider what types of visuals we can include in our own editorials to strengthen our arguments and drive home our point of view for the reader.

Turn back to your Speaking My Mind graphic organizer and review the various reasons you plan to include in your argument. Think aloud about and list the types of images that would complement or enhance the point of view stated in your model editorial. For example, for the model editorial about pet ownership, images to consider using include:

- Dogs locked in shelters
- Dogs in need of homes

- Happy dogs playing with a family
- Happy dogs out for a walk with a family

Model for students how to look for or create these images. Use the chart below to guide your decision about including the low-tech or high-tech option.

Goal	Low-Tech	High-Tech
Students locate or create visual images to enhance or support any aspect of the point of view stated in their editorial. (Note: Take care to allow students to only use images from outside sources that don't require permissions.)	Students photocopy images found in the print resources they have used for research during the reading lesson set, or students draw the images themselves.	Students use drawing software to create original images, or students conduct a search for existing images using Google Images, Flickr, or another stock photography resource.

Once you have a set of images to consider, think about *where* each of these images should be included.

> When I think about our mentor editorials, I noticed that there weren't too many images. An editorial is still mostly about the text, so I want to be careful to only include those images that really drive my point home. Let me use my Speaking My Mind graphic organizer to help. By looking back carefully at each part of my editorial, I can decide if I need an image at all, and if I do, what image would work best. I can jot down my idea on my graphic organizer in the correct location to remind myself of these decisions later on.

Demonstrate rereading through your graphic organizer, stopping at each section to ask yourself: "Do I need an image here to enhance my point? If so, what image would be most powerful?" Jot your decisions down on the graphic organizer to refer to later. Explain how students are to store their visuals for later use. **ELL** Provide Comprehensible Input—Models. This model will be what your ELLs will refer to when working independently. Think of what you can provide given their varied language proficiencies.

Try Guide students to quickly rehearse what they need to learn and do in preparation for practice

Instruct students to take out their own Speaking My Mind graphic organizers. Provide students with several minutes to review their plan, stopping at each section to ask themselves: "Do I need an image here to enhance my point? If so, what image would be most powerful?" Remind students to jot their ideas in a list to refer to later.

As students review their graphic organizers, circulate and support student thinking. Listen for examples of strong ideas to share with the class.

Clarify Briefly restate today's teaching objective and explain the practice tasks

> Including strong images in specific places within your editorial can help to make your writing more powerful. Today, finish thinking about a list of images you'd like to consider incorporating into your work, using your graphic organizer as a guide. Then, search for and create these images. Finally, think about exactly where these images will fit best into your work, recording your ideas on your graphic organizer.

Practice Students work independently or in small groups to apply today's teaching objective

Students work independently to generate a list of images to consider incorporating into their editorials. Once students have sought out or created these resources, they should work to make decisions about where to include them, recording relevant notes on their graphic organizer.

Wrap Up Check understanding as you guide students to briefly share what they have learned and produced today

Gather the class, asking each of them to bring an example of a strong visual image they have discovered or created. Have students share their image with a partner and explain the image itself as well as how it will enhance their editorial. Then, ask several students to share their work and thinking with the entire class.

Writing Lesson 7

▼ Teaching Objective

Writers draft organized and logical arguments to support their opinion.

▼ Standards Alignment

W.5.1a, W.5.4, W.5.5, W.5.7, W.5.8, SL.5.1a–d, L.5.1, L.5.6

▼ Materials

- "The Importance of Owning a Dog" (see Appendix 5.2, Sample Editorial)
- Elements of a Strong Editorial chart (created during Reading Lesson 7)

▼ Procedure

Warm Up Gather the class to set the stage for today's learning

Review the Elements of a Strong Editorial chart that you began with students during Reading Lesson 7. Ask students to recap what they have learned about the introductions to editorials by studying a variety of mentor texts. **ELL** Frontload the Lesson—Activate Prior Knowledge. This is another opportunity for ELLs to ask questions and clarify their thinking as you launch into a new lesson.

Teach Model what students need to learn and do

Reinforce that there are several strong ways to introduce a topic or issue for an editorial. Share, explain, and give an example of each type of introduction (as it relates to your editorial topic), adding each type of introduction to your chart as necessary. **ELL** Provide Comprehensible Input—Organizers. Provide Comprehensible Input—Models.

- A summary of the issue or topic addressed: This strategy often incorporates one or two strong statistics.
  - The Humane Society estimates that somewhere between 6 and 8 million pets enter animal shelters each year.

- A strong image: This strategy uses words to paint a clear picture of the topic or issue being discussed.
  - Imagine a puppy who has spent the last year living in a small cage. His nose pokes through the bars, his eyes stare up at you, begging you to take him home. You see his tail begin to wag as you pause by his cage, and you realize in that moment that you could change this puppy's life.

- A personal story: This strategy shares an experience from the author's life that illustrates the topic or issue being discussed in a way that helps to reinforce the opinion stated.
  - Before I was a dog owner, I came home every night to a house full of people who were all too busy doing their own thing to even say hello. My husband sat reading the paper, my children were in their rooms getting a head start on their homework. But now that we have Gabby, everything is different. Now, I come home to cheerful house filled with laughter and activity. The dog runs to greet me as my children trail after her, anxious to go outside for our ritual family walk together.

So, how do you choose which type of introduction is right for your editorial? Well, it's important to consider your intended audience. Who are they and which tactic will have the largest impact on them? Remember, this is your opportunity to make a first impression with your writing.

Demonstrate thinking aloud about your intended audience and the type of introduction you have chosen to pack the most punch. Now, share your introduction with the class, displaying your writing as you simultaneously read it aloud. Highlight for students your chosen introduction as well as where you included your statement of opinion. **ELL** Provide Comprehensible Input—Models. This will be a model that your ELLs refer to when working

Try Guide students to quickly rehearse what they need to learn and do in preparation for practice

Ask students to work in pairs. Each student should share a brief description of his or her intended audience as a way to initiate a discussion about the best type of introduction for that specific group of people. Partners should work collaboratively to reach a decision. This lesson represents an excellent opportunity to reinforce several essential speaking and listening skills, such as careful listening and asking questions or making comments that aid the speaker in reaching a decision. In response, students review the comments made and draw a conclusion as to which type of introduction would be the most powerful. (SL.5.1b-d)

Clarify Briefly restate today's teaching objective and explain the practice tasks

As we reflect on what we have learned about the introductions to editorials and we begin to make decisions about the direction of our own writing, it is essential to consider the intended audience for our editorials. Which type of introduction will be the most powerful and create the strongest first impression with this specific group of people?

Instruct students to work independently to craft their introductions. Students should be prepared to share and discuss their work at the end of this lesson. (SL.5.1a)

Practice Students work independently or in small groups to apply today's teaching objective

Student work independently to craft a strong introduction to their editorial modeled after a specific type of introduction discussed during the Teach portion of this lesson.

Wrap Up Check understanding as you guide students to briefly share what they have learned and produced today

Ask students to return to the same partner they worked with during the Try portion of this lesson. Each student should take turns sharing their work.

Partners should aid the writer in revising, editing, or rewriting this section as necessary.

Then, ask one or two students to share their work with the entire class. In addition to reading their work aloud, students should define their intended audience for the class and explain why they chose this particular type of introduction for their editorial.

> Ah, don't say that you agree with me. When people agree with me I always feel that I must be wrong.
>
> — Oscar Wilde

Writing Lesson 8

▼ Teaching Objective

Writers draft organized and logical arguments to support their opinions.

▼ Standards Alignment

W.5.1a–c, W.5.4, W.5.5, W.5.7, SL.5.1a–d, L.5.1, L.5.6

▼ Materials

- "The Importance of Owning a Dog" (see Appendix 5.2, Sample Editorial)
- Elements of a Strong Editorial chart (created during Reading Lesson 7)
- Speaking My Mind graphic organizer (see Appendix 5.8)
- Charting supplies or interactive whiteboard
- Pre-made chart of transitional phrases

▼ To the Teacher

This lesson focuses on students drafting the body or argument of their editorials. Your students have worked with a variety of resources to collect a range of research and facts to support their thinking. Today, students must integrate this information, organizing it into a logical flow of reasons. This is sophisticated work! As a result, this lesson may be best implemented across more than one day, providing students with adequate time to draft, share, and revise their work.

▼ Procedure

Warm Up Gather the class to set the stage for today's learning

Review the Elements of a Strong Editorial chart that you began with students during Reading Lesson 7. Ask students to recap what they have learned about the arguments put forth in editorials by studying a variety of mentor texts. **ELL** Frontload the Lesson—Activate Prior Knowledge. As in previous lessons, this is an opportunity to clarify thinking and create connections for your ELLs. Often the wait time during this activity will offer a chance for them to explain their thinking.

Teach Model what students need to learn and do

Reinforce that there are a couple of aspects students should consider including in their arguments. Share, explain, and give an example of each (as it relates to your editorial topic), adding relevant notes to your chart as necessary. **ELL** Provide Comprehensible Input—Organizers. **ELL** Provide Comprehensible Input—Models.

- A logically organized series of reasons: Reasons are typically organized from strongest to second strongest to least strong.

  I want organize my reasons logically, putting the strongest one first to grab the reader at the outset. Let me look back at the Speaking My Mind graphic organizer and put a 1 next to the strongest reason I want to use first, a 2 next to my second reason, and a 3 next to the reason that I want to save for last.

- A paragraph that addresses the opposing point of view: It's important to acknowledge this point of view and dismiss it using intelligent reasoning, not just declaring it ridiculous.

  I know that people opposed to adopting pets might mention the money and time required to care for a dog. I certainly can't say that it won't cost any time or money—that's not true. Instead I have to acknowledge this point and then defuse this argument by including a positive spin on these realities.

Transitional words and phrases are crucial to organizing your argument and linking ideas together. Outline several types of transitional words and phrases students can use to craft a smoother argument. Cluster these transitional phrases by purpose and display them on a chart for students to refer back to. See the Core Phrases section of this lesson set for examples.

Now, share the body of your editorial (the argument) with the class, displaying your writing as you simultaneously read it aloud. Highlight each of your reasons for students and show where you refute the opposition. Then, take the time to point out the transitional phrases you incorporated into your writing and discuss how these phrases link together your ideas, creating a more flowing argument. **ELL** Provide Comprehensible Input—Models. You can offer a paper copy of transitional phrases at the level of your ELLs to support them while they are working independently.

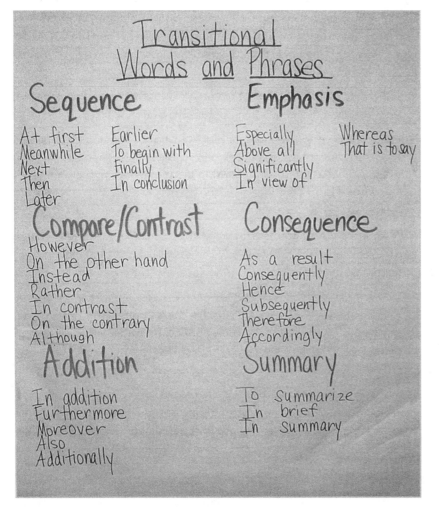

Transitional Words and Phrases

Sequence
At first   Earlier
Meanwhile   To begin with
Next   Finally
Then   In conclusion
Later

Compare/Contrast
However
On the other hand
Instead
Rather
In contrast
On the contrary
Although

Addition
In addition
Furthermore
Moreover
Also
Additionally

Emphasis
Especially   Whereas
Above all   That is to say
Significantly
In view of

Consequence
As a result
Consequently
Hence
Subsequently
Therefore
Accordingly

Summary
To summarize
In brief
In summary

Try Guide students to quickly rehearse what they need to learn and do in preparation for practice

Ask students to take out their Speaking My Mind graphic organizers and independently reflect on their own reasoning. Each student organizes their reasons, putting the strongest reason first, and indicates their decisions with numbers on their graphic organizer.

As students work, circulate and support their decision making. Choose one or two students to share their opinion statements, the organization of their reasoning, as well as the rationale behind unfolding their arguments in this way.

Clarify Briefly restate today's teaching objective and explain the practice tasks

As we reflect on what we have learned about how to craft strong arguments within our editorials, it is essential to organize our reasons so that they will unfold logically for our readers.

Instruct students to work independently to craft the body of their editorial. Students should be prepared to share and discuss their work at the end of this lesson. (SL.5.1a)

Practice Students work independently or in small groups to apply today's teaching objective

Students work independently to draft the argument portions of their editorials, including both reasons that support their point of view as well as an acknowledgment of the opposing point of view.

Wrap Up Check understanding as you guide students to briefly share what they have learned and produced today

Ask students to work with a partner. Each student should take turns sharing their work. Partners should aid the writer in revising, editing, or rewriting this section as necessary.

This lesson represents an excellent opportunity to reinforce several essential speaking and listening skills such as careful listening and the ability to ask questions or make comments that aid the writer in refining his or her argument. In response, students should review the comments made and draw conclusions as to how to revise and strengthen their arguments. (SL.5.1b–d)

 Collect and analyze student work at the end of this lesson. Determine whether students need additional support with logically organizing their reasoning, fully developing their reasoning, expressing their ideas clearly, or using transitional words and phrases effectively. Use this information to direct your instruction on subsequent days as students continue to draft their arguments. **ELL** Assess for Content and Language Understandings—Formative Assessment. This is the time you will understand the language supports and scaffolds needed for upcoming work.

Milestone Performance Assessment

Composing Effective Editorials

Use this checklist to assess student editorials at this point.

Standards Alignment: W.5.1a–c, W.5.4, W.5.5, W.5.7, W.5.7, SL.5.1a–d

	Achieved	Notes
Lead is engaging.		
Introduction provides useful background information about the topic.		
Make a clear, strong opinion statement.		
Provide three reasons to support the opinion.		
Develop reasons with evidence and research.		
Use transitional words and phrases to link and clarify ideas.		

Writing Lesson 9

▼ Teaching Objective

Writers craft strong, relevant conclusions.

▼ Standards Alignment

W.5.1d, W.5.4, W.5.5, W.5.7, W.5.8, SL.5.1a–d, L.5.1, L.5.6

▼ Materials

- "The Importance of Owning a Dog" (see Appendix 5.2, Sample Editorial)
- Elements of a Strong Editorial chart (created during Reading Lesson 7)
- Editorials Checklist (Appendix 5.9)

▼ Procedure

Warm Up Gather the class to set the stage for today's learning

Review the Elements of a Strong Editorial chart that you began with students during Reading Lesson 7. Ask students to recap what they have learned about the conclusions to editorials by studying a variety of mentor texts. **ELL** Frontload the Lesson—Activate Prior Knowledge.

Teach Model what students need to learn and do

Reinforce that there are several strong ways to conclude an editorial. Share, explain, and give an example of each type of conclusion (as it relates to your editorial topic), adding each type of conclusion to your chart as necessary. `ELL` Provide Comprehensible Input—Organizers. `ELL` Provide Comprehensible Input—Models. These examples can be offered for personal use and easy reference for your ELLs through smaller personal copies of these conclusion examples.

- A summary of the issue or topic addressed: This strategy often incorporates one or two strong statistics. This is not the best choice if students used this type of introduction.

  - The Humane Society estimates that somewhere between 6 and 8 million pets enter animal shelters each year.

- A rhetorical question: This strategy definitely leaves your reader thinking.

  - If you don't step forward to save the life of a dog in need, who will?

- A strong quotation from a reliable source.

  - "If you choose to take in a stray dog, you will likely have a dog that will be loyal for life" (www.dogrescuers.org).

So, how do you choose which type of conclusion is right for your editorial? Well, just like we did when choosing the most effective type of introduction, it's important to consider your intended audience. Who are they and which tactic will have the biggest impact on them? Remember, this is your opportunity to create a lasting impression in the mind of your reader.

Demonstrate thinking aloud about your intended audience and the type of conclusion you have chosen to pack the most punch. Now, share your conclusion with the class, displaying your writing as you simultaneously read it aloud. Highlight for students your chosen conclusion as well as where you included your statement of opinion. `ELL` Provide Comprehensible Input—Models.

Try Guide students to quickly rehearse what they need to learn and do in preparation for practice

Ask students to work in pairs. Each partner should share a brief description of his or her intended audience as a way to initiate a discussion about the best type of conclusion for that specific group of people.

Partners should work collaboratively to reach a decision. This lesson represents an excellent opportunity to reinforce several essential speaking and listening skills, such as careful listening and the ability to ask questions or make comments that aid the speaker in reaching a decision. In response, students review the comments made and draw a conclusion as to which type of conclusion would be the most powerful. (SL.5.1b–d)

Clarify Briefly restate today's teaching objective and explain the practice tasks

As we reflect on what we have learned about the conclusions to editorials and begin to make decisions about the direction of our own writing, it is essential to consider the intended audience for our editorials. Which type of conclusion will be the most powerful and create a lasting impression in the minds of our readers?

Instruct students to work independently to craft their conclusions. Students should be prepared to share and discuss their work at the end of this lesson. (SL.5.1a)

Practice Students work independently or in small groups to apply today's teaching objective

Students work independently to craft strong conclusions to their editorials modeled after specific types of conclusions discussed during the Teach portion of this lesson.

Wrap Up Check understanding as you guide students to briefly share what they have learned and produced today

Ask students to return to the same partner they worked with during the Try portion of this lesson. Students should take turns sharing their work. Partners should aid the writer in revising, editing, or rewriting this section as necessary. Partners can rely on the Editorials Checklist to guide their work together. Then, ask one or two students to share their work with the entire class.

Writing Lesson 10

▼ Teaching Objective

Writers publish and respond to editorials.

▼ Standards Alignment

W.5.6, W.5.7, W.5.8, SL.5.1a–d, SL.5.4, SL.5.6, L.5.1, L.5.2, L.5.3, L.5.6

▼ Materials

- Student editorials
- Computer access
- One mentor editorial from www.sciencenewsforkids.org
- Charting supplies or interactive whiteboard

▼ To the Teacher

Today's lesson is meant to be celebratory and help students build important reflection skills. Emphasize with students that making their voices heard in effective ways is an important skill and they now have some tools for sharing their point of view. The particulars of this day of recognition will be influenced by your choice of either the low-tech or high-tech option.

Goal	Low-Tech	High-Tech
Students share their editorials with their intended audiences and their classmates.	Students type up their editorials and submit them to relevant publications for consideration or ask to have them displayed in relevant locations. Teachers combine student editorials into one class newspaper to distribute to parents and the school community. Consider inviting responses to editorials.	Students post their editorials on a class blog. Students read and respond to the editorials of at least two other students. Students read and record their editorials, combining the audio with a series of powerful images using SmileBox, iMovie, or another similar application.

▼ Procedure

Warm Up Gather the class to set the stage for today's learning

> Today we will share our voices and opinions with the outside world.

Teach Model what students need to learn and do

Explain to students your chosen method for publishing and sharing their work with the world (see previous chart). Use your own editorial to model the process, charting key steps and guidelines for students to refer back to as you go. Be sure to emphasize the importance of keyboarding skills by reminding students of the expectation that they can type two pages of text in a single sitting. Take a moment and share your final product with the class, discussing your process along the way.

Try Guide students to quickly rehearse what they need to learn and do in preparation for practice

Prepare students for the possibility of receiving a response to the message they are putting out into the world.

> You may receive responses to your work from people who agree with you, which is a wonderful feeling. However, you may also receive a response from someone who disagrees with everything you have to say and that's OK, too. We are lucky to be able to welcome such debate and it is a sign of your maturity to be able to take in the opposition, consider their points, and ultimately stay true to your opinions and beliefs (or refine them). Similarly, we may encounter a classmate's opinion with which we strongly disagree. Again, that is OK. It is not OK, however, to attack that author personally.

Guide students in creating thoughtful and respectful responses to the opinions of others by crafting a class shared response to one of the mentor editorials you have been working closely with for the last few weeks.

Clarify Briefly restate today's teaching objective and explain the practice tasks

Refer back to the process chart that outlines how you would like students to finalize and share their editorials. Allow students the time and opportunity to ask questions and clarify their responsibilities.

Practice Students work independently or in small groups to apply today's teaching objective

Students work to finalize, publish, and share their editorials.

Wrap Up Check understanding as you guide students to briefly share what they have learned and produced today

Have students read and respond to the editorials written by at least two of their classmates. Remind them of the need to respond thoughtfully and respectfully.

 Collect students' final editorials and responses to classmates and use the writing rubrics to analyze their work.

ELL Assess for Content and Language Understanding—Summative Assessment. This is a great time to reflect on your ELLs' language proficiency from the beginning of the unit until the end. Take this time to compare their writing from lesson 1 to this assessment to reflect on how you taught into their language needs. This is also an opportunity to think about their needs and how to support their language proficiency in upcoming work.

Language Companion Lesson

This lesson is best taught shortly after students have established the topics for their editorials.

▼ Teaching Objective

Writers use content-specific words to make their writing stronger.

▼ Common Core State Standards Alignment

L.5.6, W.5.1c

▼ Materials

- Student copies of alpha-box chart with selected academic transition words already filled in
- Enlarged copy of the same chart
- Reading material for students' individual topics

▼ To the Teacher

This lesson focuses on the importance of using academic vocabulary and topic-specific words to strengthen writing. Many students overuse conversational language in their writing, avoiding general academic and domain-specific words and phrases that would clarify and strengthen their message. This lesson helps them gather and use words to enhance their editorial writing.

▼ Procedure

Warm Up Gather the class to set the stage for today's learning

Present the following two passages to the students to read with these questions in mind:

- What do both passages have in common?
- What are the differences between the two passages?

- Which passage provides the most information to the audience?
- Which passage do you think would be most convincing to the audience?

Editorial Passage 1	Editorial Passage 2
Our town needs a skate park. More and more kids like to skateboard, but there is no place for them to go. We need a park with lots of stuff to do on our skateboards. A park would let us learn new tricks and become better skaters. Not as many kids would get hurt. Not as many kids would get in trouble for skating and hanging out in places like shopping malls and the steps in town because they would have a good place to go in town. Maybe kids in town can help find money to do this.	Riverville needs a skateboard park. Skateboarding has become very popular in recent years with our citizens, but the town has no recreational facility for skaters with the jumps, ramps, and other obstacles that skaters need. A skate park would allow boarders to build their skills and practice key maneuvers like spins, flips, and turns. Skate park architects follow strict safety regulations. Consequently, fewer skaters suffer injuries. In addition, not as many skateboarders would get in trouble for skating and loitering in places like shopping malls and public staircases because they would have an appropriate facility in the community. Perhaps young townspeople could hold fundraisers to help pay for a new skate park in Riverville.

After reading, engage students in a discussion about their responses to the questions. Guide students to notice the academic phrases and topic-specific vocabulary in the second passage. Then discuss the benefits of using academic vocabulary:

- It sounds more formal, which is important when appealing to others in writing.
- Phrases like "In addition" and "Consequently" help connect ideas logically.
- Using specific words clarifies the message to the audience.
- The writer sounds more like an expert on a topic when including specific vocabulary.

Teach Model what students need to learn and do

I am going to introduce you to a tool that will help you gather academic vocabulary to use in your editorials.

Present an enlarged alpha-box chart to the class. There should be some general academic phrases already filled in on the chart, as in the sample in Appendix 5.6. (See the Core Words and Core Phrases in the introduction of this lesson set for additional ideas.)

What are some of the topic-specific words or phrases that the author of Passage 2 used?

Fill these in on the chart under the appropriate letter. Do not try to get them all. A few will suffice to illustrate how to organize words on the chart. Explain that writers can use the alpha-box chart to gather topic-specific vocabulary in advance. The alpha-box chart then becomes a word bank students can use when it is time to write.

Try Guide students to quickly rehearse what they need to learn and do in preparation for practice

Distribute alpha-box charts to all students. Ask students to try to think of specific words that could be important when writing about their topics. They should fill in three to five ideas under the appropriate letters.

Explain that sometimes it is challenging to just think of words, but we can also get ideas from reading about our topics. We can borrow words from these topic-related sources.

Clarify Briefly restate today's teaching objective and explain the practice tasks

Explain that students will spend time reading about their topics. As they read, they should be on the lookout for topic-specific words that might be useful for their editorial writing. They should fill these in on the alpha-box chart.

Practice Students work independently or in small groups to apply today's teaching objective

Students read and gather topic-specific vocabulary.

Wrap Up Check understanding as you guide students to briefly share what they have learned and produced today

Have a few students shared some of the words they gathered.

- What words did you find?
- How do you imagine you might use that word in your editorial?

Restate the benefits of using academic vocabulary in editorial writing. *Important*: Save the alpha-box charts to use as reference during the writing process.

Academic Language Alpha-Box

A	B	C Consequently	D
E	F Furthermore For example For instance	G	H However
I In addition I have argued that	J	K	L Likewise
M Most of all	N	O On the other hand	P
Q	R	S Similarly Specifically	T
U	V	W X	Y Z

> " There is no good in arguing with the inevitable. The only argument available with an east wind is to put on your overcoat.
>
> — James Russell Lowell

GLOSSARY

Acknowledge: to admit or recognize the truth, existence, or validity of a point of view.

Argument: a discussion in which there is disagreement along with presentation of various sides of an issue.

Conclude: to bring to an end; finish or complete.

Editor: a person who prepares written materials for publication or film for viewing.

Editorial: an article or commentary, as in a newspaper or on television, that expresses an opinion or viewpoint.

Evidence: the basis for belief; that which constitutes proof of something.

Opinion: what one thinks about a person or matter, especially a judgment not necessarily based on fact alone.

Opposition: the act or state of opposing, or the state of being opposed or opposite to; those on the other side of an argument.

Ordering: the way something is organized or arranged in space or time.

Periodical: a publication composed of issues that appear at regular intervals.

Position: the appropriate location of a person or thing.

Stance: the opinions or attitude of someone with regard to something.

Support: to provide evidence for; prove with facts and reasoning. Courtesy of the author

PD **pd** TOOLKIT™

Accompanying *Core Ready* for Grades 3–5, there is an online resource site with media tools that, together with the text, provides you with the tools you need to implement the lesson sets.

The PDToolkit for Pam Allyn's *Core Ready* Series is available free for 12 months after you use the password that comes with the box set for each grade band. After that, you can purchase access for an additional 12 months. If you did not purchase the box set, you can purchase a 12–month subscription at **http://pdtoolkit.pearson.com.** Be sure to explore and download the resources available at the website. Currently the following resources are available:

- Pearson Children's and Young Adult Literature Database
- Videos
- PowerPoint Presentations
- Student Artifacts
- Photos and Visual Media

- Handouts, Forms, and Posters to supplement your Core-aligned lesson plans
- Lessons and Homework Assignments
- Close Reading Guides and Samples
- Children's Core Literature Recommendations

In the future, we will continue to add additional resources. To learn more, please visit **http://pdtoolkit.pearson.com.**

In this unit we are going to be making some new friends. We are going to spend time reading within a series of books. A series is a set of books, written by the same author, that share the same characters and same type of stories. Once you read a few books from a series, you'll start to feel like those characters are old friends. You will be working in teams for this lesson set. I've put each of you into a Core Crew. Together, you will choose and study a series together. It's going to be your job to get to know everything about your series—the settings, the plots, and the themes you might find—so you can prove to the class that your series is the best, the most interesting, the funniest, or the most important for third graders to read.

APPENDIX 3.2 Story Elements Graphic Organizer

Name: ______________________________ Date: ______________

Title: ______________________________

____

____

Author: ______________________________

____

____

Character(s): ______________________________

____

____

Setting(s): ______________________________

____

____

Problem: ______________________________

____

____

Solution: ______________________________

____

____

Plot (Key Events): ______________________________

____

____

Name: _____ Date: _____

THEME
Be on the lookout for . . .

What characters do	What characters say	How characters change

Text Evidence of the Theme

What characters learn	These items go hand in hand with the theme

Name: _____   Date: _____

I usually enjoy books and series in the following genres (mystery, adventure, fantasy, realistic fiction, etc.):

I usually enjoy books and series with the following types of settings (school, magical worlds, sporting events, etc.):

I usually enjoy books and series with plots and themes about (friendship, seeking adventure, overcoming hardships, fighting evil, etc.):

Even though I don't normally choose this type of book or series, I plan to expand my reading and try (describe a different type of book or series to try):

List specific books, authors, or series for your future reading list:

Judy Moody Gets Famous

Have you ever had your picture in the paper? In **Judy Moody Gets Famous**, by Megan McDonald, we see just how far Judy will go to see her name in print. While Judy may be famous in her family for her many melo-dramatic moods, and famous in her third-grade class for getting white cards, she has never had her picture in the local newspaper. Judy doesn't know what she's missing until her classmate, Jessica Finch, informs her that not only did she have her picture in the paper as champion of the re-gional spelling bee, but she even won a tiara. Judy is jealous. Since she is not a very talented speller, she soon realizes that she won't be getting famous anytime soon for her spell-ing. She tries to think of other ways to become famous, and her failed attempts are always hilarious. In the end, Judy does not become famous, or at least not in the way she first imagined.

I enjoyed this book because it was really witty and Judy is a lovable character. The author, Megan McDon-ald, has a sharp sense of humor that makes this book very entertaining. For example, when Judy hears about her classmate's success at the spelling bee spelling the word **artichoke**, Judy thinks about how she can barely spell **meatloaf**. She "felt about as famous as a pencil." Determined to become fa-mous, Judy tries out all sort of zany things. She carves "GW" on a chewed-up cherry pit and claims it belonged to the tree George Washington chopped down. She has her cat make toast in a talent competition for pets, but the closest she comes to fame is getting her elbow in the corner of a picture in the newspaper.

The ending of this book came as a surprise to me, because Judy does not exactly get famous. Instead she does something generous and thoughtful for someone else without getting any credit for it. She does a good deed but remains anonymous. This seems to be more satisfying to her than get-ting her picture in the paper for some-thing small and silly, and it makes for a much more interesting story. This was a fun book with a helpful lesson at the end.

Name: _____ Date: _____

Book Title: _____

Important characters	Connections to your life (*it reminds me of . . .*)
Setting	Compliments for the author (with explanation)
Important parts of the plot • Opinion 1 with example(s) from the story	Compliments for the illustrator (with explanation)
• Opinion 2 with example(s) from the story	To whom you would recommend the book
• Opinion 3 with example(s) from the story	

The Knights of the Kitchen Table

The Knights of the Kitchen Table, by Jon Scieszka, is about three boys. Their names are Joe, Fred, and Sam. The boys discover that a magic book given to them by Joe's uncle gives them the power to travel back in time. Poof! They travel back to the time of King Arthur. The rest of the story is about how they try to find the magic book so they can get back to their own time period. This is the first book in the Time Warp Trio series, and I think it is great because it is full of adventure and is very funny.

I loved how the book is full of adventure. For example, in the beginning, Joe, Fred, and Sam fight the Black Knight. The fight is very exciting and makes you wonder if they will win or lose. They win! They also meet other knights who take them to fight a smelly giant and an angry dragon. Sam tricks the giant by telling him the dragon said he was a weakling, so the giant and the dragon fight each other. The giant and dragon kill each other with a big explosion!

After that, people think the boys are heroes. They even do card tricks for Queen Guinevere and get knighted by King Arthur! Finally, Merlin the magician helps them get back to their own time.

The Knights of the Kitchen Table is also hilariously funny. One of my favorite lines was when the boys were about to get stabbed by the knight's lance. Joe says "three regular guys happened to find themselves facing death by shish-kebab." Another hysterical part was when the dragon makes fire at the same time the giant passes gas, and they both get blown up! In addition, it was really funny when the boys teach the stable boys baseball, and the ball accidentally flies into Merlin's tower.

Every chapter of The Knights of the Kitchen Table makes you wonder what will happen next and keep reading. It can even teach you about a new time period in a fun way. If you like funny books with lots of adventure about time travel, this is definitely the book for you!

Name: _____   Date: _____

Revising	Yes or No	Notes
Did I include a strong lead?		
Did I include an introduction with a brief summary (without solution)?		
Did I include at least one opinion statement with specific support from text?		
Did I include a strong conclusion?		
Did I use transitional phrases to connect ideas?		
COPS Editing Checklist		
Capitals—I remembered to use capitals correctly.		
Order and usage of words: I have reread my sentences, and they all sound right and make sense.		
Punctuation–I have used correct punctuation.		
Spelling–I have corrected my spelling errors.		

Standards Alignment: RL.3.2, RL.3.5, RL.3.9, W.3.4, SL.3.2

Reading Lesson 4
Milestone Performance Assessment: Creating Succinct Summaries

Use this checklist to assess student summaries.

Name: _____   Date: _____

	Achieved	Notes
Summary includes key characters.		
Summary includes setting.		
Summary includes problem.		
Summary includes solution.		
Summary includes key events in plot in sequence.		
Summary is succinct (not a retelling).		

Standards Alignment: RL.3.1, RL.3.2, RL.3.5, RL.3.9

Reading Lesson 6
Milestone Performance Assessment: Determining Theme with Text Evidence

Use this checklist to assess student work on the Thinking about Theme graphic organizer.

Name: _____   Date: _____

	Achieved	Notes
Identify a theme present in the text.		
Provide text evidence of the theme (connected to what characters say, do, and learn, and how they change).		

Standards Alignment: RL.3.1, RL.3.5, RL.3.9, W.3.4, W.3.10

Reading Lesson 7

Milestone Performance Assessment: Comparing Multiple Texts in a Series

Use this checklist to assess student work comparing texts with a Venn diagram.

Name: _____ Date: _____

	Achieved	Notes
Venn diagram includes setting, plot, and theme for each book.		
Venn diagram indicates items both texts have in common.		
Make a broad statement about the series that connects to what is common across multiple texts.		

Standards Alignment: RL.3.1, RL.3.2, RL.3.5, RL.3.9, W.3.4, W.3.8, SL.3.1a-b, SL.3.3, SL.3.4, SL.3.6, L.3.1, L.3.6

Reading Lesson 9

Milestone Performance Assessment: Comparing Elements across Texts

Use this checklist to assess student presentations on their study of a series.

Name: _____ Date: _____

	Achieved	Notes
Include an accurate summary of each text.		
Articulate themes suggested across the series with relevant examples from the text.		
Make a broad statement about the series that connects to what is common across multiple texts.		
Include relevant information about the author and how this information connects to the content of the series.		
Collaborate effectively with group in preparing and presenting the material.		

Standards Alignment: RL.3.1, RL.3.4, W.3.1a, W.3.10, SL.3.1a

Writing Lesson 2
Milestone Performance Assessment: Articulating Strong Opinions of a Text

Use this checklist to assess student Strong Opinion T-charts.

Name: _____ Date: _____

	Achieved	Notes
Articulate three or more strong opinions of the text.		
Mention specific text elements, structure, or author's writing.		

Standards Alignment: W.3.1a, W.3.1b, W.3.4, W.3.10

Writing Lesson 5
Milestone Performance Assessment: Writing Persuasive Book Reviews

Use this checklist to assess student book review drafts at this point.

Name: _____ Date: _____

	Achieved	Notes
Draft includes a strong lead.		
Draft includes an introduction with a succinct summary (without solution).		
Draft includes at least one opinion statement with specific support from text.		

Standards Alignment: W.3.1a-d, W.3.6, W.3.10, SL.3.6, L.3.1, L.3.2, L.3.3

Writing Lesson 9
Milestone Performance Assessment: Writing Persuasive Book Reviews

Use this checklist to assess student book reviews.

Name: _____   Date: _____

Revising	Yes or No	Notes
Include a strong lead.		
Include an introduction with a succinct summary (without solution).		
Include at least one opinion statement with specific support from text.		
Include a strong conclusion.		
Use transitional phrases to connect ideas.		
Follow teacher-directed procedures to publish review.		
COPS Editing Checklist		
Correct **c**apitalization.		
Correct **o**rder and usage of words.		
Correct **p**unctuation.		
Correct **s**pelling.		

Writing Lesson 10
Milestone Performance Assessment: Writing to Persuade

Use this checklist to assess students' persuasive writing pieces.

Name: _____   Date: _____

	Achieved	Notes
Include an engaging lead.		
Introduction answers question.		
Provide strong and precise reasons to support thinking.		
Use transitional words and phrases to connect ideas.		
Include a strong conclusion.		

The following checklist provides observable Core Standards–aligned indicators to assess student performance as speakers and listeners. Use it in its entirety to gather performance data over time or choose appropriate indicators to create a customized checklist to match a specific learning experience.

Student's Name: _____ **Topic of Study:** _____ **Time Frame:** _____

Performance Indicator	Achieved	Notes
Actively engages in collaborative discussions in a variety of settings (student partnerships, student groups, teacher-led). [SL.3.1]		
Prepares for discussions in advance and uses this preparation to enhance discussion. [SL.3.1a]		
Follows agreed-upon rules for discussions (active listening, taking turns to speak, etc.). [SL.3.1b]		
Contributes to discussions by commenting on the ideas of others, asking questions, and explaining ideas. [SL.3.1c, SL.3.1d]		
Demonstrates understanding of the main idea from a given source such as read-aloud or other media and formats. [SL.3.2]		
Asks and answers questions in detail using information from a speaker. [SL.3.3]		
Reports on a topic, story, or experience with focus and accurate detail. [SL.3.4]		
Speaks clearly and at an understandable pace. [SL.3.4]		
Creates engaging audio recordings that demonstrate reading fluency. [SL.3.5]		
Uses visual displays to enhance presentations. [SL.3.5]		
Elaborates in complete sentences appropriate to the task and situation. [SL.3.6]		

Did you ever find you had something to say but you weren't sure how to say it? Did you ever find you were full of ideas and weren't sure how to share them? Did you ever find you were inspired by something and wanted to make your own version? Poetry is the perfect small package for our messages to the world. In this lesson set, we're going to read poems and think about what we like about them, what we don't, what we can learn from them, and how we can find poems to honor through our own writing. This lesson set is about reading poems closely and carefully to consider all the things the writer is trying to tell us in such a small space. This lesson set is also about writing our own poems, and modeling them after poems that speak to us. Finally, this lesson set is about discussing, debating, and persuading others to agree with what you think poems *really* mean.

Words Free as Confetti

Come, words, come in your every color.
I'll toss you in storm or breeze.
I'll say, say, say you,
Taste you sweet as plump plums,
bitter as old lemons,
I'll sniff you, words, warm
as almonds or tart as apple-red,
feel you green
and soft as new grass,
lightweight as dandelion plumes,
or thorngray as cactus,
heavy as black cement,
cold blue as icicles,
warm as *abuelita*'s yellowlap.
I'll hear you, words, loud as searoar's
Purple crash, hushed
as *gatitos* curled in sleep,

as the last goldlullaby.
I'll see you long and dark as tunnels,
bright as rainbows,
playful as chestnutwind.
I'll watch you, words, rise and dance
and spin.
I'll say, say, say you
in English,
in Spanish,
I'll find you.
Hold you.
Toss you.
I'm free too.
I say *yo soy libre*,
I am free
free, free,
free as confetti.

Source: Words Free as Confetti a poem from Confetti Poems for Children text copyright © 1996 by Pat Mora. Permission arranged with LEE & LOW BOOKS INC., New York, NY 10016.

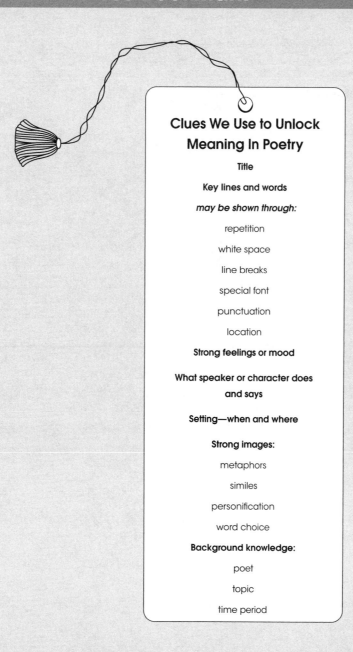

Clues We Use to Unlock Meaning In Poetry

Title

Key lines and words

may be shown through:

repetition

white space

line breaks

special font

punctuation

location

Strong feelings or mood

What speaker or character does and says

Setting—when and where

Strong images:

metaphors

similes

personification

word choice

Background knowledge:

poet

topic

time period

Name: _____   Date: _____

Structures	Poems in which structure can be found
• Repetition	
• White space	
• Line breaks	
• Special font	
• Punctuation	
• Location	

Fog

The fog comes

on little cat feet.

It sits looking

over harbor and city

on silent haunches

and then moves on.

Source: Chicago Poems by Carl Sandburg, Henry Holt and Company, New York: NY 1916.

The New Colossus

Not like the brazen giant of Greek fame,

With conquering limbs astride from land to land;

Here at our sea-washed, sunset gates shall stand

A mighty woman with a torch, whose flame

Is the imprisoned lightning, and her name

Mother of Exiles. From her beacon-hand

Glows world-wide welcome; her mild eyes command

The air-bridged harbor that twin cities frame.

"Keep, ancient lands, your storied pomp!" cries she

With silent lips. "Give me your tired, your poor,

Your huddled masses yearning to breathe free,

The wretched refuse of your teeming shore.

Send these, the homeless, tempest-tossed to me,

I lift my lamp beside the golden door!"

Source: The Poems of Emma Lazarus, Volume I, pages 202–203, Houghton, Mifflin and Company. New York, NY 1899.

XXXIII.

IN THE GARDEN.

A bird came down the walk:
He did not know I saw;
He bit an angle-worm in halves
And ate the fellow, raw.

And then he drank a dew
From a convenient grass,
And then hopped sidewise to the wall
To let a beetle pass.

He glanced with rapid eyes
That hurried all abroad,—
They looked like frightened beads, I thought;
He stirred his velvet head

Like one in danger; cautious,
I offered him a crumb,
And he unrolled his feathers
And rowed him softer home

Than oars divide the ocean,
Too silver for a seam,
Or butterflies, off banks of noon,
Leap, plashless, as they swim.

Source: "In the Garden," from *Poems by Emily Dickinson, Series Two*, Section III, Nature, Poem XXIII. Edited by T. W. Higginson and
Mabel Loomis Todd, Boston: Roberts Brothers 1892.

Name: _____ **Date:** _____

Please *honestly* answer the following questions about poetry.

1. How much do you like poetry on a scale of 1 to 5 (1 being you really don't like it and 5 being you like it a lot)? Please explain. _____
   _____
   _____

2. What is the title of your favorite poem? _____
   _____
   _____

3. What is the name of your favorite poet? _____
   _____
   _____

4. Please list any other poets' names that you know: _____
   _____
   _____

5. What do you *like* about poetry? _____
   _____
   _____

6. What do you *dislike* about poetry? Please explain. _____
   _____
   _____

7. Have you ever written poetry? _____
   _____
   _____

8. How much of a poet do you consider yourself (1 being not at all and 5 being a lot)? Please explain._____
   _____
   _____

Tribute: "Swimming in a Lake on a Sunny Afternoon"

On the lake, calm waters I have found.
Floating, listening to water's sound;
Time leaves me be while I linger here
Rocking and bobbing as waves come round.

The motor boats that pass me by
Must shake their heads and wonder why
I stay still, not moving or rushing
Sparkling surface, sun in the sky.

They pass near and give a wave
Wondering if I am theirs to save.
I turn my face into the breeze
Warm and delivering a scent I crave.

The water is gentle, strong and true.
But I am not an island, things come due
And the current draws me back to land,
And the current draws me back to land

Standards Alignment: RL.4.5, SL.4.2

Reading Lesson 3
Milestone Performance Assessment: Examining Poetic Structures

Use this checklist to assess student work in identifying and explaining the importance of structures in poetry.

Name: _____   Date: _____

	Achieved	Notes
Accurately identify one or more structures in a poem.		
Provide logical explanations of how the structure was important to the poem.		

Standards Alignment: RL.4.1, RL.4.4

Reading Lesson 5
Milestone Performance Assessment: Examining Poetic Images

Use this checklist to assess student work with identifying strong images in poetry.

Name: _____   Date: _____

	Achieved	Notes
Accurately identify a strong image in a poem.		
Provide logical explanations of how the image was important to the poem.		

Standards Alignment: RL.4.1, SL.4.1c, SL.4.1d

Reading Lesson 7
Milestone Performance Assessment: Determining Poet's Purpose

Use this checklist to assess student work in determining a poet's purpose.

Name: _____   Date: _____

	Achieved	Notes
Identify a logical purpose for writing the poem.		
Provide relevant evidence to support thinking about the poet's purpose.		

Standards Alignment: RL.4.1, RL.4.2, RL.4.4, RL.4.5, SL.4.1b, SL.4.1d

Reading Lesson 8
Milestone Performance Assessment: Comparing and Contrasting Poems

Use this checklist to assess student work comparing and contrasting poems.

Name: _____   Date: _____

	Achieved	Notes
Describe what both poems are saying.		
Identify key elements of each poem: content, structure, mood, strong images, what characters say and do, and poet's purpose (May be uneven, but student should identify most of the elements.).		
Highlight similarities between the poems.		

Standards Alignment: W.4.1a-d, W.4.4, W.4.10

Reading Lesson 10
Milestone Performance Assessment: Reflection on Core Questions

Use this checklist to assess student work on written reflections on the core questions.

Name: _____   Date: _____

	Achieved	Notes
Include an opening that introduces the topic of the reflection.		
Accurately answer selected core question.		
Provide examples and evidence for thinking from texts or experiences during lesson set to support ideas.		
Use transitional words and phrases to link ideas.		
Conclude with summarizing thought.		

Standards Alignment: W.4.4, W.4.6, W.4.10

Writing Lesson 4
Milestone Performance Assessment: Using Strong Imagery in Poetry

Use this checklist to assess student tribute poems with strong images.

Name: _____   Date: _____

	Achieved	Notes
Compose a tribute poem based on an original poem.		
Attempt to create a strong image in the poem.		
Choose words that effectively convey the image.		

Standards Alignment: W.4.1a, SL.4.1a-d, L.4.3

Writing Lesson 6
Milestone Performance Assessment: Forming Opinions About Poetry Meaning

Use this checklist to assess student work in developing opinions.

Name: _____   **Date:** _____

	Achieved	Notes
Express an opinion about the meaning of the poem.		
Use appropriate academic language to express opinion (phrases).		
Demonstrate an understanding of how to form an interpretation using knowledge from previous lessons.		

Standards Alignment: W.4.1b-d, SL.4.1a-d, L.4.1, L.4.3

Writing Lesson 7
Milestone Performance Assessment: Forming and Defending Opinions about Poetry Meaning

Use this checklist to assess student work on developing opinions.

Name: _____   Date: _____

	Achieved	Notes
Express an opinion about the meaning of the poem.		
Use appropriate academic language to express opinion (phrases).		
Use evidence from the poem to support opinion.		

This following checklist provides observable Core Standards–aligned indicators to assess student performance as speakers and listeners. Use it entirely to gather performance data over time or choose appropriate indicators to create a customized checklist to match a specific learning experience.

Student's Name: _____   Topic of Study: _____   Time Frame: _____

COMPREHENSION AND COLLABORATION

Performance Indicator	Achieved	Notes
Actively engages in collaborative discussions in a variety of settings (student partnerships, student groups, teacher-led). [SL.4.1]		
Prepares for discussions in advance and uses this preparation to enhance discussion. [SL.4.1a]		
Follows agreed-upon rules and roles for discussions (active listening, taking turns to speak, etc.). [SL.4.1b]		
Contributes to discussions by commenting on the ideas of others, asking and answering questions and explaining ideas. [SL.4.1c-d]		
Paraphrases from a given source such as read-aloud or other media and formats. [SL.4.2]		
Identifies reasons and evidence a speaker provides to support a point. [SL.4.3]		

PRESENTATION OF KNOWLEDGE AND IDEAS

Reports on a topic, story, or experience with organization, focus and accurate detail. [SL.4.4]		
Speaks clearly and at an understandable pace. [SL.4.4]		
Provides audio recordings and/or visual displays that effectively enhance ideas or themes of presentations. [SL.4.5]		
Uses either formal or informal English appropriate to task and situation. [SL.4.6]		

It is your turn to speak out and make your voices heard, rationally, logically, and persuasively. How often have you heard or read a story on the news and thought to yourself, "I have something to say about that"? Or how many times have you listened to adults discuss an issue that concerns *you*, but they never ask your opinion? Well today is your day. Not only are we going to spend the next few weeks identifying the topics that concern you the most, we are also going to learn how you can effectively and powerfully put your opinions out into the world and be heard.

The Importance of Owning a Dog

The Humane Society estimates that somewhere between 6-8 million pets enter animal shelters each year. 3-4 million of those animals are euthanized. Another 3-4 million are adopted by loving families. Your family can be one of those loving families! In my opinion, adopting a dog seems like a no brainer because there are too many dogs currently living in shelters that need a good home and too many reasons why having a dog can make your life better.

First things first, kids are constantly told to get fresh air and exercise instead of watching TV. It's true, we only have one body and if it's going to last until we're 100 years old it better be strong and healthy. Walking, running and playing with a playful puppy are excellent and fun ways to get daily exercise. These walks are also a perfect opportunity for grown-ups to get outside and spend time with their children. Kids aren't the only ones who need exercise, you know.

Another great thing about dogs is that they make excellent listeners and secret keepers. Researchers have found that having a pet in the house makes children better communicators and more self-confident. That means spending time with a loving dog causes kids to feel proud to be who they are instead of worrying what others think of them. It also improves social skills like listening and understanding body language. So far, no research has shown that broccoli makes children better listeners.

Sometimes as kids, we lose things (our shoes), we break things (by accident) or we forget to clean up after ourselves. Dogs do all of these things, too! By learning how to properly care for a dog - cleaning up after them, remembering to feed them at breakfast AND dinner - kids become more responsible. So you won't have to ask if we've brushed our teeth before bed and your flower vases will last longer!

The last thing that must be mentioned is how much fun it is to be around a dog. This may not be as scientific as the other points but it isn't hard to believe that families with a dog must smile and laugh more often. Think about the silly things a dog might do: chase its tail, perform silly tricks, dress in silly rabbit ears on Halloween, these are just a few examples. We have all heard the saying, "laughter is the best medicine," and research confirms that this is true. Laughing lowers blood pressure, reduces stress, and exercises muscles in the stomach, face and back.

Some people might say that owning a dog is actually a *bad* idea for families because of the amount of money and time caring for a dog requires. It's true that dogs cost money – you have to buy food, bring them to the vet, and make sure they have a toy or two. However, talking about how to save money, budget for expenses, and search for good deals makes a wonderful learning opportunity for parents and children. As for the time caring for a dog requires? Well, think about all the ways you spend your time right now. Do you really need to watch more TV or do you think it might be more fun and rewarding to take care of a furry, lovable friend?

Certainly owning a dog is a big decision that must be carefully considered. However, the many positive benefits of a canine companion will surely be rewarding. Taking in a stray dog will give you a loyal friend for life. Somewhere a dog is wagging his tail, waiting for you to finish reading so he can lick your face and sleep on your lap.

Big Food, Big Soda: Ban Supersized Drinks

If I told you there was something you could drink that tasted good but if you bought it in a huge container and drank too much of it your health would be seriously hurt, don't you think most people would agree you shouldn't be able to buy it in a big container? Of course. But when that thing is soda, people insist that they should be able to buy as big a size serving as they want. Allowing them to do this leads to diabetes and other serious medical conditions. The sale of supersized sodas should be stopped.

There can be no doubt that the sugar in soda leads to diabetes and other health problems (http://www.diabetes.org/diabetes-basics/type-2/). Americans have been gaining weight steadily for the past two decades, and a large part of this move toward obesity can be traced to the sugar in sodas. "In addition to weight gain, higher consumption of SSBs is associated with development of metabolic syndrome and type 2 diabetes." (Malik et al., 2011).

We Americans drink more soda than almost anybody else on earth. "More than 15 billion gallons were sold in 2000. That works out to at least one 12-ounce can per day for every man, woman and child." (Squires, 2000). And the sugar in all that soda is making us sick. Stopping people from buying huge sized sodas won't prevent them from drinking soda – it will just help them keep the amount they drink to a reasonable level.

As for those who point to the United States Declaration of Independence and the part about "life, liberty, and the pursuit of happiness", (1776) you can still pursue happiness by buying a lot of regular sized sodas if you really fell you must drink a huge amount of soda to be happy. But you won't find yourself in the situation of guzzling a huge soda just because it is there and you are trying to finish it.

Also, higher rates of diabetes and obesity not only make us much less healthy as a nation, they make health care costs go up to treat these ailments, so we all end up paying the cost for supersized sodas.

So ban the sale of giant sodas. It will help make us much healthier as a country. And maybe some people will even start thinking about drinking something better for them.

References:

American Diabetes Association, Inc. (2006). *American Diabetes Association*. Retrieved from http://www.dia s.org/diabetes-basics/type-2/

Malik, V. S., Popkin, B. M., Bray, G. A., Despres, J. P., Willett, W. C., & Hu, F. B. (2010). Sugar sweetened beverages and risk of metabolic syndrome and type 2 diabetes: a meta-analysis. *Diabetes Care, 33*, 2477–83.

Squires. S. (2001). *Soft Drinks, Hard Facts*. Retrieved from http://www.washingtonpost.com/wp-dyn/content/article/2005/07/12/AR2005071200783.html

U.S. Declaration of Independence, 1776.

Texting Instead of Talking: Are Text Messages Destroying Communication?

"How r u 2day?" If that question makes sense to you, chances are you're an expert at sending text messages. Some people (mostly grownups) are alarmed by the amount of time young people spend on cell phones, and the spelling and grammar they use within their text messages. Even though not every text message is a masterpiece, they are an important tool for communication.

Like them or not, text messages are here to stay. In fact a recent Pew Internet & American Life Project study showed that teenagers send over three thousand text messages per month! (Lenhart, Ling, Campbell, & Purcell, 2010). You may think texting is just a way to be silly with your friends, but they are actually teaching us to communicate our thoughts in a short, straight to the point way. This is not easy to do! No one wants to read a whole paragraph when all they need to know is where their mom put their clean gym shorts! Sometimes it takes creativity – and yes, made up words – to write our messages in a short and simple way, but this is good exercise for our brains.

Of course if we are sending so many text messages, this means we are spending less time using our phones for their original purpose – making phone calls. However, text messages don't *replace* human interaction, and sometimes it isn't possible to make a phone call anyway. For example, if we are in a library it would

be rude (and against the rules!) to make a loud phone call. A text message allows us to say a quick hello, or to let our mom know we made it across the street safely. Come to think of it, mothers should be *glad* that kids are so great at texting! It's also important to note that most of the time we use text messages to arrange a time to meet our friends in person: "Are you free tonight? Let's go see a movie!" See? Text messages bring us together.

Now, I suppose the point about poor grammar and spelling must be addressed. There *is* a special language used in text messages that would be unacceptable to use for a school assignment or to communicate with anyone other than our friends

and family members. However, when we are communicating outside of school or work, we should be allowed to have fun with the English language! As long as we are responsible and make sure to use only proper English outside of text messages, there is no harm in having fun with friends on our cell phones.

Finally, let's go back to that surprising fact from earlier: teenagers send over three thousand text messages each month. That is six text messages every hour. It is hard to believe that anyone would need to send that many messages in such a short amount of time. Sure, it gives a lot of time to practice the art of text messaging, but we should not let any activity consume our lives or take up too much of our time. Text messaging is fine in small or medium amounts, and we can, and should cut back the amount of time we spend texting by asking ourselves, "Does this message contain

important information that must be sent right now?" If the answer is no, put that phone down, do u hear me?

In conclusion, don't panic, text messages are not destroying our ability to communicate with each another. Texting make us creative, and able to say what we really need to say quickly and simply. Yes, it is amazing how quick and easy it is to check in with our friends, but we should not go crazy and send more messages than we really need to. This way we can be good company for the people that are right in front of us, and we can pay attention to our surroundings. Trust me, you'll be thankful when you *don't* walk into a street sign or trip over a crack in the sidewalk because your nose was stuck in a phone!

Reference:

Lenhart, A., Ling, R., Campbell, S. & Purcell, K. (2010). Teens and Mobile Phones. Pew Internet and American Life Project. Retrieved from http://pewinternet. org/Reports/2010/Teens-and-Mobile-Phones.aspx

Zoos: Good for Animals and People

Have you ever seen, in front of your very eyes, an animal with an eight foot long tail that eats for twenty hours a day and is strong enough to kill a lion? Well, if you've ever been to a zoo, chances are you can answer yes to this question, so long as the zoo had a giraffe exhibit If we didn't have zoos in the United States, most of us would never see such amazing animals, let alone see them up close and in a safe environment. The Association of Zoos and Aquariums (AZA), receives more than 175 million visitors annually, which is more visitors annually than NFL, NBA, NHL, and MLB attendance combined (http://www.aza.org/visitor-demographics/) Zoos are beneficial to people and animals in many ways.

Keeping Animals Happy and Healthy

It might sound surprising to hear that animals benefit from being kept in a zoo. In fact, zoos get a lot of criticism for keeping wild animals in captivity. A lot of  people think living in cages makes animals unhappy and bored. Actually, the cages in a zoo are more like an animal's real habitat in the wild, with similar plants, trees and food! The zookeepers also give the animals a lot of attention and take great care of their health, making sure they have toys to play with and get enough exercise.

Speaking of the animal's health, the zoo is actually a really great place for an animal to get sick. Zookeepers are highly educated animal doctors and scientists. If a lion has a cough or a cheetah hurts his leg, the zookeepers can nurture the animals back to health. In the wild a sick animal might not survive and would be vulnerable to predators.

Protecting the Species

What's even better is that zoos are able to save animals from endangerment or extinction. Unfortunately, in the wild there are people, called poachers, who hunt animals illegally because they can get a lot of money from selling animal products, like furs and ivory tusks. If too many animals are killed they might disappear from our planet forever. One success story is when zoos were able to save the California condor, a type of bird that almost went extinct. At one time there was less than two dozen California condors but the Los Angeles and San Diego zoos offered the birds shelter and safety. San Diego Zoo Global mentions on their website that "as of April 30, 2012, the population of California condors had grown to 405, including 226 condors living in the wild" (http://www.sandiegozooglobal.org/overview).

Educating Communities

Now how do zoos benefit people and communities? Most importantly, zoos teach us how to care for the magnificent creatures that share our planet. Almost all zoos have educational programs to teach visitors about animal conservation. That means we learn how to take better care of the environment, and when the environment is healthy, animals are more likely to be healthy. This makes us better friends to animals, and we can feel proud of ourselves for being responsible.

Another benefit of having a zoo or opening a zoo in a city is tourism. The San Diego zoo attracts five million visitors every year (sandiegozoo.org). Tourists

(continued)

spend money, not just at the zoo, but at local businesses who rely on a steady stream of customers to make a profit to *stay* in business.

As long as zoos treat their animals humanely, the animals will be safe, healthy and happy in their specially designed habitats, and will bring more tourists into town. More importantly, zoos will inspire all who visit to take care of the world and the creatures big and small that walk the Earth.

References:

Association of Zoos and Aquariums. Retrieved October 2, 2012, from http://www.aza.org/visitor-demographics/

San Diego Zoo Global. Retrieved October 1, 2012, from http://www.sandiego-zooglobal.org/overview

San Diego Zoo. Retrieved October 2, 2012, from http://www.aza.org/visitor-demographics/

Nearshore Oil Drilling Editorial

Imagine that Florida, instead of having white, beautiful beaches, had black and desolate shorelines from an oil spill! Florida must ban nearshore oil drilling permanently!

According to www.stateofflorida.com, Florida has 2,276 miles of shoreline, of which 663 miles are famous beaches. Nearshore oil drilling would harm the beauty and the environment along Florida shorelines. Besides, an oil spill would destroy the wildlife, and would devastate the tourism, fishing and water-sport industries. These industries are sources of major income to Florida. According to Visit Florida, tourism alone brought about 1 million jobs and $65.5 billion revenue to Florida in 2007. It generated $3.9 billion sales tax to Florida government that year. Florida cannot risk losing these vital industries and its most beautiful resource, its shorelines and beaches.

For the above reasons, Florida must prohibit nearshore oil drilling.

Source: © 2011 Kim-Anh Vo. Reprinted with permission of the author.

APPENDIX 5.7 Analysis of an Editorial Graphic Organizer

Name: ______________________________ Date: ______________

Title: ______________________________

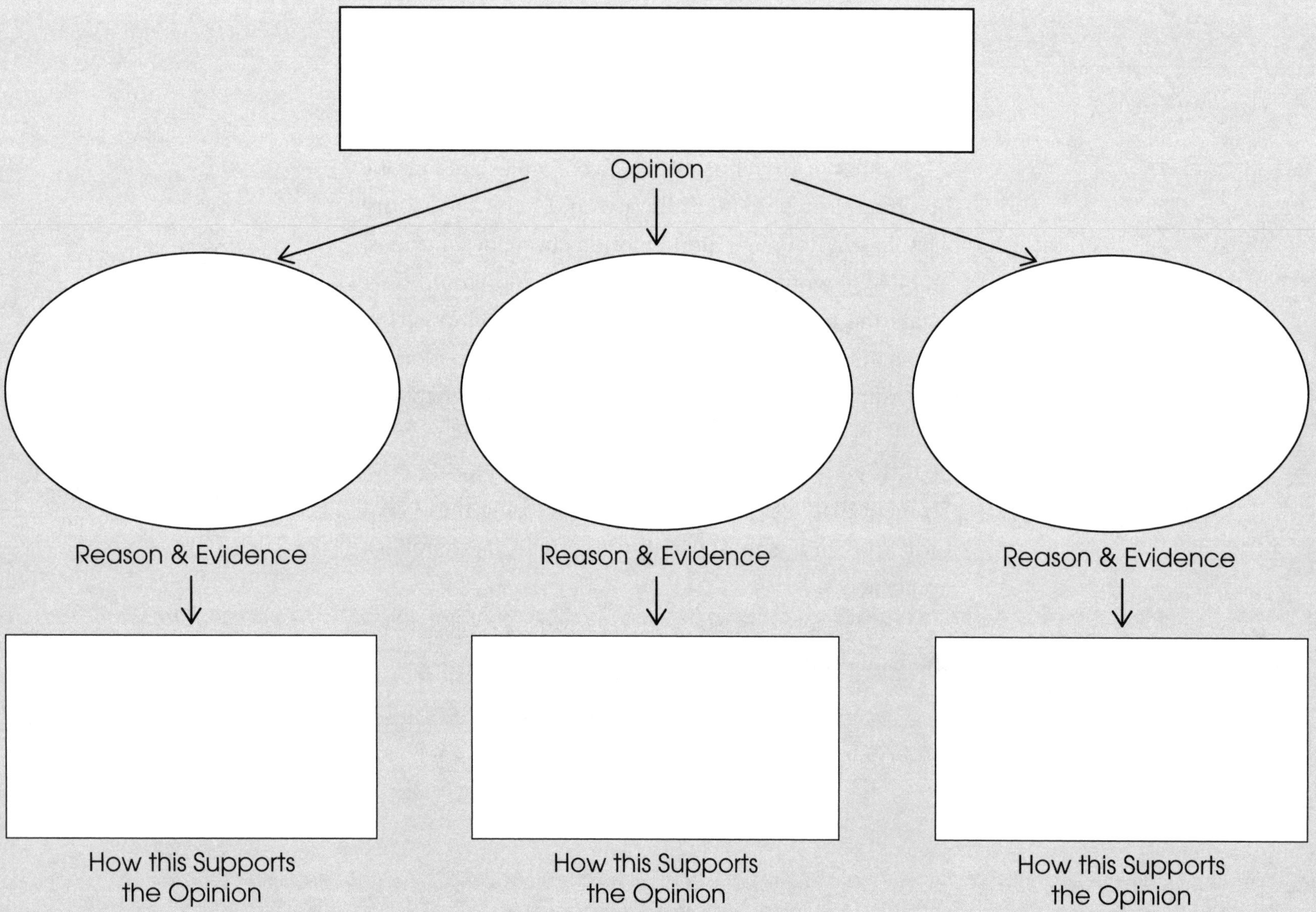

Opinion
Reason & Evidence
Reason & Evidence
Reason & Evidence
How this Supports the Opinion
How this Supports the Opinion
How this Supports the Opinion

Name: _____ Date: _____

Title of editorial:

Author's opinion:

Reason and evidence 1:

Reason and evidence 2:

Reason and evidence 3:

Name: _____ Date: _____

Statement of opinion: Use strong language to clearly state your opinion. This is your chance to get the audience ready for the argument you are about to present.

Argument: The argument in an editorial is made up of a series of logically organized reasons. These reasons are usually based in research.

Reason 1:

Reason 2:

Reason 3:

Name: _____ Date: _____

Revising	Yes or No	Notes
Will my lead grab readers' attention and make them want to keep reading?		
Does my introduction provide the reader necessary background information?		
Do I include a clear, strong opinion statement?		
Do I include three strong reasons to support my opinion?		
Do I support my reasons with well-developed evidence and research?		
Do I include a strong conclusion using an effective concluding technique?		
Do I use transitional words and phrases to clarify and connect my ideas?		
COPS Editing Checklist		
Capitals—I remembered to use capitals correctly.		
Order and usage of words—I have reread my sentences, and they all sound right and make sense.		
Punctuation—I have used correct punctuation.		
Spelling—I have corrected my spelling errors.		

✂ -

Standards Alignment: RI.5.1, RI.5.7, RI.5.10, W.5.4, W.5.7, W.5.8, W.5.10, SL.5.1a, SL.5.1b, L.5.6

Reading Lesson 4
Milestone Performance Assessment: Note-Taking Strategies

Use this checklist to assess student notes at this point.

Name: _____   **Date:** _____

	Achieved	Notes
Develop a system to organize notes.		
Paraphrase information from sources.		
Record direct quotes from sources; use quotes and credits source.		
Keep a list of sources used.		

✂ -

Standards Alignment: RI.5.10, W.5.4, W.5.10, SL.5.1a–d, L.5.1, L.5.6

Reading Lesson 10
Milestone Performance Assessment: Reflection on Core Questions

Use this checklist to assess student work on written reflections on the core questions.

Name: _____   **Date:** _____

	Achieved	Notes
Include an opening that introduces the topic of the reflection.		
Accurately answer the selected core question.		
Provide examples and evidence for thinking from texts and/or experiences during lesson set to support ideas.		
Conclude with summarizing thought.		
Use transitional words and phrases to link ideas.		

Standards Alignment: RI.5.8, RI.5.10, W.5.1, W.5.4, W.5.6, W.5.9a, W.5.10, SL.5.1a–d, L.5.1, L.5.6

Writing Lesson 2
Milestone Performance Assessment: Analyzing Editorial Components

Use this checklist to assess student Taking a Closer Look Graphic Organizers

Name: _____ Date: _____

	Achieved	Notes
Identify the opinion(s) expressed in the editorial.		
Identify evidence and reasons that support the opinion(s).		
Explain how reasons or pieces of evidence support the opinion(s).		

Standards Alignment: W.5.1b, W.5.4, W.5.5, W.5.7, W.5.8, SL.5.1a–d, L.5.1, L.5.6

Writing Lesson 5
Milestone Performance Assessment: Planning for Effective Editorials

Use this checklist to assess student Speaking My Mind Graphic Organizers.

Name: _____ Date: _____

	Achieved	Notes
Express a strong opinion statement.		
Provide at least three logical reasons to support opinion.		
Develop reasons with evidence and research.		

Standards Alignment: W.5.1a-c, W.5.4, W.5.5, W.5.7, W.5.7, SL.5.1a-d

Writing Lesson 8
Composing Effective Editorials

Use this checklist to assess student editorials at this point.

Name: _____   **Date:** _____

	Achieved	Notes
Lead is engaging.		
Introduction provides useful background information about the topic.		
Make a clear, strong opinion statement.		
Provide three reasons to support the opinion.		
Develop reasons with evidence and research.		
Use transitional words and phrases to link and clarify ideas.		

The following checklist provides observable Core Standards–aligned indicators to assess student performance as speakers and listeners. Use it entirely to gather performance data over time or choose appropriate indicators to create a customized checklist to match a specific learning experience.

Student's Name: _____   Topic of Study: _____   Time Frame: _____

COMPREHENSION AND COLLABORATION

Performance Indicator	Achieved	Notes
Actively engages in collaborative discussions in a variety of settings (student partnerships, student groups, teacher-led). [SL.5.1]		
Prepares for discussions in advance and uses this preparation to enhance discussion. [SL.5.1a]		
Follows agreed-upon rules and roles for discussions (active listening, taking turns to speak, etc.). [SL.5.1b]		
Contributes to discussions by commenting on the ideas of others, asking and answering questions. [SL.5.1c]		
Reviews key ideas and conclusions generated by discussion. [SL.5.1d]		
Summarizes ideas from a given source such as read-aloud or other media and formats. [SL.5.2]		
Identifies main points and links to supporting evidence provided by a speaker. [SL.5.3]		

PRESENTATION OF KNOWLEDGE AND IDEAS

Performance Indicator	Achieved	Notes
Reports on a topic or text or presents opinion with organization, focus, and accurate detail. [SL.5.4]		
Speaks clearly and at an understandable pace. [SL.5.4]		
Provides multimedia components and visual displays that effectively enhance ideas or themes of presentations. [SL.5.5]		
Uses either formal or informal English appropriate to task and situation. [SL.5.6]		

References

Allington, D. (2012). Private experience, textual analysis, and institutional authority: The discursive practice of critical interpretation and its enactment in literary training. *Language and Literature*, 21(2).

Carrier, K. A., & Tatum, A. W. (2006). Creating sentence walls to help English-language learners develop content literacy. *The Reading Teacher*, 60(3), 285–288.

Ehri, L. C., Dreyer, L. G., Flugman, B., & Gross, A. (2007). Reading rescue: An effective tutoring intervention model for language-minority students who are struggling readers in first grade. *American Educational Research Journal*, 44, 414–448.

Fountas, I. C., & Pinnell, G. S. (1997). *Guided reading, good first teaching for all children.* Portsmouth, NH: Greenwood Press.

Goldenberg, C. (2008). Teaching English Language Learners: What the research does—and does not—say. American Educator, 32(2), 8–23, 42–44.

Lewis, M. (1993). *The lexical approach: The state of ELT and the way forward.* Hove, England: Language Teaching Publications.

Mora, P. (1999). "Words Free As Confetti." *Confetti: Poems for Children.* Illustrated by Enrique O. Sanchez. New York: Lee and Low.

Nattinger, J. R. (1980). A lexical phrase grammar for ESL. *TESOL Quarterly*, 14(3), 337–334.

PARCC. (2011). *PARCC model content frameworks: English language arts/literacy, grades 3–11.*

Index